WOMEN IN MEDIA

WOMEN IN MEDIA:

A DOCUMENTARY SOURCE BOOK

By MAURINE BEASLEY and SHEILA SILVER

Women's Institute for Freedom of the Press

Washington, D.C.

Acknowledgment is made for permission to excerpt from the following: Columns by "Grace Greenwood," *New York Times*, Feb. 1, 1873 and July 9, 1877, copyright © 1873-77 by the New York Times Company, reprinted by permission; "Front Page Girl" from *Ladies of the Press* by Ishbel Ross, copyright © 1936 by Ishbel Ross, reprinted by permission of Harper & Row, Publishers; chapter II from *Purple Heart Valley* by Margaret Bourke-White, copyright © 1944, 1971 by Margaret Bourke-White, reprinted by permission of Simon & Schuster, a Division of Gulf & Western Corporation; "Guidelines for Creating Positive Sexual and Racial Images in Educational Material," copyright © 1975 by The Macmillan Publishing Co., Inc., reprinted by permission of the publisher; excerpts on feminists and the media from *The Politics of Women's Liberation*, copyright © 1976 by Jo Freeman, reprinted by permission of the author and the publisher, David McKay, Inc.: excerpts on programming and employment from the *Report of the Task Force on Women in Public Broadcasting*, 1975, reprinted with permission of the Corporation for Public Broadcasting; excerpts from Nora Magid's "The Heart, the Mind, the Pickled Okra: Women's Magazines in the Sixties," appear by permission of *The North American Review*, copyright © 1970 the University of Northern Iowa; portions of "Advertising and Women: A Report on Advertising Portraying or Directed to Women" appear by permission of the National Advertising Review Board; The United Methodist Women's monitoring study, *Sex Role Stereotyping in Prime Time Television*, is excerpted here by permission of the Women's Division Board of Global Ministries, the United Methodist Church. The statement of objectives of the editors of *off our backs* appears with their permission; excerpts from *"Ms.: A Personal Report,"* copyright © 1972 Ms. Magazine Corp., are reprinted by permission; "My Last Hurrah: Occupying the *Ladies Homes Journal*," appears by permission of Vivien Leone and William Haddad, Manhattan Tribune Syndicate Service; recommendations excerpted from *Women in the CBC: Report of the Task Force on the Status of Women*, copyright © 1975 Canadian Broadcasting Corporation, appear by permission of the CBC.

Printed in the United States of America by Anaconda Press, Catherine Bilzor, Proprietor, 1320 14th Street, N.W., Washington, DC 20005.

Library of Congress Catalog Card Number: 77-82376
International Standard Book Number: 0-930470-00-1

Published and distributed by
WOMEN'S INSTITUTE FOR FREEDOM OF THE PRESS
3306 Ross Place, N.W., Washington, DC 20008. (202) 966-7783

For our mothers

Maurine Hieronymus Hoffman

and

Georgina Parrish Amenta

CONTENTS

INTRODUCTION

The Women's Institute for Freedom of the Press has several very good reasons for being pleased to publish this book.

The first reason is, of course, the rapidly growing women's media movement itself, which has created the strong demand for information about women and media. As never before, women are doing a lot of thinking about the structure and influence of mass media on the lives of all of us.

There are new women's media groups and "new (and old) girl" networks springing up in every major city; the media women's professional organizations are discussing new professional concerns; and there is a host of new media businesses, profit and nonprofit: film companies, video, cable, theater groups, artists' collectives, periodicals, recording companies and publishing houses. New organizations of women writers are forming, and conferences and festivals are being held to discuss ways to help each other.

Nor is the phenomenon limited to this country. It is happening with equal vigor all over the world.

Yet almost none of this information is available to the general public — and especially to the female half of the general public who might be most interested in knowing about it — nor is it presently available to the students in journalism and communications schools, or women's studies departments, where it is their function to be studying such phenomena.

Yet, while they may not know the extent, or even the issues, of this new movement, students are aware that something is happening and they want to know more about it. For example, a poll of approximately half of the students in the College of Journalism and Communication at the University of Florida, Gainesville, showed that 139 women and 65 men would either definitely or probably enroll in a course on women and mass communications if one were offered. In raw numbers, this would provide students for many semesters to come and for a great variety of courses. In terms of percentages, 73% of the women and 24% of the men said they would probably or definitely take such a course.

We are happy to publish material that will be helpful to such students, and their teachers who want to bring their teaching material up to date. Dr. Beasley and Ms. Silver, out of their experience in teaching this subject, in both general courses and in their "Women and Mass Communications" course, have discovered the kinds of documents that are most needed by students and that best tell the story of this new development in communications. They have selected and arranged their documents to describe that historical development from 1790 to the present. The first 15 documents are selections from history that bring us to the point which so many women have seen as the nadir for women in media portrayal and employment. Indeed, it was the situation that then gave rise to the women's media movement. Documents 16 through 24 illustrate the various ways women began to take action for change. Documents 25-29 are examples of the response by the media industry (including the alternative media) to constructively bring about change. Document 30 looks to the movement's possible future.

Unfortunately no beginning book — when there is so much catching up to do — can cover all the long-missing information. Documents on film, on music, on theater or the arts, all extremely important media, will have to await the next volume, as will more information about the valuable contributions of minority women, other than the Black women journalists covered in Document 8. The next volume will also have to include more on the equally lively media movements of women in Canada and other countries.

Yet we are pleased to publish this volume for what it does contribute as a first-of-its-kind presentation of material that is not available generally. Some of the documents are not available to the public at all. For example, try to find the report of the Equal Employment Opportunity Commission on sex discrimination at the *Washington Post*. Imagine trying to locate copies of the 1972 Petition to Deny WABC-TV's broadcast license renewal. How many will be able to obtain a copy of the agreement between the Los Angeles Women's Coalition for Better Broadcasting and KNBC-TV? The fact that these are not available in the "public" press means not only that students cannot study them and learn from them but that others cannot know about these important facets of the women's media movement. They cannot support or join it, they cannot make their special contribution to it.

The Women's Institute for Freedom of the Press, itself a part of the new women's media movement, has included its Associates Statement, reprinted here beginning on page 196. It, too, is a document for the future.

Therefore, we are pleased to publish this book, finally, because we believe it will be a contribution to that movement as well as to those in the various schools where such developments are the subjects of their study. We believe that these documents will provide stimulating discussions in the movement, in the classrooms, and outside of both, and that the result in the years to come will carry us further toward a communication system that includes everyone.

Donna Allen

July 22, 1977   Women's Institute for Freedom of the Press

CHAPTER 1

Mary Katherine Goddard: Petition to U.S. Senate

When the Continental Congress arranged for the first official printing of the Declaration of Independence in 1777, it picked a woman, Mary Katherine Goddard of Baltimore, to do the job. Although this seems surprising today, it attracted no attention at the time. Colonial women acted both as printers and newspaper publishers, frequently following their husbands or relatives into these occupations. About thirty colonial women are known to have been printers, publishers or typesetters, aside from an uncounted number of others who helped male printers in varying degrees. Of the thirty women, six served as official printers for colonial governments and one for a city government, while sixteen published newspapers, pamphlets and tracts.

Among the most outstanding was Mary Katherine Goddard, a member of a prominent printing family. Both her mother, Sarah Updike Goddard, and her brother, William Goddard, were printers and newspaper publishers in Providence, Rhode Island. Working beside them, Mary Katherine Goddard picked up the printing trade in Rhode Island and later managed her brother's printing plant in Philadelphia. She moved to Baltimore when her brother asked her to take over the *Maryland Journal*, Baltimore's first newspaper, which he had founded in 1773. She ran the newspaper while he traveled through the colonies setting up the forerunner of the present postal service.

Mary Katherine Goddard scored impressive achievements during the Revolution. In addition to printing the Declaration of Independence, she made the *Maryland Journal* one of the most vigorous voices of the rebellious colonies, acted as Baltimore's chief printer and ran bookselling and bookbinding businesses on the side. She also occupied the responsible position of Baltimore postmistress, giving her a claim to being the first woman ever appointed to federal office.

Described as an "expert and correct compositor of types," she functioned both as a craftsman and a publisher. In the winter of 1777, the Continental Congress, forced by the British to flee from Philadelphia to Baltimore, authorized her to print the first copy of the Declaration of Independence with the names of the signers attached. It was not easy to publish a newspaper during the Revolution but Mary Katherine Goddard persisted in spite of paper shortages, inflation and battles over freedom of the press, making the *Maryland Journal* among the best in the colonies. A keen judge of news, she published "extras" or "extraordinaries," as she called them, on significant events including the battle of Bunker Hill and the Continental Congress's call for arms.

Her efforts failed to bring a just reward. William Goddard was not content to let his sister continue operation of the newspaper after it became successful and managed to resume control in 1784, leading to a permanent split between the two. In addition, after fourteen years as postmistress she was removed in a case of sex discrimination. In 1789 a new Postmaster General directed that she be replaced with a man. No reason was given initially although later it was explained that the Baltimore post office might be given supervision over other offices and "more travelling might be necessary than a woman could undertake."

More than 200 leading citizens petitioned Postmaster General Samuel Osgood to retain her and she made personal appeals to both President George Washington and the U. S. Senate. They were to no avail and she was forced to leave office, even though the plan to expand the functions of the post was never carried out. As postmistress, she had been entitled to 20 per cent of the postal receipts, but she had held office during the war when the position had not been profitable. Naturally she resented being stripped of her post when it started to be lucrative, just as she resented losing the newspaper when it began to make money. She continued to support herself as a bookseller and storekeeper until 1816 when, at the age of 78, she died in Baltimore.

Her unsuccessful petition to the U. S. Senate in 1790 to retain her office as postmistress of Baltimore is reprinted below. In the style of the day it was written in the third person.

Petition

To the Honorable Senate of the United States.

The Representation of Mary Katherine Goddard humbly sheweth, That She kept the Post Office at Baltimore from the Dissolution of the old Government till the Month of November last, a term of fourteen years and upwards — That from the Non-importation Agreement, and various other causes incident to the Revolution, the Income of the Office was inadequate to its disbursements, as will appear by the Schedule hereunto annexed, and in order to accomplish this undertaking, she was obliged to advance hard money to defray the Charges of Post-Riders for several years, when they were not to be procured on any other terms; during which period, the whole of her labour and industry was necessarily unrewarded; therefore, she with great deference hoped, that having thus established and continued the Office when it was worth no Person's acceptance, She would be considered as worthy of being retained whenever it became more valuable.

That She hath been discharged without the smallest imputation of any Fault, and without any previous notice whatever, till an Order arrived from Mr. Burrell whilst at Baltimore, to deliver up the Office to Mr. White, the Bearer of his note, & although he remained several Days in town, yet he did not think proper to indulge her with a personal interview, whereby she might learn (therein) of her removal, or to what motives, it could possibly be ascribed. Such a Procedure contrasted with her conduct in Office, and the approbation of the public, testified by the number and respectability of these, who addressed Messrs. Osgood & Burrell on her behalf, leave no room to question, either her inclination or ability to discharge the duties of her appointment.

That sundry public and private applications, prior to the 19th of November last, were made to the above Gentlemen, praying that She might be restored, but no answer was returned, till the latter End of January when a Mr. Osgood wrote to the Merchants of Baltimore, that the Evil was irremediable by him. During this Interval She flattered herself that so long a consideration of the Subject would have infallibly terminated in her favour; but she has since learned that the neglect proceeded more from contempt than a desire of redress.

She also represents that taking her Office, contrary to the Sense & Expectation of the whole Community, and delaying a determination of her Fate so long, whether she should be restored or not, has greatly augmented her anxiety and distress — these are but poor rewards indeed for fourteen Years faithful Services, performed in the worst of times, and acknowledged in the most public manner by all her Co-temporaries & Superiors in Office in these words, "that no change could possibly be for the benefit of the public."

And further, as it has been universally understood that no Person should be removed from Office under the present Government, unless manifest misconduct appeared, and as no such charge could possibly be made against her, with the least colour of Justice, she was happy in the Idea of being secured both in her employ & the protection of all those who wished well to the federal Cause: And if it should so happen that she should be obliged to make room for one of more worth, or interest, that she would notwithstanding be allowed a reasonable time to prepare for the Event.

And although Mr. White who has succeeded her might doubtless have been highly meritorious, in the different Offices, he has sustained, yet, she humbly conceives, he was not more worthy of public notice & protection in his Station, than She has uniformly been in hers. It must therefore become a matter of serious importance to her, if Government can find no means of rewarding this Gentleman's Services, but by taking her little Office, established by her own Industry in the best years of her life, & whereon depended all her future Prospects of subsistence. In old Countries, People come in & go out, with the Minister of the day & his party; but here She never could suppose that any Minister, Party, or Individual, would deign to cast a wishful Eye upon so small an Object, whilst in the Hands of such a Professor. Various reasons have from time to time been assigned & abandoned, to sanction her removal, but the only one worthy of either notice or belief, is to the following Effect, though equally fallacious with the rest; . . . , That the Deputy at Baltimore will hereaforth be obliged to ride & regulate the Offices to the Southward, but that with great deference to the Post Master General will be found altogether impracticable; because the business of that Office will require his constant attendance, as no other than the Principal alone could possibly be relied on, or give satisfaction to the Merchants who frequently make large remittances by post. If therefore the duties of Mr. Burrell's Office are to be performed by any other than himself, it cannot well be attempted by a Deputy, fully occupied with his own; and if two Persons must be employed, according to his new Plan, She apprehends herself, at least, as well qualified to give the necessary Instructions to the Riding Post Master, as Mr. White, or any other person heretofore unexperienced in such business.

That although it has been suggested that the Income of her Office, for a few years last past, has made her amends for her former assiduity care and expence, yet She would beg leave to observe, that from the many failures which have distressed this Community since the Peace, She has met with her Share of losses and misfortunes, a Truth well known to all her Neighbours; And now to deprive her of this Office, to which She has a more meritorious & just claim than any other person, is a circumstance, pregnant with that Species of aggravation, which a Sense of Ingratitude inspires & which is much easier felt than described.

She therefore humbly hopes that the honorable the Senate will take her case into their serious Consideration & grant her such Assistance, as may be in their Power, in restoring her to the public Confidence & the Enjoyment of her former Office, & She will ever pray . . . . . .

Baltimore 29th Jan. 1790.

M. K. Goddard

CHAPTER 2

Anne Royall: Political Journalism

In the early nineteenth century opportunities dwindled for women in printing and publishing. Yet the colonial tradition of women journalists did not die out entirely. One especially remarkable woman, Anne Royall, published newspapers in the nation's capital from 1831 until 1854.

As a poverty-stricken young woman from the frontier, Anne Royall had made a Cinderella-like marriage to William Royall, a Revolutionary War hero and Virginia aristocrat. Although she inherited his comforable estate, his relatives managed to break the will, and at the age of fifty-five she found herself penniless again. Refusing to beg a pittance from the family, she took an amazing step for a woman of her times, traveling by stagecoach over the raw new nation while writing and marketing thirteen travel books describing her experiences.

Living partially on the charity of the Masons, her husband's fraternal brothers, she assailed evangelical groups that were stimulating the anti-Masonic fervor of the day. This led to her conviction in 1829 on the charge of being a "common scold." Two newspapermen paid her fine, saying they acted to uphold freedom of the press.

When she was sixty-one (in 1831), she settled in Washington and started the first of her two newspapers, *Paul Pry*. It lasted five years and was followed immediately by *The Huntress*, which continued until three months before her death in 1854. Both papers showed her commitment to democratic government and to investigative journalism. As an editor, Anne Royall served as a watchdog of public morals, exposing graft and wrong-doing, campaigning for internal improvements, sound money, states' rights, free schools, free thought and free speech, and against the Bank of the United States.

Judged by some other Washington journalists as a comic figure, she was miserably poor throughout her long career, and died, as she wrote in the last issue of *The Huntress* with "but thirty-one cents in the world."

Anne Royall's vigorous personal style and zeal to expose wrong-doing are illustrated in her farewell editorial in the final issue of *Paul Pry*, November 19, 1836. Two of her chief concerns, fear for her country in the face of the coming Civil War and worry over her poverty, were voiced in the last issue of *The Huntress*, July 24, 1854. The *Paul Pry* editorial and excerpts from the final issue of *The Huntress* are reprinted here.

FROM *PAUL PRY,* NOVEMBER 19, 1836

This is the last appearance of Paul Pry. Its first appearance was sudden and unexpected — perhaps unwelcome to many. Its exit is likewise sudden, and probably unlamented: like its namesake in the play, it was no doubt an unwelcome visitor by popping in where it was least looked for.

But while the Editress, noways concerned for the frowns and winks of the enemies of poor Paul, would draw a veil over its errors, she must say in its defence, it has done more for its friends than they have done for Paul; and they will repent their neglect of its admonitions too late. Had they attended to the warnings of Paul Pry, their country would not, as it is, be overrun with public swindlers and land gamblers. Nor has Paul been paid for its labors. Like its great predecessor, *Paul Jones,* it has been treated with ingratitude and shameful neglect![1]

Delinquents, we speak to you. If you have hearts, do not suffer this to pass unheeded. Remember the widow, whose husband spent seven years for you, on the fields of your revolutionary battles, and this at his own cost.

Always in the van of the editorial corps, and attacking the enemies of its country in their strong holds, Paul Pry dragged them into open day, and pointed them out to the people!

Paul Pry was the first to sound the alarm that traitors were in the camp. It was the first to proclaim the abandonment of reform by Gen. Jackson. It was the first that discovered, and the first to challenge the Post Office loans and the Post Office frauds. It was the first to challenge the organization of the office-holders as a party, at the 4th of July celebration in Pittsburg and Brownsville in 1833. It was the first that challenged the Indian land frauds of the great land companies, and the perfidy of the Southern Jackson men in selling the country to Mr. Van Buren and his political intriguers, to conceal those frauds. Paul Pry was the first to put a stop to the enormous swindling of a knot of "God's people," as they impiously call themselves. That is, "good, sound Presbyterian yankees," under the

[1]John Paul Jones was an American naval hero of the Revolution, who died in poverty.

lead of a certain Mr. WM. A. BRADLEY. Millions of dollars were swallowed up by this concern, (thank God for removing two of them out of the way,) under pretence of drawing money for corporation debts from Congress.[2] Paul Pry was the first to trace those pious rogues to their den, and drag them forth. (May a speedy vengeance overtake them.) And it is to Paul Pry the citizens of Washington are chiefly indebted for the last act of Congress in behalf of their Holland debt, by putting it out of the power of this pious Bradley and his friends, to finger the cash.

In return, we are proud to acknowledge that the citizens of Washington have ever been the able, willing, and untiring friends of Paul Pry. A thousand years of service of ten such papers, rendered to such people, would not, nor could not repay them!!!!

The Editress has only to say, that if the people will do their duty to themselves as faithfully as she has done by them, all will yet be well! But let no man sleep at his post. Remember, the office-holders are desperate, wakeful and vigilant.

FROM *THE HUNTRESS*, JULY 24, 1854

Perhaps we may never publish another paper. Life is uncertain, though we are at the present writing in perfect health.

We return many thanks to our friends in Philadelphia for their kindness in sending us their papers, viz: the Post, American Courier, and Saturday Evening Mail — without any return. This is too much kindness, especially as we can get them at Shillington's for a trifle. Gentlemen, do not kill us with kindness.

CONGRESS,——We trust in heaven for three things. First—that members may give us the *means to pay for this paper*, perhaps three or four cents a member—a few of them are behind hand; but the fault was not theirs; it was owing to Sally's sickness. Others again have paid us from two to six dollars. Our printer is a poor man, and we have but thirty-one cents in the world, and for the first time since we have resided in the city, (thirty years,) we were unable to pay our last month's rent, only six dollars. Had not our landlord been one of the best of men, we should have been stript by this time; but we shall get that from our humble friends.

Second—That Washington may escape that dreadful scourge, the Cholera.

Our third prayer is that the Union of these States may be eternal.

[2]The former mayor of Washington, William A. Bradley, was a political and personal foe, whom she accused of profiting unjustly from Congressional appropriations to pay debts of the District of Columbia.

CHAPTER 3

Jane G. Swisshelm: Abolitionist Newspaper

Desire to reform society brought a group of independent-minded women into journalism before the Civil War. Their causes included temperance, "moral purity" (elimination of prostitution), dress reform, suffrage and higher education for women, but the abolition movement drew the greatest concern. Although their periodicals were sometimes greeted with alarmed outcries, the reformers refused to give up.

One of the most determined, Jane G. Swisshelm, had begun her career in journalism by submitting contributions to Pennsylvania newspapers. These articles attracted so much attention that it was considered unlikely a woman wrote them, and a rumor circulated that the real author was a member of the state legislature.

In 1848 she started the Pittsburgh *Saturday Visiter* in sympathy with the Liberty (anti-slavery) party. This paper made her one of the best-known abolitionists in the nation.

In 1850, she became the first woman Washington correspondent when Horace Greeley engaged her to write for the *New York Tribune*. Although her stay in the capital was brief, she won equal rights to sit in the Senate Press Gallery with men — despite Vice-President Millard Fillmore's warning that "the place would be very unpleasant for a lady."

Separating from her husband in 1857, she took her only child, a daughter, and pioneered on the Minnesota frontier, where she founded another abolitionist newspaper, the St. Cloud *Democrat*, and lectured on behalf of abolition.

During the Civil War, she returned to Washington, served as Washington correspondent for her St. Cloud paper, and also took employment as one of the first women clerks in the federal government.

Her autobiography, *Half a Century,* was completed in 1880 when she was sixty-eight, and she died in 1884.

Chapters 21 and 22 from *Half a Century* (Chicago: Jansen, McClurg and Co., 1880), detailing the founding of the *Saturday Visiter*, follow:

CHAPTER XXI.

Pittsburgh Saturday Visiter

After the war, abolitionists began to gather their scattered forces and wanted a Liberty Party organ. To meet this want, Charles P. Shiras started the *Albatross* in the fall of '47. He was the "Iron City Poet," author of "Dimes and Dollars" and "Owe no Man a Dollar." He was of an old and influential family, had considerable private fortune, was courted and flattered, but laid himself and gifts on the altar of Liberty. His paper was devoted to the cause of the slave and of the free laborer, and started with bright prospects. He and Mr. Fleeson urged me to become a regular contributor, but Mr. Riddle objected, and the *Journal* had five hundred readers for every one the *Albatross* could hope.[1] In the one I reached the ninety and nine unconverted, while in the other I must talk principally to those who were rooted and grounded in the faith. So I continued my connection with the *Journal* until I met James McMasters, a prominent abolitionist, who said sorrowfully: "Well, the last number of the *Albatross* will be issued on Thursday."

"Is it possible?"

"Possible and true! That is the end of its first quarter, and Shiras gives it up. In fact we all do. No use trying to support an abolition paper here."

While he spoke a thought struck me like a lightning flash, and he had but finished speaking, when I replied:

"I have a great notion to start a paper myself."

He was surprised, but caught at the idea, and said:

"I wish you would. You can make it go if anybody can, and we'll do all we can to help you."

I did not wait to reply, but hurried after my husband, who had passed on, soon overtook and told him the fate of the *Albatross*. For this he was sorry, for he always voted a straight abolition ticket. I repeated to him what I had said to Mr. McMasters, when he said:

"Nonsense!" then reflected a little, and added, "Well, I do not know after all but it would be a good idea. Riddle makes lots of money out of your letters."

---

[1] Robert M. Riddle was editor of the *Pittsburgh Commercial Journal*, which printed occasional letters by Swisshelm against the Mexican war and slavery.

When we had talked about five minutes, he turned to attend to business and I went to the *Journal* office, found Mr. Riddle in his sanctum, and told him the *Albatross* was dead; the Liberty Party without an organ, and that I was going to start the *Pittsburg Saturday Visiter*; the first copy must be issued Saturday week, so that abolitionists would not have time to be discouraged, and that I wanted him to print my paper.

He had pushed his chair back from his desk, and sat regarding me in utter amazement while I stated the case, then said:

"What do you mean? Are you insane? What does your husband say?"

I said my husband approved, the matter was all arranged, I would use my own estate, and if I lost it, it was nobody's affair.

He begged me to take time to think, to send my husband to him, to consult my friends. Told me my project was ruinous, that I would lose every dollar I put into it, and begged, entreated me to take time; but all to no purpose, when a bright idea came to him.

"You would have to furnish a desk for yourself, you see there is but one in this room, and there is no other place for you. You could not conduct a paper and stay at home, but must spend a good deal of time here!"

Then I suddenly saw the appalling prospect thus politely presented. I had never heard of any woman save Mary Kingston working in an office. Her father, a prominent lawyer, had employed her as his clerk, when his office was in their dwelling, and the situation was remarkable and very painful; and here was I, looking not more than twenty, proposing to come into the office of the handsome stranger who sat bending over his desk that he might not see me blush for the unwomanly intent.

Mr. Riddle was esteemed one of the most elegant and polished gentlemen in the city, with fine physique and fascinating manners. He was a man of the world, and his prominence had caused his name to become the target for many an evil report in the bitter personal conflicts of political life. I looked the facts squarely in the face and thought:

"I have been publicly asserting the right of woman to earn a living as book-keepers, clerks, sales-women, and now shall I shrink for fear of a danger any one must meet in doing as I advised? This is my Red Sea. It can be no more terrible than the one which confronted Israel. Duty lies on the other side, and I am going over! 'Speak unto the children of Israel that they go forward.' The crimson waves of scandal, the white foam of gossip, shall part before me and heap themselves up as walls on either hand."

So rapidly did this reflection pass through my mind, or so absorbed was I with it, that there had been no awkward pause when I replied:

"I will get a desk, shall be sorry to be in your way, but there is plenty of room and I can be quiet."

He seemed greatly relieved, and said cheerfully:

"Oh yes, there is plenty of room, I can have my desk moved forward and take down the shutters, when there will be plenty of light. Heretofore you have been Jove thundering from a cloud, but if you will come down to dwell with mortals we must make a place for you."

Taking down the shutters meant exposing the whole interior of the room to view, from a very public street; and after he had exhausted every plea for time to get ready, he engaged to have the first copy of the *Visiter* printed on the day I had set. He objected to my way of spelling the word, but finding I had Johnson for authority, would arrange the heading to suit.

I was in a state of exaltation all forenoon, and when I met my husband at dinner, the reaction had set in, and I proposed to countermand the order, when he said emphatically:

"You will do no such thing. The campaign is coming, you have said you will start a paper, and now if you do not, I will."

The coming advent was announced, but I had no arrangements for securing either advertisements or subscribers. Josiah King, now proprietor of the *Pittsburg Gazette* and James H. McClelland called at the *Journal* office and subscribed, and with these two supporters, the *Pittsburg Saturday Visiter*, entered life. The mechanical difficulty of getting out the first number proved to be so great that the forms were not on the press at 3 P.M. By five the streets were so blocked by a waiting crowd, that vehicles went around by other ways, and it was six o'clock, Jan. 20th, 1848, when the first copy was sold at the counter. I was in the editorial room all afternoon, correcting proof to the last moment, and when there was nothing more I could do, was detained by the crowd around the doors until it was after eleven.

Editors and reporters were gathered in the sanctum, and Mr. Riddle stood by his desk pointing out errors to some one who should have prevented them, when I had my wraps on ready to start. Mr. Fleeson, then a clerk on the *Journal*, stepped out, hat in hand, and bowing to the proprietor, said:

"Mr. Riddle, it is your privilege to see Mrs. Swisshelm to her lodgings, but as you seem to decline, I hope you will commission me."

Mr. Fleeson was a small man and Mr. Riddle had drawn himself to his full height and stood looking down at him saying:

"I want it distinctly understood that Mrs. Swisshelm's relations in this office are purely those of business. If she requires anything of any man in it, she will command him and her orders shall be obeyed. She has not ordered my attendance, but has kept her servant here all the evening to see her to her friend's house, and this should be sufficient notice to any gentleman that she does not want him."

During the ten years we used the same editorial-room. Mr. Riddle was often absent on the days I must be there, and always secured plenty of light by setting away the shutters when I entered. He generally made it necessary for me to go to his house and settle accounts, and never found it convenient to offer his escort to any place unless accompanied by his wife.

The *Visiter* was three years old when he turned one day, examined me critically, and exclaimed:

"Why do you wear those hideous caps? You seem to have good hair. Mrs. Riddle says she knows you have, and she and some ladies were wondering only yesterday, why you do make yourself such a fright."

The offending cap was a net scarf tied under the chin, and I said, "You know I am subject to quinsy, and this cap protects my tonsils."

He turned away with a sigh, and did not suspect that my tonsils had no such protection outside the office, where I must meet a great many gentlemen and make it apparent that what I wanted of them was votes! votes!! Votes for the women sold on the auction block, scourged for chastity, robbed of their children, and that admiration was no part of my object.

Any attempt to aid business by any feminine attraction was to my mind revolting in the extreme, and certain to bring final defeat. In nothing has the church of Rome shown more wisdom than in the costume of her female missionaries. When a woman starts out in the world on a mission, secular or religious, she should leave her feminine charms at home. Had I made capital of my prettiness, I should have closed the doors of public employment to women for many a year, by the very means which now makes them weak, underpaid competitors in the great workshop of the world.

One day Mr. Riddle said:

"I wish you had been here yesterday. Robert Watson called. He wanted to congratulate us on the relations we have for so long maintained. We have never spoken of it, but you must have known the risk of coming here. He has seen it, says he has watched you closely, and you are an exception to all known law, or the harbinger of a new era in human progress."

Robert Watson was a retired lawyer of large wealth, who watched the world from his study, and philosophized about its doings; and when Mr. Riddle had given me this conclusion, the subject was never again referred to in our years of bargaining, buying and selling, paying and receipting.

CHAPTER XXII.

Reception of the Visiter

While preparing matter for the first number of the *Visiter*, I had time to think that so far as any organization was concerned, I stood alone. I could not work with Garrison on the ground that the Constitution was pro-slavery, for I had abandoned that in 1832, when our church split on it and I went with the New School, who held that it was then anti-slavery. The Covenanters, before it was adopted, denounced it as a "Covenant with death and an agreement with hell." I had long ago become familiar with the arguments on that side, and I concluded they were fallacious, and could not go back to them even for a welcome into the abolition ranks.

The political action wing of the anti-slavery party had given formal notice that no woman need apply for a place among them. True, there was a large minority who dissented from this action, but there was division enough, without my furnishing a cause for contention. So I took pains to make it understood that I belonged to no party. I was fighting slavery on the frontier plan of Indian warfare, where every man is Captain-lieutenants, all the corporals and privates of his company. I was like the Israelites in the days when there was no king, and "every man did that which was right in his own eyes."

It seemed good unto me to support James G. Birney, for President, and to promulgate the principles of the platform on which he stood in the last election. This I would do, and no man had the right or power to stop me. My paper was a six column weekly, with a small Roman letter head, my motto, "Speak unto the children of Israel that they go forward," the names of my candidates at the head of the editorial column and the platform inserted as standing matter.

It was quite an insignificant looking sheet, but no sooner did the American eagle catch sight of it, than he swooned and fell off his perch. Democratic roosters straightened out their necks and ran screaming with terror. Whig coons scampered up trees and barked furiously. The world was falling and every one had "heard it, saw it, and felt it."

It appeared that on some inauspicious morning each one of three-fourths of the secular editors from Maine to Georgia had gone to his office suspecting nothing, when from some corner of his exchange list there sprang upon him such a horror as he had little thought to see.

A woman had started a political paper! A woman! Could he believe his eyes? A woman! Instantly he sprang to his feet and clutched his pantaloons, shouted to the assistant editor, when he, too, read and grasped frantically at his cassimeres, called to the reporters and pressmen and typos and devils, who all rushed in, heard the news, seized their nether garments and joined the general chorus, "My breeches! oh, my breeches!" Here was a woman resolved to steal their pantaloons, their trousers, and when these were gone they might cry "Ye have taken away my gods, and what have I more?" The imminence of the peril called for prompt action, and with one accord they shouted, "On to the breach, in defense of our breeches! Repel the invader or fill the trenches with our noble dead."

"That woman shall not have *my* pantaloons," cried the editor of the big city daily; "nor my pantaloons," said the editor of the dignified weekly; "nor my pantaloons," said he who issued manifestos but once a month; "nor mine," "nor mine," "nor mine," chimed in the small fry of the country towns.

Even the religious press could not get past the tailor shop, and "pantaloons" was the watchword all along the line. George D. Prentiss took up the cry, and gave the world a two-third column leader on it, stating explicity, "She is a man all but the pantaloons." I wrote to him asking a copy of the article, but received no answer, when I replied in rhyme to suit his case:

> Perhaps you have been busy
> Horsewhipping Sal or Lizzie,
> Stealing some poor man's baby,
> Selling its mother, may-be.
> You say — and you are witty —
> That I — and, tis a pity —
> Of manhood lack but dress;
> But you lack manliness,
> A body clean and new,
> A soul within it, too.
> Nature must change her plan
> Ere you can be a man.

This turned the tide of battle. One editor said, "Brother George, beware of sister Jane." Another, "Prentiss has found his match." He made no reply, and it was not long until I thought the pantaloon argument was dropped forever.

There was, however, a bright side to the reception of the *Visiter*. Horace Greeley gave it respectful recognition, so did N. P. Willis and Gen. Morris in the *Home Journal.* Henry Peterson's *Saturday Evening Post, Godey's Lady's Book*, Graham's and Sargent's magazines, and the anti-slavery papers, one and all, gave it pleasant greeting, while there were other editors who did not, in view of this innovation, forget that they were American gentlemen.

There were some saucy notices from "John Smith," editor of *The Great West*, a large literary sheet published in Cincinnati. After John and I had pelted each other with paragraphs, a private letter told me that she, who had won a large reputation as John Smith, was Celia, who afterwards became my very dear friend until the end of her lovely life, and who died the widow of another dear friend, William H. Burleigh.

In the second number of the *Visiter*, James H. McClelland, as secretary of the county convention, published its report and contributed an able article, thus recognizing it as the much needed county organ of the Liberty Party.

CHAPTER 4

Margaret Fuller: Foreign Correspondence

Horace Greeley described Margaret Fuller as "the most remarkable and in some respects the greatest woman whom America has yet known." An intimate of Ralph Waldo Emerson and Henry Thoreau, she won literary fame as an author, critic, feminist and Transcendentalist philosopher. Her journalistic career is less well-known, but she deserves the title of the first woman foreign correspondent.

Traveling to Europe in 1846 as a writer for Greeley's *New York Tribune*, Fuller reported on social conditions in the British Isles, France and Italy, and interviewed leading literary and political figures. In Italy, she covered an unsuccessful revolution, thwarted by a French siege of Rome. Her first-person accounts of the French bombardment made her the first woman war correspondent.

A precocious child who read Virgil in the original Latin at the age of seven, she played a major role in New England intellectual life as a teacher, writer and conversationalist with notables of the Transcendentalist movement. She became a co-editor of *The Dial*, a quarterly literary journal of the Transcendentalists, in 1840. Four years later Greeley hired her as his first woman staff member, naming her literary critic for the *Tribune*. She also wrote exposés on public institutions and promoted a home for freed women convicts.

Before she went abroad, she published *Woman in the Nineteenth Century*, a classic book on American feminism that helped lay the foundation for the Seneca Falls convention on women's rights in 1848. In her book she pointed out that those who claimed "women were too delicate to participate in politics totally overlooked their exploitation in the labor force." As she noted: "Those who think the physical circumstances of Woman would make a part in the affairs of national government unsuitable, are by no

15

means those who think it is impossible for negresses to endure fieldwork, even during pregnancy, or for sempstresses (original spelling) to go through their killing labors."

Fuller's Roman experiences brought her both personal happiness and tragedy. A love affair with a Roman nobleman, Giovanni Angelo, Marchese d'Ossoli, absorbed her in revolutionary activities, including direction of an emergency hospital. They apparently were married in the summer of 1849, almost a year after the birth of a son who was left with a nurse in the mountains during the revolution.

After Rome fell, the couple was reunited with the child and lived in Florence until 1850 when, returning to the United States, all three lost their lives in a shipwreck outside of New York harbor, a few weeks after her 40th birthday.

Margaret Fuller's European dispatches to the *New York Tribune* were collected by her brother, Arthur B. Fuller, after her death and published in *At Home and Abroad or Things and Thoughts in America and Europe*. Excerpts of her account of the siege of Rome dated July 6, 1849, and sent to the *Tribune* are reprinted here.

LETTER XXXIII

Rome, July 6, 1849.

If I mistake not, I closed my last letter just as the news arrived here that the attempt of the democratic party in France to resist the infamous proceedings of the government had failed, and thus Rome, as far as human calculation went, had not a hope for her liberties left. An inland city cannot long sustain a siege when there is no hope of aid. Then followed the news of the surrender of Ancona, and Rome found herself alone; for, though Venice continued to hold out, all communication was cut off.

The Republican troops, almost to a man, left Ancona, but a long march separated them from Rome.

The extreme heat of these days was far more fatal to the Romans than to their assailants, for as fast as the French troops sickened, their place was taken by fresh arrivals. Ours also not only sustained the exhausting service by day, but were harassed at night by attacks, feigned or real. These commonly began about eleven or twelve o'clock at night, just when all who meant to rest were fairly asleep. I can imagine the harassing effect upon the troops, from what I feel in my sheltered pavilion, in consequence of not knowing a quiet night's sleep for a month.

The bombardment became constantly more serious. The house where I live was filled as early as the 20th with persons obliged to fly from the

Piazza di Gesu, where the fiery rain fell thickest. The night of the 21st-22nd, we were all alarmed about two o'clock, A. M. by a tremendous cannonade. It was the moment when the breach was finally made by which the French entered. They rushed in, and I grieve to say, that, by the only instance of defection known in the course of the siege, those companies of the regiment Union which had in charge a position on that point yielded to panic and abandoned it. The French immediately entered and intrenched themselves. That was the fatal hour for the city. Every day afterward, though obstinately resisted, the enemy gained, till at last, their cannon being well placed, the city was entirely commanded from the Janiculum, and all thought of further resistance was idle.

It was true policy to avoid a street-fight, in which the Italian, an unpractised soldier, but full of feeling and sustained from the houses, would have been a match even for their disciplined troops. After the 22nd of June, the slaughter of the Romans became every day more fearful. Their defences were knocked down by the heavy cannon of the French, and, entirely exposed in their valorous onsets, great numbers perished on the spot. Those who were brought into the hospitals were generally grievously wounded, very commonly subjects for amputation. My heart bled daily more and more at these sights, and I could not feel much for myself, though now the balls and bombs began to fall round me also. The night of the 28th the effect was truly fearful, as they whizzed and burst near me. As many as thirty fell upon or near the Hotel de Russie, where Mr. Cass has his temporary abode.[1] The roof of the studio in the pavilion, tenanted by Mr. Stermer, well known to the visitors of Rome for his highly-finished cabinet pictures, was torn to pieces. I sat alone in my much exposed apartment, thinking, "If one strikes me, I only hope it will kill me at once, and that God will transport my soul to some sphere where virtue and love are not tyrannized over by egotism and brute force, as in this." However, that night passed; the next, we had reason to expect a still more fiery salute toward the Pincian, as here alone remained three or four pieces of cannon which could be used. But on the morning of the 30th, in a contest at the foot of the Janiculum, the line, old Papal troops, naturally not in earnest like the free corps, refused to fight against odds so terrible. The heroic Marina fell, with hundreds of his devoted Lombards. Garibaldi saw his best officers perish, and himself went in the afternoon to say to the Assembly that further resistance was unavailing.

The Assembly sent to Oudinot, but he refused any conditions,—refused even to guarantee a safe departure to Garibaldi, his brave foe. Notwithstanding, a great number of men left the other regiments to follow the leader whose courage had captivated them, and whose superiority over difficulties commanded their entire confidence. Toward the evening of Monday,

---

[1] Lewis Cass, Jr., was the United States charge d'affaires in Rome.

the 2d of July, it was known that the French were preparing to cross the river and take possession of all the city. I went into the Corso with some friends; it was filled with citizens and military. The carriage was stopped by the crowd near the Doria palace; the lancers of Garibaldi galloped along in full career. I longed for Sir Walter Scott to be on earth again, and see them; all are light, athletic, resolute figures, many of the forms of the finest manly beauty of the South, all sparkling with its genius and ennobled by the resolute spirit, ready to dare, to do, to die. We followed them to the piazza of St. John Lateran. Never have I seen a sight so beautiful, so romantic, and so sad. Whoever knows Rome knows the peculiar solemn grandeur of that piazza, scene of the first triumph of Rienzi, and whence may be seen the magnificence of the "mother of all churches," the baptistery with its prophyry columns, the Santa Scala with its glittering mosaics of the early ages, the obelisk standing fairest of any of those most imposing monuments of Rome, the view through the gates of the Campagna, on that side so richly strewn with ruins. The sun was setting, the crescent moon rising, the flower of the Italian youth were marshalling in that solemn place. They had been driven from every other spot where they had offered their hearts as bulwarks of Italian independence; in this last strong-hold they had sacrificed hecatombs of their best and bravest to that cause; they must now go or remain prisoners and slaves. *Where* go, they knew not; for except distant Hungary there is not now a spot which could receive them, or where they can act as honor commands. They had all put on the beautiful dress of the Garibaldi legion, the tunic of bright red cloth, the Greek cap, or else round hat with Puritan plume. Their long hair was blown back from resolute faces; all looked full of courage. They had counted the cost before they entered on this perilous struggle; they had weighed life and all its material advantages against liberty, and made their election; they turned not back, nor flinched, at this bitter crisis. I saw the wounded, all that could go, laden upon their baggage cars; some were already pale and fainting, still they wished to go. I saw many youths, born to rich inheritance, carrying in a handkerchief all their worldly goods. The women were ready; their eyes too were resolved, if sad. The wife of Garibaldi followed him on horseback. He himself was distinguished by the white tunic; his look was entirely that of a hero of the Middle Ages,— his face still young, for the excitements of his life, though so many, have all been youthful, and there is no fatigue upon his brow or cheek. Fall or stand, one sees him a man engaged in the career for which he is adapted by nature. He went upon the parapet, and looked upon the road with a spy-glass, and, no obstruction being in sight, he turned his face for a moment back upon Rome, then led the way through the gate. Hard was the heart, stony and seared the eye, that had no tear for that moment. Go fated, gallant band! and if God care not indeed for men as for the sparrows, most of ye go forth to perish. And Rome, anew the Niobe! Must she lose also these beautiful and brave, that promised her regeneration, and would have given it, but for the perfidy, the overpowering force, of the foreign intervention?

I know that many "respectable" gentlemen would be surprised to hear me speak in this way. Gentlemen who perform their "duties to society" by buying for themselves handsome clothes and furniture with the interest of their money, speak of Garibaldi and his men as "brigands" and "vagabonds." Such are they, doubtless, in the same sense as Jesus, Moses, and Eneas were. To me, men who can throw so lightly aside the ease of wealth, the joys of affection, for the sake of what they deem honor, in whatsoever form, are the "respectable." No doubt there are in these bands a number of men of lawless minds, and who follow this banner only because there is for them no other path. But the greater part are the noble youths who have fled from the Austrian conscription, or fly now from the renewal of the Papal suffocation, darkened by French protection.

As for the protectors, they entirely threw aside the mask, as it was always supposed they would, the moment they had possession of Rome. I do not know whether they were really so bewildered by their priestly counsellors as to imagine they would be well received in a city which they had bombarded, and where twelve hundred men were lying wounded by their assault. To say nothing of the justice or injustice of the matter, it could not be supposed that the Roman people, if it had any sense of dignity, would welcome them. I did not appear in the street, as I would not give any countenance to such a wrong; but an English lady, my friend, told me they seemed to look expectingly for the strong party of friends they had always pretended to have within the walls. The French officers looked up to the windows for ladies, and, she being the only one they saw, saluted her. She made no reply. They then passed into the Corso. Many were assembled, the softer Romans being unable to control a curiosity the Milanese would have disclaimed, but preserving an icy silence. In an evil hour, a foolish priest dared to break it by the cry of *Viva Pio Nono!*[2] The populace, roused to fury, rushed on him with their knives. He was much wounded; one or two others were killed in the rush. The people howled then, and hissed at the French, who, advancing their bayonets, and clearing the way before them, fortified themselves in the piazzas. Next day the French troops were marched to and fro through Rome, to inspire awe in the people; but it has only created a disgust amounting to loathing, to see that, with such an imposing force, and in great part fresh, the French were not ashamed to use bombs also, and kill women and children in their beds.

---

[2]Long Live the Pope! (Pius IX)

CHAPTER 5

Sarah J. Hale:
Godey's Lady's Book

Aside from resolute individuals like Anne Royall and Jane Swisshelm, most middle-class women in pre-Civil War America led lives restricted to the home and family. Although millions of women, both slaves and immigrant whites, labored unceasingly, the eyes of society saw only one image of womanhood: The lady, a wan, modest creature who reflected her husband's glory and encased her mind in a sentimentality as stifling as the corset in which she laced her body.

This myth of the lady and its attendant cult of domesticity, endorsed by clerical opinion, was disseminated in a new kind of sex-segregated journalism that developed during the period. More than twenty-five publications aimed at women were founded between 1806 and 1849 with women as editors or associate editors. Most, like the tearful novels aimed at women readers, reinforced the social proprieties limiting women to the home.

The most famous, *Godey's Lady's Book*, was founded in Philadelphia in 1830 by Louis A. Godey and edited for 40 years by Sarah Josepha Hale, the foremost woman journalist of her day. A New England widow who turned to journalism to support her five children, Mrs. Hale carefully stayed within the bounds of convention. Although she composed sermons on wifely duties, she labored valiantly to advance the position of women, believing them to be finer and purer than men. She also published stories and articles by a large number of women writers.

Sarah Hale supported higher education for women, campaigned to improve their nutrition and health in an era that romanticized female weakness, fought for retention of property rights by married women, pioneered for day nurseries and advocated that young women prepare to support themselves if, due to the death or incapability of male relatives, it became necessary. She argued that public school teaching, missionary work and medicine were particularly appropriate fields for women because of their superior sensibilities. However, she did not support woman suffrage.

Serving as editor until the age of ninety, she retired in 1877 and died the following year.

In the "Editors' Table" each month in *Godey's Lady's Book*, Sarah J. Hale expressed her own opinion on issues affecting women. The following editorial appeared in January, 1853.

EDITORS' TABLE

There is an old legend that the nineteenth century is to be the "Century of Woman."

A late English writer, commenting on this, says: "Whatever the wisdom or the foolishness of our forefathers may have meant by this, English women know but too well that, up to this time (1851), the middle of the century, it has not been theirs. Those who deny are perhaps even better aware of it than those who allow."

Now, we differ in opinion with this English writer. The century, thus far, has been marked as woman's above any or all preceding ages. Even in the times of chivalry, when men worshipped her charms, they had little respect for her intellect or her intelligence. The mass of men were ignorant; physical force, diplomatic cunning, and religious superstitions ruled the world. There was no organ of public opinion, by which woman as woman could be heard, or through which she could make her powers of mind apparent. And the writer we have quoted above acknowledges this, as he goes on to say—

"In no century, perhaps, has so much freedom, nay, opportunity, been given to woman to cultivate her powers, as best might seem to herself. Man leaves her room and space enough. She is no longer called pedantic, if her powers appear in conversation. The authoress is courted, not shunned. Accordingly, the intellectual development of English women has made extraordinary progress. But, as the human being does not move both feet at once, except he jumps, so, while the intellectual foot has made a step in advance, the practical foot has remained behind. Woman stands askew. Her education for action has not kept pace with her education for acquirement. The woman of the eighteenth century was, perhaps, happier, when practice and theory were on a par, than her more cultivated sister of the nineteenth. The latter wishes, but does not know how to do many things; the former, what she wished, at least that she could do.

"What then? Shall we have less theory? God forbid! We shall not work better for ignorance. Every increase of knowledge is a benefit, by showing us more of the ways of God. But it was for the increase of 'wisdom,' even more than of knowledge, that David prayed—for wisdom is the practical application of knowledge.

" 'Not what we know, but what we do, is our kingdom,' and woman, perhaps, feels that she has not found her kingdom."

No, woman has not yet attained her kingdom; but she is preparing for it. This intellectual education was a necessary preliminary; she could not do the work of an educator properly till she was herself educated. And this has been accomplished since the present century began. Woman is now prepared for a sphere of activity, and, in our country, this sphere is already opened. Within the last twenty-five years, the teacher's office in schools, as well as at home, has been passing into her hands. There are, probably, at this time, from sixty to one hundred thousand female teachers of public and private schools in the United States. Women are editors, authors, and artists, and a few have entered the arena—where their greatest honors as public benefactors are yet to be won—of medical science.

Now, let no reader imagine we are about setting up for "Woman's Rights." God has given her the care of humanity in its helplessness of infancy—in its sorrows and sicknesses. She should be educated as the Conservator of health, physical as well as morally—as the Preserver, Teacher, Inspirer.

The need of her aid is now felt and acknowledged by the wise and good men of our land. They call her to the Mission field. Since this century commenced, about twelve hundred American women have gone as missionaries to the heathen. Is not this a wonderful advance in her sphere? Since the days of the Apostles and the early fathers of the church, never has the helping power of woman in the church been thus permitted. Her office of Deaconess—instituted by the Apostles—had been nearly suppressed, till within this present century it is again revived, or reviving. Let us hope every Christian church will soon have its Deaconesses, to take care of the poor and sick of their own sex.

But the idea that seems to have met the most pressing need of the missionary and progressive spirit of the century is that of "FEMALE MEDICAL MISSIONARIES." This was first advanced in the "Lady's Book" of March last, and steadily advocated through the year.

But it is said, "Woman cannot go abroad to attend the sick—their domestic employment precludes them from practice. What shall they do, when they are called for and cannot go?" Just what the male doctor does when he is called for, and cannot go—stay at home. Just what everybody else does, when he is asked to do a thing and cannot—let it alone. "But the people will not employ them if you make them doctors." Very well, then, let them employ others. We don't expect people to employ those whom they do not choose to employ; and we are willing to say that, if woman never practices medicine, she would be amply repaid for studying it. Another says, "You will break up the medical profession, you will drive all the men out of it, and even those who are now in it will starve." They may as well starve as the women. They have as much physical strength, and as many hands and feet, to earn their daily bread, as women have, and, if they cannot cope with women in the medical profession, let them take an humble occupation, in which they can.

We admit that woman has her own sphere in which to act, as much as man. She is better calculated for some duties than for others, and we maintain that there are none, within the whole range of these duties, for which she could have been better designed, or more in her sphere of usefulness, than in this of medicine. Tell about this being the appropriate sphere of man, and his alone! With tenfold more plausibility and reason might we say, it is the appropriate sphere of woman, and hers alone. The order of nature—the constitution of families—the nature of human society—the earthly origin of the race—the commission of the child first to the care of woman—the delicacy of females—all these proclaim her fitness to be the good physician.

CHAPTER 6

Suffrage Newspapers:
The Revolution
Woman's Journal

It was not sexual bondage itself that turned a few outspoken women into the first feminists in the United States. When women abolitionists found their crusades against slavery hampered by sex discrimination, they revolted and demanded equality with men, including the right to vote. The delegates at the Seneca Falls convention of 1848 disagreed with the view that women ought to be kept legally inferior because they were thought to be mentally inferior to men. One of the prime organizers was Elizabeth Cady Stanton who soon teamed up with Susan B. Anthony in a half-century collaboration to improve women's status.

After the Civil War, Stanton and Anthony insisted that suffrage be extended to women as well as Negro men, and succeeded in securing the introduction of a woman's suffrage amendment. It did not pass, but while the two were campaigning for it in Kansas, they met a wealthy supporter, George Francis Train, who offered to back them in a weekly newspaper.

The Revolution was that paper. Published in New York, it began in January, 1868 and lasted two and one-half years. Anthony was the publisher and Stanton was a co-editor. The 16-page paper espoused easy divorce, condemned prostitution, and, among other positions, opposed the Fifteenth Amendment, contending that it should not pass giving the vote to Negro men without women also being included. Supporting the equal rights efforts of women on all fronts — in unions, professions, education, and organized religion — it made a spirited contribution to women's cause. Most of its editorials were written by Stanton and signed ECS.

The Revolution did not suit conservative supporters of the women's vote, including Lucy Stone, abolitionist and wife of another abolitionist, Henry Blackwell, both of whom felt strongly that suffrage campaigns for women and Negro men should be entirely separate. When in 1869 Stanton and Anthony organized the National Woman Suffrage Association limited to women, the Stone group established the American Woman Suffrage Association, open to men and representatives from "recognized" (or "respectable," that is, more moderate) suffrage organizations, and launched its own newspaper, the *Woman's Journal*, financed by a joint stock company and published in Boston.

The Stone Association garnered a majority of the nation's suffragists with a moderate platform giving priority to votes for Negro men and calling for women to work for the vote on the state and local levels, assuming that national suffrage would result eventually. Milder in tone than *The Revolution*, the *Woman's Journal* reported on local enfranchisement activities and served as the voice of middle-class professional and club women. Its success marked the demise of *The Revolution.*

In existence until 1914, the *Woman's Journal* was edited for most of its long life by Lucy Stone, Henry Blackwell and their daughter, Alice Stone Blackwell. Other distinguished writers contributed to it, including Julia Ward Howe, author of "Battle Hymn of the Republic," who wrote the newspaper's first editorial on its appearance, January 8, 1870.

An editorial by Elizabeth Cady Stanton from *The Revolution,* dated February 5, 1868 follows. It is paired with the "Salutatory" by Julia Ward Howe from the first issue of the *Woman's Journal*.

INFANTICIDE AND PROSTITUTION

Scarce a day passes but some of our daily journals take note of the fearful ravages on the race, made through the crimes of Infanticide and Prostitution.

For a quarter of a century sober, thinking women have warned this nation of these thick coming dangers and pointed to the only remedy, the education and enfranchisement of woman; but men have laughed them to scorn. Let those who have made the "strong-minded" women of this generation the target for the gibes and jeers of a heedless world repent now in sackcloth and ashes, for already they suffer the retribution of their folly at their own firesides, in their sad domestic relations. Wives sick, peevish, perverse, children deformed, blind, deaf, dumb and insane; daughters silly and wayward; sons waylaid at every corner of the streets and dragged down to the gates of death, by those whom God meant to be their saviors and support. Look at these things no longer as necessary afflictions, sent to wean us from earth as visitations from Providence; but as the direct results of the violation of immutable laws, which it was our duty to study and obey. In the midst of all these miseries, let us regard ourselves as guilty sinners and not helpless saints. God does not wink, even at the sins of ignorance.

We ask our editors who pen these startling statistics to give us their views of the remedy. We believe the cause of all these abuses lies in the degradation of women.

Strike the chains from your women; for as long as they are slaves to man's lust, man will be the slave of his own passion.

Wonder not that American women do everything in their power to avoid maternity; for, from false habits of life, dress, food and generations of disease and abominations, it is to them a period of sickness, lassitude, disgust, agony and death.

What man would walk up to the gallows if he could avoid it? And the most helpless aspect of this condition of things is that our Doctors of Divinity and medicine teach and believe that maternity and suffering are inseparable.

So long as the Bible, through the ignorance of its expounders, makes maternity a curse, and women, through ignorance of the science of life and health find it so, we need not wonder at the multiplication of these fearful statistics. Let us no longer weep, and whine, and pray over these abominations; but with an enlightened conscientiousness and religious earnestness, bring ourselves into line with God's just, merciful and wise laws. Let every thinking man make himself today a missionary in his own house. Regulate the diet, dress, exercise, health of your wives and daughters. Send them to Mrs. Plumb's gymnasium, Dr. Lewis's school, or Dr. Taylor's Swedish movement cure, to develop their muscular system, and to Kuczkowski to have the rhubarb, the sulphur, the mercury and "the sins of their fathers" (Exodus XX:5) soaked out of their brains.

ECS

SALUTATORY

The New Year had just stepped across its threshold, and after it, clinging closely to its skirts, comes our new enterprise. We begin the year's work with the year, hoping that both may prosper. We have begun many new years with this same vision of work and of usefulness, never quite realized. But the progress of time makes our tasks clearer to us, and we may say that never was work more joyous to us than that which at present stands ready to our hand.

The cultivation of wide and tender relations with the beings nearest to us in nature and sympathy, the removal of a thousand barriers of passion and prejudice, the leaping out of the whole heart of womanhood towards a new future, a future of freedom and of fullness — our prospectus shows us such things as these. To see them even in a dream is blessed, but these are of the prophetic dreams that enjoin their own fulfillment.

We who stand beside the cradle of this enterprise are not young in years. Our children are speedily preparing to take our place in the ranks of

society. Some of us have been looking thoughtfully towards the final sum-
mons, not because of ill health or infirmity, but because, after the establishment of our families, no great object intervened between ourselves and that
last consummation. But these young undertakings detain us in life. While
they need so much of care and of counsel, we cannot consent to death. And
this first year, at least, of our journal, we are determined to live through.

The classic *"plaudite omnes"* was looked for at the end of the drama.
Our *"adjurate omnes"* comes more properly at the beginning. "Call no man
happy till he is dead," said Solon, very wisely. But beginnings of life and
works are greeted with congratulation because they open up new hopes and
new chances. So we say to you, friends, that you may not indeed dare to
call us entirely fortunate until our work shall have done its work. But fortunate we are in being able to make a beginning, and in this good fortune we
ask you to rejoice with us. Be friendly to our babe. Inquire for it often,
and when you have good things to share, send us some of them. A newspaper, you know, is not clever for nothing. It eats up silver, and gold, and
brains. It is tended by tutelary devils, who also must eat. Be mindful of
this. The need and the hands willing to supply it being met and announced,
do not suffer the want of material support to hinder the two from a helpful
yoking together. So, help us, friends of men and women! Help us, you who
from your larger or lesser means reserve always a certain proportion for the
needs of humankind.

We must not promise too much, but we may promise that the trust
confided to us in the WOMAN'S JOURNAL shall be administered by us in
the interests of humanity, according to our best understanding of them. As
we claim admission to life in its largeness and universality, it will not become us to raise side issues and personal griefs. Too much labor lies before
us to allow us time for complaints and criminations, were such utterances
congenial to us. Our endeavor, which is to bring the feminine mind to bear
upon all that concerns the welfare of mankind, commands us to let the dead
past bury its dead. The wail of impotence becomes us no longer. We must
work as those who have power, for we have faith, and faith is power. We implore our sisters, of whatever kind or degree, to make common cause with
us, to lay down all partisan warfare and organize a peaceful Grand Army of
the Republic of Women. But we do not ask them to organize as against
men, but as against all that is pernicious to men and to women. Against su-
perstition, whether social or priestly, against idleness, whether aesthetic or
vicious, against oppression, whether of manly will or feminine caprice. Ours
is but a new manoeuvre, a fresh phalanx in the good fight of faith. In this
contest, the armor of Paul will become us, the shield and breastplate of
strong and shining virtue. And with one Scripture precept we will close our
salutation. With sisterly zeal and motherly vigilance, "Let brotherly love
continue."

J.W.H.

CHAPTER 7

Lippincott and Ames: Washington Correspondence

The Civil War enlarged opportunities for women in many areas including journalism. Women left the confines of their homes to serve as nurses, to organize relief activities and to teach the newly-freed slaves. When the war ended, they continued their activities in teaching, welfare work and education.

In the field of journalism, one group of women established national reputations as Washington correspondents, often using pen names, as was common in those days, to sign their contributions to leading publications. Coming from abolitionist backgrounds, they defended the Negro and civil rights and attacked the excesses of Gilded Age politics. But as soon as there was a sizable number of women Washington correspondents, they were barred from the Capitol press galleries.

In 1879 the Congressional Directory listed 20 women correspondents entitled to gallery privileges, about 12 per cent of the total of 166 correspondents. Within two years after the rules change that excluded the women and others not considered "bona fide" journalists from the galleries, women correspondents began increasingly to be relegated to society gossip instead of covering politics.

Two of the most outstanding of the early women correspondents were Mary Clemmer Ames, who wrote for *The Independent* in New York, an influential weekly, and Sara Clarke Lippincott, who wrote as "Grace Greenwood" for the *New York Times* in the 1870's. Others were Emily Edson Briggs, the "Olivia" of the *Philadelphia Press,* and Mary Abigail Dodge, whose pen name was "Gail Hamilton," of the *New York Tribune.*

The life of Mary Clemmer Ames, said to be the highest-paid newspaperwoman of her day, illustrated the cultural conflict besetting a woman living in the Victorian age and trying to maintain her image as a "respectable home-loving lady" at the same time as she climbed to the top of a competitive masculine occupation. A nurse in Union hospitals during the war, Mary Ames turned to a literary career when the war ended and her marriage to a Methodist minister failed.

Launching her first "Woman's Letter from Washington," in the *Independent* in 1866, she continued this highly-acclaimed column until her death in 1884 at the age of fifty-three. Yet, shortly after she began it, she told her readers that fame held no appeal to her as a refined woman who modestly shrank from public notice and preferred the domestic scene to the political arena. She justified her journalistic career, however, by holding that women writers had a moral duty to purify politics even if their efforts brought unwelcome attention.

From 1869 to 1872, she wrote for the *Brooklyn Daily Union* as well as the *Independent*, so impressing Henry C. Bowen, publisher of both, that he paid her a record $5,000 a year. A foe of the scandal-ridden Grant administration, she defended the press against attacks from those exposed as corrupt. Following her divorce, she wrote under her maiden name, Clemmer, which she continued to use after her marriage to Washington journalist Edmund Hudson.

Sara Clarke Lippincott first came to Washington as a young woman before the Civil War and worked as an assistant editor on an abolition newspaper, *The National Era*. As "Grace Greenwood," she was one of a number of women writers in the 1850's who gained success under a floral pseudonym to suit the era of sentimental literature.

Returning to the capital following a successful career as a writer of children's books and lecturer on patriotic themes, she wrote a series of columns for the *New York Times* from 1873 until 1878. In her columns, Grace Greenwood attacked corruption, supported the cause of women government workers and was appalled by the willingness of the Hayes administration to permit the return of white supremacy in the South.

A supporter of woman suffrage, she opposed divorce even though her own marriage proved tragic. Her husband, Leander Lippincott, was indicted in a conspiracy to file false land claims and disappeared in 1878 while she was traveling abroad to provide her only child, a daughter, with a musical education. A prolific author of newspaper and magazine articles, she continued to write almost up to the day of her death in New Rochelle, New York, at the age of eighty.

Excerpts from two of Sara Clarke Lippincott's "Grace Greenwood" columns written for the *New York Times* from Washington are reprinted here. One dates from 1873 and the other, 1877. Accompanying them is an excerpt from Mary Clemmer's "A Woman's Letter from Washington" in *The Independent*, March 7, 1878.

WASHINGTON NOTES

By Grace Greenwood

Tuesday, Jan. 20, 1873

A newspaper paragraph tells me that the late earthquake in Idaho lifted one man "two feet into the air." The feelings of that poor man can be readily realized by every member of Congress implicated in this unfortunate dis-Credit Mobilier. The disclosure seems to come to them as a sudden shock — to surprise and bewilder them — a fact which to my mind is a proof that they were, none of them, in the first place, consciously and perversely dishonest in the transaction. But the absolute ignorance, in some cases, of the fact of owning stock of this sort at all is a singular feature of the case. What poor heads for business these patriots and statesmen have! How forgetful and inaccurate are they in pecuniary matters. Why, women could scarcely do any worse. I am not going to preach a lay-sermon to our unfortunate brothers who have so suddenly passed from the warm sunshine of wordly favor into the cold shadow of suspicion and obloquy. In the discredited word of some of them, I have a faith as tenacious as that of the little boy who in a dispute with his sister exclaimed, "It's true, for ma said so; and if ma says it's so, it's so, if it ain' so." I am sorry for them all, but I can only say "the pity of it," and hope for a good deliverance. One thing, however, has forcibly struck me, as it doubtless has many others: it is that those have fared best in this business who have been the most daring and outspoken. Next to blamelessness is fearlessness. Next to absolute moral purity is moral courage. We know there can be courage without purity, but it is difficult to believe there can be purity without courage. I like to see a man face the music, even if it play the "Death March," or worse, the "Rogue's March." As politic as plucky were the honorable gentlemen who simply said, "Yes, I took some of the stock, and am only sorry I had not the means to take more."

For them the storm has blown over. The world may set them down as defiant and morally obtuse, but it can neither pity nor laugh at them. Open confession is good for the soul, but it must be of the prompt, unhesitating sort. Neither gracious nor efficacious is a late, reluctant avowal, like that of the Yankee deacon under church discipline, who obstinately fought the charge, prevaricated and doubled on his tracks till the close of his trial, then rose, in the last ditch of his pew, and said, "Brethren, if you will have it so, I plead guilty. I own up, for I don't think it is the part of a good Christian to hold out when a thing is fairly proved agin him."

But if a tithe of what is charged is true, surely something is out of joint; there must be serious deficiencies in pay and privileges, if any of our faithful servants in Congress "needs must play such pranks as these." Let the country look to it that they be no more so sorely tempted. The proposition to increase their salaries is most timely. Do that, and double their mileage, conserve the franking privilege, and make their railroad passes transferable, so that they can turn a penny now and then by disposing of them. Let us, the people, make any sacrifice to secure moral immunity to these representative men, who dwell in "a city set on a hill, which cannot be hid" — who are lights set in the great brazen candlesticks of the nation. To be able to meet their needs, let a deaf ear be once more turned to the demand of the poor clerks of the departments for an increase of salary; refuse yet again the humble petition of the women for equal pay for equal services. *They* are used to refusal, to waiting, to disappointments — as well used as is the *anquilla* to being skinned or the *astacus* to being boiled. Let us economize in every way, whatever it may cost us; let us do without statues to our dead heroes, the only heroes we are sure of — though no grist goes to the Mills, *pere et fils*, and more than one lady sculptor models in vain, and sits herself like Patience on a monument smiling at the Library Committee; let us sell the marble of the Washington Monument; let us dismiss the Board of Public Works. Only make Congress thoroughly comfortable, and all these good things shall be added. While this beloved body is in its present impecunious and unprotected state, exposed to the seductive wiles of shrewd men of the world and heartless adventurers, there can be no peace or security, political or moral, for any of us.

A stern Democratic statesman said to me the other day, "The disgrace of this transaction, Madam, will cling to the descendants of these men for generations." I shuddered, but disposed, as I always am, to look on the bright side of things, replied, "Ah, no; let us hope that in those times there will be so much bigger jobs of the sort, more undeniable and disreputable bargains and sales, that this will sink into insignificance and be forgotten." Progress is the law of the universe. I doubt not that they had their modest little Credit Mobilier affairs in the time of Jefferson and the elder Adams. Talleyrand, that Solomon of profane history, says: "The present age has produced a great many new things, but not a new mankind."

I, as a woman, am disposed to be especially charitable. If I had been born to regard the world as "mine oyster," to believe money and power my right, as one of the irresponsible lords of creation — if I had been a poor struggling politician, an underpaid patriot voting and office-seeking, and going to Congress for a century or so, I might thus have been tempted, might thus have succumbed — in a sort of a way — been subsidized and Mobilier-ized without knowing it. Let us women not "think of ourselves more highly than we ought to think," but be humble and thankful. The pious Mohammedan father says to his son, while pointing to the profane Frank, "But for the mercy of God, thou mightest have been as one of these."

THE NEW ORDER OF THINGS

From Our Special Correspondent

WASHINGTON, Tuesday, July 3, 1877

Many times during the past six months I have been called to account in various quarters for my political utterances, denominated "heresies" and "vagaries." Sometimes I have been strangely misunderstood, but often too well understood for the pleasure of my critics, especially of the reformed Republican school. I have been sharply rebuked by my brothers, as an indiscreet sister — "speaking out in meeting," and revealing the secrets of the vestry, the deacons, the elders, and holy men generally. I have been roughly reminded that I was a woman, and told that I ought to be sternly remanded by public opinion to woman's proper sphere, where the eternal unbaked pudding and the immemorial unattached shirt-button await my attention. That same sphere is a good one to fall back upon. I can "rastle" with cooking and sewing as well as any of my gentler sisters, but just at present I confess I prefer serving up a spicy hash of Southern Democratic sentiment to concocting a pudding, and pricking with my pen "the bubble reputation" of political charlatans to puncturing innocent muslin with my needle. I hear I am accused of "making war on the civil service reform." I deny the charge. I attack only the poor pretense, the idle parade, the misleading semblance of reform. Of the great system of moral and political reform in Government service, which is the text of so many eloquent leaders, which is to so many political enthusiasts "the substance of things hoped for, and the evidence of things not seen," we really know little here, where it is popularly supposed to be making such magnificent headway — and perhaps is. It works out of sight in the deeps of Cabinet councils and departmental negotiations and diplomacies — "caverns measureless to men."

A WOMAN'S LETTER FROM WASHINGTON

By Mary Clemmer

I do not presume to say that all-night sessions are never necessary. 'Tis a pity that, if ever necessary, they are equally demoralizing. It is a hard strain, even on a man's nerves (and, wonderful to tell, some men have nerves), to sit for seventeen consecutive hours in the dulling, deadening atmosphere of the Senate. Instead of doing the sensible thing, as we may be sure nine out of ten common-sense women would do — proceed to get a comfortable dinner, at a reasonable hour — through all the hours they fill their unfortunate stomachs with odds and ends of tobacco, hard apples, etc., washed down by brandy, whisky, and wine, till they find themselves in a sufficiently unhappy and perverted condition of body and soul to enable them to draw up a code of laws for the lower Pandemonium. They have only to visit the cloak-room a sufficient number of times to be, in common parlance, "ready for anything." They pull off their boots, take off their coats, stretch themselves at full length in their stocking-feet on the sofas; or they strut, swagger, and reel about the floor, lean over their desks, and repeat the dubious stories of the cloak-room to their comrades, or, filled with "fight," they mumble, blubber, and bluster in vain attempt to utter one coherent sentence. The majority of the senators do none of these things. I would gladly give the names of many who would not, were it not for the shame of their comrades. Whatever the strain, there are men who meet it patiently, faithfully, honorably, like the gentlemen that they are. But, if twelve senators are drunk, and act accordingly, the number is quite sufficient to cast disrepute upon the entire Senate. When the story is told in the public journals, the heading is not "Twelve Senators Drunk." It is "The Senate on a Drunk." This is a heading that I have read in one of the leading journals of the land. I am so utterly imbued with the futility of attempting to make the crooked straight that my impulse was not to mention the matter. The Capital teems with tales of "the glorious past," of Daniel Webster's "drunks," of the toddies and tantrums of many other illustrious men. Why take up the burden of the old sullied strain and proclaim to the land? Still the Senate gets drunk. Though women struggle to the van, shutting up grog-shops, striving, with voices full of tears, with these very senators; still they get drunk, and the world is no better than it used to be. This was the instinctive feeling. I was ashamed for these men, who had such reason to be ashamed of themselves, and, for the sake of the women who loved them, did not want to mention their names. Nor do I now. I refer to the fact already disgracefully public, because, in spite of it, after all, on the whole, I do believe the world to be better than it used to be. In Daniel Webster's day, if the entire Senate had lain drunk under its desks, it would not have sent the thrill of disapprobation, disgust, and shame through the land which moves it now it knows that twelve or fifteen senators were drunk enough in public convocation to make asses of themselves. To-day not only the many senators who did not drink at all, but the drunkards themselves, are ashamed as they recall that night. One generation ago it was quite the common thing. To-day no one is more certain than the participants that such a scene cannot be repeated with impunity; that, if it comes, it will be followed not more surely by disgrace than by defeat.

The opposite was true once. But now people in power are no longer afraid to set the seal of their disapprobation upon promiscuous liquor-drinking. This is true at the White House. It is true also of Speaker Randall, who does not even offer it to his guests. There are Cabinet ministers, also, who do not provide liquors at their public entertainments. These facts mark a new and higher era in official example. It is but the feeling of the masses reaching a climax. The spirit of the people is turned against the sum of horrors entailed by liquor-drinking. The Senate has yet to set the seal of its power on this damning traffic; the seal of its example on tippling and drunkenness. Think of the inspired tones, the tender eloquence of Frances Willard poured in vain on these drunken legislators, as it was, not two weeks ago! Think of the thousands of temperance petitions fluttering through the length of the land into this Senate Chamber, only to drop unheeded from senatorial hands! How could it be otherwise? one asked in that night session, as he counted thirty-five brandy-bottles with empty tumblers in one cloakroom, as he gazed upon the "spreads" set out in the Sergeant-at-Arms's room, as he gazed at a senator vomiting over the costly furniture of the Secretary's room, and at other senators who seemed to be mounting the air, or pawing the ground, or lying back in their seats telling ribald stories to shouting men who were perfectly sober. There was one senator, of long experience and national repute, so drunk he could not stand unsupported at his desk. Even his faithful handkerchief, which almost never fails him, dropped from his hand. Two men, one on either side, held him up, prompting him to utter his "amendment," which he slowly mumbled out, amid shrieks of laughter. At last he sank down in a drunken stupor. His amendment was voted down; when he awoke, arose, and repeated it, amid the wildest mirth of the Senate, who gathered around him almost crazy with merriment. In the middle aisle stood Blaine, perfectly sober, shaking his finger and shouting at a third senator, who bears an honored name in a great state, who a moment later staggered to the cloak-room, helped on by beneficient chairs, that saved him from the floor, and who only reached a sofa to sink at once into a drunken sleep, where he slept, while two feet away another senator thundered at him simple and easy questions, which he was too drunk even to hear. When he awoke, at last, another senator, as drunk as he was, staggered up in front of him, clapping both uncertain hands upon his shoulder; and the two stood thus wavering together like two swinging pendulums, gazing and muttering at each other in the most maudlin manner. The ludicrous picture was too much for the most serious, and both gallery and Senate leaned back and shouted aloud with amusement. There was another senator, who has a reputation for refinement of dress and manner. His personal friends assure me that he "is as sensitive as a woman"; which is unfortunate as he insists on the masculine prerogative of getting "tight." This night he perambulated the Senate Chamber as if "his feet were caught in a skein of sewing silk," and he, in the effort to disentangle them, was disjointing at the knees, with a terrific bump threatening to annihilate the back of his curly head. His affections were of such a lively character that he insisted on hugging and kissing every senator whom he fell against. He was also burdened with a wild desire to speak. His best friend could not keep him still. He broke in, with unintelligible sentences, upon every speaker, and when he attempted to vote fell over his desk.

All this, and a thousand deal more, went on in the Senate Chamber, with the Senate of the United States in full session. With all these senatorial bacchanals afloat, not even sixty sober senators could redeem the aspect of the legislative chamber or make it look other than a convocation of men engaged in the wildest spree.

There was not a senator from New York nor from New England who was intoxicated. There were many senators from the West and from the South who were perfectly sober. Yet the liquor lunatics were all from the South and the West. The masculinity in public life needs a thorough purging of some kind. Making utter exception of perfectly honorable men, whom I know and honor, I am still profoundly impressed with the low tone of public morality and by the utter necessity of its purifying and uplifting. A coarseness which amounts to filthiness always and to brutality often is everywhere apparent in public places. You see it even in the huge spittoons, which should be hung around the neck, as they set at the feet of every doorkeeper, e' en of the Ladies' Gallery. A lady speaks to one of these men, and until he disburdens his jaws and empties his mouth of a nasty squid, which he does before her face, he cannot even answer her! As masculine muscle still prevents my casting my vote on this subject, I demand (with not a tear in my voice) that no man who makes a public use of tobacco shall ever be appointed to wait upon American ladies in the Capitol. If senators choose to get drunk and to disport upon the Senate floor as buffoons, let not the door of the upper gallery, through which ladies pass, to behold them, be defiled even by tobacco. Let the drunkenness and the nastiness be all shut below, while it is given up to men. Do you wonder that the senators shrank so utterly from the invasion of the Senate Chamber by women? The best senators think that politics are not high enough for women. They show such a very decided fondness for them themselves that they continue to monopolize them entirely; but they are not good enough for "my wife." "Do you think I could bear to see my wife in such a place as the Senate Chamber was on Friday night?" said a senator, who has been besieged by suffrage women for the past month, in pathetic tones. "No! no!" with a mournful shake of the head. "Politics are not high enough for women." My friend is utterly sincere. There are many other senators, who never get drunk, who are equally so. Nevertheless, I pass through the "thinness" of their argument as if it had not fell upon me. It is too light for me even to feel its touch. You are honorable, fine-minded men. I admire you considerably; but I don't mind you, not I! You are no freer from nonsense than your brethren are from cant. You know a thing or two — here and there a language, and considerable about law. You are perfectly certain what you want, and what you don't want; but, bless me, you don't know half as much as you think you do. Some of the subtle forces forcing the human race up the path of progression are beyond your ken. Remember, brother, you abide on the plane of tobacco-juice, brandy-bottles, and doubtful stories. They are not yours, you may not tell them; but you live where they are, so you must not take on airs to me. You can't awe me, simply because you are a man. You can arouse my reverence only through exalted qualities. Greatness never assumes. Greatness never says: "I am great; thou art small." Greatness says: "Mine is the human nature; so, too, is thine. Inspire me. I will not hinder thee. Freer by nature than thou, I will not add the smallest weight to thy lifting hands. Use as I use the great gift of human life, according to thine impulse and thy power. What am I, to assume to dictate to thee?" The other sort of senator, who turns his back on woman in politics— save as she appears there in the lobby, or in worse places — is the senator who gets drunk, who wants the brandy-bottles, the "spreads" in the Sergeant-at-Arms's room, the sprees, the dirty stories, all to himself. In such flights an elegant lady might be in the way, you know. When you falteringly say "It would be degrading to the lady herself," I am constrained to answer: "That is all bosh!" A thousand doorkeepers more than I already encounter, with spittoons around their necks, or ten thousand drunken senators, making gyrations to the invisible, could not degrade me an atom, nor any lady. I should immediately proceed to help make a law that would keep the senators sober or keep them at home, and the tobacco-imbibing doorkeepers would suddenly grow invisible. They should certainly provide for their numerous small children and serve their country outside of its Capitol. A humiliating sight, and so humiliating that I shall not witness it again, is that of women pleading, begging of such men for that political equality, which no company of men will ever grant; which, when it comes, as come it will, must come through that greater development and education of men, which can come only by women. When women as a sex are great enough to make men more humble as men, great enough to fill any position to which they aspire, a few women will not have to plead. Let petitions to Congress from tens of thousands of women continue to come in to Congress. In spite of Father Christiancy, who don't want them to come, yet says "he will vote for woman suffrage when the majority want it," let them continue to come, that he may not be left in ignorance of that "majority"; and, at dignified intervals, let a great woman make a great speech, to back the petitions. But don't use the weapons of weakness. For mercy's sake, don't "gad-fly" the men. The Lord never made a man that will not run from that sort of operation; and who can blame him? The masculine creature has an instinctive aversion to being nagged. And I, who have an equal compassion for the weaknesses of both sides of humanity, for one, don't want him nagged. His lovely neighbor, who may wear to his delight the rose of womanhood for him, or be a jabbing thorn stuck in his side, will never make out much in her own behalf, while his muscles unfortunately continue tougher than hers, if she persists in irritating him in any way. Even his tremendous "judgment" will go under if you make him "mad." And as for you and your "cause," it is lost the moment you make yourself ridiculous. That moment he ensconces himself on the throne of his masculine prerogative, into which the ridiculous finds it not impossible to enter. But never mind. If through your weakness he is on that throne, your beating against it will only be the wave breaking on the rock. So don't appoint "female prayer-meetings" in the Senate lobby; and, when you have said one brave, broad, honest say, *say no more*, but go home and stay there. It weakens your influence, it harms your cause to pursue senators and representatives, as they have been pursued for the last month. Thoughtful men will not forget the heroic utterances of Elizabeth Cady Stanton; Dr. Thompson, of Oregon; Mrs. Lawrence, of Massachusetts; and other ladies who addressed the Senate Committee of Privileges and Elections, in January.

* * *

As, for the first time this winter, I have written slightly of woman suffrage, letters are coming in to me addressing me concerning "My Cause." Let me assure my friends that I have no "cause" but the cause of human nature. I simply believe in the equality of humanity; that every creature God has made has an equal right to make the most and the best of itself, of all its powers; and that in the struggles of growth it should not be hindered in the slightest by law, by so-called religion, nor by human selfishness.

I do not care more for the rights of women than for the rights of men. If I speak more tenderly of women, it is because ages of physical servitude have put them at such great disadvantage. We lean toward the worsted side — the side weakened by suffering. But a woman should be femininely strong, as a man should be masculinely brave. "Superior to her sex" is a phrase that should be blotted from English speech. Because I believe in the future of the human race, I believe in the growth, the perfect development, the emancipation of woman, for the sake of the whole.

Washington, D.C., Feb. 27, 1878

CHAPTER 8

The Journalist:
Black writers
"The Newspaper Woman"

In 1870, the first year in which the U. S. Census listed journalists by sex, only 35 of the reported total of 5,286 were women. By 1880 the number had increased to 288 out of 12,308 persons, and by 1900 to 2,193 out of a total of 30,098. These statistics, however, listed only those who made their living solely from journalism, omitting many who contributed editorial content on a regular basis but were not considered full-time employees.

The Journalist, a trade publication, estimated in 1886 that 500 women worked regularly on the editorial side of American newspapers while two years later it estimated there were 200 on New York newspapers alone. In 1889 the weekly publication devoted an entire issue to women journalists, including biographical sketches of 50 individuals, 10 of whom were Black, representing all geographical areas of the country. In praising their achievements, the editor noted that all women journalists were still "true women" even though they supported themselves by wielding a pencil instead of a needle to sew on buttons for the "lords of creation." Many of the Black women mentioned sold articles to both Black and white publications.

Of the Black group, Ida Wells, later Ida Wells-Barnett, achieved the most distinguished career. Born to slave parents, she called for equal rights for her race; she brought a test case in Memphis that challenged segregated railroad cars, and she criticized the inadequate Memphis schools for Negroes. When this latter act caused the loss of her job as a teacher in Memphis, she became an owner of the *Memphis Free Speech* and devoted herself to her journalistic career.

After three of her friends were lynched in 1892, she wrote eloquent editorials against the crime of lynching. Her newspaper office was destroy- a result, and she moved to New York to work for the *New York*

Age and continued to write editorials against lynching. She founded both Negro women's clubs and anti-lynching societies and lectured widely in the United States and abroad. Following her marriage in 1895 to Ferdinand L. Barnett, lawyer and editor, she lived in Chicago and published several newspapers up to her death in 1931.

In spite of the success which *The Journalist* attributed to the 50 woman journalists, it also acknowledged — in an editorial in the same issue written by Flora McDonald, herself a newspaperwoman — that women reporters could not hope to be treated equally with men.

Reprinted here is the section titled "Some Female Writers of the Negro Race," written by Lucy Wilmot Smith in *The Journalist,* January 26, 1889. It is followed by the Flora McDonald editorial entitled "The Newspaper Woman: One Side of the Question."

SOME FEMALE WRITERS OF THE NEGRO RACE

The Negro woman's history is marvelously strange and pathetic. Unlike that of other races, her mental, moral, and physical status has not found a place in the archives of public libraries. From the womb of the future must come that poet or author to glorify her womanhood by idealizing the various phases of her character, by digging from the past, examples of faithfulness and sympathy, endurance and self-sacrifice and displaying the achievements which were brightened by friction. Born and bred under both the hindrances of slavery and limitations of her sex, the mothers of the race have kept pace with the fathers. They stand at the head of cultured, educated families whose daughters clash arms with the sons. The educated Negro woman occupies vantage ground over the Caucasian woman of America, in that the former has had to contest with her brother every inch of the ground for recognition; the Negro man, having had his sister by his side on plantations and in rice swamps, keeps her there, now that he moves in other spheres. As she wins laurels he accords her the royal crown. This is especially true in journalism. Doors opened before we knock, and as well equipped young women emerge from the class-room the brotherhood of the race, men whose own energies have been repressed and distorted by the interposition of circumstances, give them opportunities to prove themselves; and right well are they doing this by voice and pen. On matters pertaining to women and the race, there is no better author among our female writers than

MRS. N.F. MOSSELL. — Her style is clear, compact and convincing. Seven years teaching in Camden, N.J. and Philadelphia, her present home, and the solid reading matter, viz.: The Bible, "Paradise Lost," The Atlantic Monthly and The Public Ledger, which was her daily food while under her father's roof, gave her a deep insight into human nature, and the clear mode of expression which makes her articles so valuable to the press. Her career began many years ago, when Bishop Tanner — then editor of The Christian Recorder — was attracted by an essay on "Influence" which he requested for publication. Short stories followed, and from then to the present, she has been engaged constantly on race journals. "The Woman's Department" of the New York Freeman was edited by her with much tact and The Philadelphia Echo is always more readable when containing something from her pen. For three yeears she has been employed on the Philadelphia Times, Independent and Philadelphia Press Republican, following the particular lines of race literature and the "Woman's Question." Mrs. Mossell's experience in journalism is that editors are among the most patient of men; that the rejection of an article by no means proves that it is a failure; that sex is no bar to any line of literary work; that by speaking for themselves women can give the truth about themselves and thereby inspire the confidence of the people. Besides newspaper work her home life is a busy one, assisting her husband, a prominent physician of Philadlephia, whose own literary life has been an incentive to her. Spare moments are given to the completion of a book, on a race question, which will soon be launched on the current of thought and society.

MRS. LUCRETIA NEWMAN-COLEMAN is a writer of rare ability. Discriminating and scholarly, she possesses to a high degree the poetic temperament and has acquired great facility in verse. Her last poem, "Lucile of Montana," ran through several numbers of the magazine Our Women and Children, and is full of ardor, eloquence and noble thought. Mrs. Coleman has contributed special scientific articles to the A. M. E. Review and other journals, which were rich in minute comparisons, philosophic terms and scientific principles. She is a writer more for scholars than for the people. A novel entitled "Poor Ben," which is the epitome of the life of a prominent A. M. E. Bishop, is pronounced an excellent production. Mrs. Coleman is an accomplished woman and well prepared for a literary life. She was born in Dresden, Ontario, went with her missionary father to the West Indies where he labored a number of years, thence to Cincinnati, O., where he was pastor of a church, and after his death she went with her mother to Appleton, Wisconsin, to take advantage of educational facilities. After graduating from the scientific course of Lawrence University, she devoted her time to literary pursuits, and now ranks with the most painstaking writers.

MISS IDA B. WELLS, (IOLA), has been called the "Princess of the Press," and she has earned the title. No writer, the male fraternity not excepted, has been more extensively quoted; none have struck harder blows at the wrongs and weakness of the race. T. T. Fortune (probably the "Prince" of the Negro press) wrote after meeting her at the Democratic Conference in Indianapolis: "She has become famous as one of the few of our women who handle a goose-quill with diamond point as easily as any man in the newspaper work. If Iola was a man, she would be a humming independent in politics. She has plenty of nerve and is as sharp as a steel trap."

Miss Wells' readers are equally divided between the sexes. She reaches the men by dealing with the political aspect of the race question, and the women, she meets around the fireside. She is an inspiration to the young writers and her success has lent an impetus to their ambition. When the National Press Convention, of which she was Assistant Secretary, met in Louisville she read a splendidly written paper on "Women in Journalism; or How I Would Edit." By the way, it is her ambition to edit a paper. She believes that there is no agency so potent as the press in reaching and elevating a people. Her contributions are distributed among the leading race journals. She made her debut with the Living Way, Memphis, Tenn., and has since written for The New York Age, Detroit Plaindealer, Indianapolis World, Gate City Press, Mo., Little Rock Sun, American Baptist, Ky., Memphis Watchman, Chattanooga Justice, Christian Index and Fisk University Herald, Tenn., Our Women and Children Magazine, Ky., and the Memphis papers, weeklies and dailies. Miss Wells has attained much success as teacher in the public schools of the last named place.

MRS. W. E. MATHEWS (VICTORIA EARLE). — Ten years ago "Victoria Earle" began taking advantage of opportunities offered for acting as "sub" for reporters employed by many of the great dailies. She has reported for the New York Times, Herald, Mail and Express, Sunday Mercury, The Earth, The Phonograpic World, and is now New York correspondent to the National Leader, D.C., The Detroit Plaindealer, and the Southern Christian Recorder. Under various *nom de plume* she has written for the Boston Advocate, Washington Bee, Richmond Planet, Catholic Tribune, Cleveland Gazette, New York Age, New York Globe, and the New York Enterprise, besides editing three special departments. Reportorial work is her forte, yet her success in story writing has been great. She contributes to the story department of Waverley Magazine, The New York Weekly and Family Story Paper. "Victoria Earle" has written much; her dialect tid-bits for the Associated Press are much in demand. She has ready several stories which will appear in one volume, and is also preparing a series of historical textbooks which will aim to develop a race pride in our youth. She is a member of the Women's National Press Association and no writer of the race is kept busier.

MISS MARY V. COOK (Grace Ermine). — Whatever honors have come to Miss Cook are the results of persevering industry. She has edited the Woman's Department of the American Baptist, Ky., and the Educational Department of Our Women and Children in such a manner as to attract much attention to them. Her writings are lucid and logical and of such a character as will stand the test of time. Aside from journalistic work her life is a busy one. She has appeared on the platform of several national gatherings and her papers for research, elegance of diction and sound reasoning were superior. She holds the professorship of Latin at the State University, her Alma Mater, yet, however great her mental ability, it is overmatched by her character. Her life is the chrystalization of womanly qualities. She moves her associates by a mighty power of sympathy which permeates her writings. She is a good news gatherer and is much quoted, is a native of Bowling Green, Ky., where her mother, a generous hearted woman who sympathizes with her aspirations, still lives. Miss Cook is interested in all questions which affect the race.

In the mild countenance of MRS. AMEILIA E. JOHNSON can be read the love and tenderness for children which was demonstrated last year by the publication of The Ivy, an eight-page journal devoted especially to the interests of our youth. It was a good paper filled with original stories and poems and information concerning the doings of the race. Mrs. Johnson is keen, imaginative and critical, story writing is her forte. It is a part of her nature to weave her thoughts into pleasing imagery. Even when a child she would follow the scratches on her desk with a pencil and tell wonderful stories of them to her seatmate. She has written many of them at different times and is now engaged in writing a story book to be used in Sunday-school libraries. Many short poems from her pen find snug resting places in corners of weeklies. There is a vein of wit and humor in her sayings – a pith and transparency which makes her articles extremely readable. Of all the writers before the public none possesses in a higher degree the elements of a skillful critic. She has contributed to the Baptist Messenger, Md., The American Baptist, Ky., and Our Women and Children magazine. Mrs. Johnson was educated in Canada – taking a thorough French course – and has taught both French and English branches in Baltimore, her present home.

LILLIAN ALBERTA LEWIS (BERT ISLEW). – Those who know much about the newspapers of the race, know something of Bert Islew's Budget of Gossip in the spicy "They Say Column" of the Boston Advocate. Bright, witty, sparkling, one would not think Bert Islew's career antedates only three years and that she was barely twenty when she caught the public ear. The early atmosphere she breathed may have developed a public spirit-edness. Was born in the home of Hon. Lewis Hayden, that good man whose name is closely associated with the Crispus Attucks monument. When but thirteen years old and in the graduating class of the Bowdoin Grammar school she entered a prize essay contest and carried off the third prize, although the other contestants were older High School pupils and graduates. This fired her ambition, and soon after graduation she wrote a novel entitled, "Idalene Van Therese," which, for lack of means is unpublished. Then came her successful career with the Advocate. In addition to her newspaper work, she has for several years been the private stenographer and secretary to the widely known Max Eliot, of the Boston Herald. This position calls for proficiency; and Bert Islew's record for taking down copy verbatim is among the highest in New England. Then, too, her position in the Herald office calls for special articles and reportorial work which she does creditably. She is recognized in all circles for her ability, and works side by side with editors and reporters without an iota of distinction being made.

To the ready pen of **MISS MARY E. BRITTON (MEB.)** is due many of the reformatory measures which have given the race equal facilities on railroads in Kentucky. The energy and resolute vim of her character is traced in her writings, especially when advocating woman's suffrage and the same moral standard for both sexes. She has studied language from the standard English and American authors and her diction is remarkably chaste. Miss Britton was editor of the "Woman's Column" of the Lexington Herald, contributes special articles to the Courant — the Kentucky educational journal — the Cleveland Gazette, The American Catholic Tribune, the Indianapolis World and Our Women and Children magazine. Her own ambition to excel prompts her to inspire others and nearly all her articles have this and was exhibited in those written for The Ivy, the children's paper. The local papers of Lexington, Ky., her home, and the Cincinnati Commercial have published and commented on her articles.

MISS IONE E. WOOD. — There is a dash of freshness, a breezyness in Miss Wood's writings, a clear, decided ring which will yet be heard in louder tones. She has very pronounced views on total abstinence and is an enthusiastic member of the Woman's National Suffrage Association. She contributed several stories to The Ivy and now edits the Temperance Department of Our Women and Children magazine. Miss Wood will make a clever reporter. She is now tutor in Greek in the Kentucky State University.

MISS KATIE D. CHAPMAN sends from her far away Dakota home, spritely poems and other contributions to racial journals. She is only eighteen, but the public is becoming familiar with her bright thoughts and unique expressions. She has read much and will write much. Her contributions have appeared principally in The Christian Recorder and Our Women and Children. Her ambition was stirred when but five years old by receiving a book as reward for committing a poem. She will devote her talent to juvenile literature.

OCCASIONAL CONTRIBUTORS. — Among those who do special work and contribute valuable articles to weeklies and monthlies are Mesdames Francis E. W. Harper and L. F. Grimke, Philadelphia, Cora C. Calhoun, former editor of the Woman's Department in the Chattanooga Justice; Olive B. Clanton, New Orleans; Lavinia E. Sneed, Ky.; Josephine Turpin Washington, Selma; Misses Georgia M. DeBaptiste, Ill.; Julia K. Mason, D.C.; Alice Henderson, Ark.; and Meta Pelham, one of the essentials on the Plaindealer staff.

EDITORS. — The Western Herald was edited by Mrs. Amos Johnson, Keokuk, Ia.; The Lancet, by Miss Carrie Bragg, Petersburg, Va.; The Musical Messenger, by Miss Amelia L. Tighlman, Montgomery, Ala.; The St. Matthew's Lyceum, by Mrs. M. E. Lambert, Detroit, Mich.; The Ivy, by Mrs. A.

E. Johnson, Baltimore, Md., and Miss A. E. McEwen is Assistant Editor of the Herald, Montgomery, Ala.

This article includes only a few of our writers. When we remember the very difficult circumstances of the past, the trials and discomforts of the present, we are indeed cheered with the prospects. In the busy hum of life it is difficult to make one's way to the front, and this is true of all races, hence, we are not at all discouraged since our sisters have had such ready access to the great journals of the land. When the edge of prejudice shall have become rusted and worn out, the Negro woman shall be heard most potently in the realm of thought; till then we shall strive.

LUCY WILMOT SMITH
1889

THE NEWSPAPER WOMAN

ONE SIDE OF THE QUESTION

By Flora McDonald

The newspaper woman is not born, she grows. The process of erection is gradual and — shades of departed martyrs! — is painful. It is death by slow torture and a slow Phoenix like rising from the dead body's ashes. She comes into the world, like other women, with a grain or two more brain than the average possibly, but with the same inherent self-distrust, the same keen, ragged-edged sensibilities, and when she has been built over, behold her! one part nerve and two parts Indian rubber. Carrie Bartlett, a young woman formerly connected with the editorial staff of the Minneapolis Tribune, now a Unitarian minister at Sioux Falls, Dak., did railroads for the Tribune, and it is told of her that every time she heard a man swear in her daily round of railroad offices, she would turn her face to the wall and weep. Notice, she never made a newspaper woman. She kept her soul alive and set to saving others. The girl who has it in her to survive for newspaper work will cry the first time a man swears at her, grate her teeth the second time, and swear back the third time. Upon my soul she will, and you tenderly nurtured female journalists sit down and hold your contradictions; you don't know anything about the inner mechanism of the creature under discussion.

Every newspaper man realizes how members of his professon are a class by themselves. They are necessarily so, for a man who works while respectable people sleep, and sleeps while respectable people work, must be something distinct from unqualified respectability, and as lines are drawn in society, if he has any identity with other human beings, it is with those who "live after midnight." Now, as lines are drawn by the same yard rule society, the newspaper woman finds she is a class by herself — a cheerful community of one. This is strictly true of her in towns outside of Chicago and New York, and, owing to the general lack of good fellowship among women, is more or less true of her everywhere. The same causes that operate to isolate men of her profession separate her from other social beings, and, further than this, her sex makes her solitary in her profession. The men among whom she works may pay her the compliment of treating her quite like "a good fellow" — and a woman struggling for her daily bread among men can have no more satisfactory treatment — they may generously make her "one of the gang," with extra privileges accorded her femininity — the privilege of being the receptacle of all the love affairs of the "Salad" reporters, of being solemnly consulted about the cloth and cut of their occasional (very occasional) new trousers, of hearing both sides of opposing factions, of being admitted, with odds in her favor, to pools on election, of losing money by "tips" on the races that the sporting editor "wouldn't give to any man but her," and of having some one of the number go no more than a block out of his way to see that she gets home safe when the day's work is done and the crowd has "fed" and discussed and settled the affairs of the nation at some chop house between 2 and 3 o'clock in the morning — she may enjoy all this and still the fact remains that she is a woman, still she suffers in a greater or lesser degree the uneasy sensations of a fish out of water. Not, mind you, that her discomfort is occasioned by the men who are companions — not a bit of it; the reason lies only in the natural order of things. "Don't have anything more to do with the men than you can help," was the advice given one girl starting out in newspaper work; "they are a bad lot." After six months' laboring among them, she refused an offer of marriage, saying it would ever more be impossible for her to content herself with loving one man, because, on the ground of analogy, she was firmly planted in devotion to newspaper men all over the world. But, though every reason for this devotion is given, any well-balanced woman who works among newspaper men, one thousand and one causes make hers the miserable experience of a freak — the "only and original one of its kind on earth." While her male associates religiously treat her like a brother, she must always be the wise brother that knows enough to make herself scarce when consideration for the peculiarities of her condition becomes a restraint. Her existence is generously tolerated rather than desired, and the most she knows of the satisfaction of being wanted anywhere is the consciousness of not being wanted.

It is outside her office relations, however, that the real wretchedness of the newspaper woman lies. On the supposition, presumably, that an animal is more familiar with the ways of its own kind than with anything else, her work lies chiefly among women. The personalities in which journalism of the present indulges are her peculiar forte. "Sassiety" is pre-eminent by her sphere of action. Life becomes to her one long-drawn-out five o'clock tea of somebody else. She is in the swim, but not of it, and, recording the slops and founders of the big fish, she in time descends to a state of mental and moral petrifaction that is simply awful. One woman says "society reporting is prostitution of brains." Oh, that it were no worse! It is prostitution of soul, too. There is at least one society reporter who is certain her chance of heaven would be considerably brightened if she could change her lot for the police run. She would turn from the ghastly horrors of an afternoon reception and find new life in the glorious details of a murder case, or, to have done with weddings forever, do hangings, and see her self-respect growing taller every day.

On gossip does she live, move, and have her being. Her only thoughts of death become plans for sending back a description of the latest thing in white robes, or of writing up some of the prominent angels and turning it in with a few old cuts for a Sunday morning feature. In Western cities, where there is no estate so high as real estate, she is alternately patronized and snubbed until the cry "why should the spirit of mortal be proud?" becomes a bitter mockery. When she is snubbed she understands how men like Spies come to exist, and when a grateful parvenue, whose entertainment she has been assigned, drags her down to the refreshment table, she knows so exactly the mortification of a menagerie under similar circumstances; she vows that never again will she stay after the circus, and watch the animals fed. The writer, one of those wretched, down-trodden society reporters whose experience doubtless is not foreign to them all, ever mindful of her lowly calling and by nature 'umble as Uriah Heep, has been taken by the arm and run out of a wedding by the gilt-edged mistress of the mansion in which the event was taking place, on various occasions, to insure a correct report of the bride's gown, has been bribed with beer or wine until the white ribbon she wears turned pink with shame; she has been fed by opulent entertainers, making the difference between her and sleeping-car porters a matter of berths and brass buttons; she has been kept out in the cold waiting for the woman who wanted it all in the paper without anybody seeing the reporter, until she positively had to talk to herself about the lake of eternal fire to keep herself from freezing to death — in short she has suffered and escaped the sweet relief of total annihilation, until, cursing her worst enemy, she would simply implore heaven to strike him a society reporter on the spot.

FLORA McDONALD
1889

CHAPTER 9

"Nellie Bly":
Stunt Reporting

With Joseph Pulitzer's *New York World* leading the way, new formulas for metropolitan newspapers emerged in the late nineteenth century, combining colorful and sensational news, crusades, illustrations and extravagant promotion. Casting off its preoccupation with politics, the press turned to human interest reporting, employing an increasing number of women reporters. Although most were restricted to the new women's and society pages, designed to capitalize on department store advertising aimed at housewives, a few women reporters were allowed to work in city rooms beside men reporters. Sally Joy White, believed to be the first woman regularly employed as a staff writer on a metropolitan paper, started on the *Boston Post* in 1870.

Editors frequently exploited the sex of capable women reporters by assigning them stunts deemed especially daring for women or making them "sob sisters," specializing in tear-jerking accounts of flamboyant events. Women reporters ascended in balloons, descended in diving bells, dressed up like beggars and waifs, feigned madness and posed as servants in the homes of society figures to pursue exciting and scandalous tidbits for their readers.

The most famous stunt reporter by-line of all, "Nellie Bly," belonged to a determined young woman from Pittsburgh, Elizabeth Cochrane. As a teenager she started reporting to support herself after her father's death, receiving her pseudonym from a Pittsburgh editor who took it from a Stephen C. Foster song. Following crusades against factory conditions in Pittsburgh, she tackled the New York journalistic scene in 1887, resolved to reach the top. It didn't take her long.

She landed a job on the *New York World* by exposing the mistreatment of patients at the Blackwell's Island insane asylum, after pretending to go berserk and being committed there. When her sensational revelations led to a grand jury investigation, Nellie Bly's career soared. More first-person accounts enthralled readers as she had herself arrested for theft to expose women's prisons, masqueraded as an invalid to investigate free medical care, toiled in department stores and factories to picture the plight of underpaid employees, posed as an unemployed servant to reveal employment agency practices and foiled the schemes of Central Park mashers who seduced young women.

But her greatest triumph came in 1889 at the age of 24 when she raced around the world to beat the record of Phineas Fogg, hero of Jules Verne's romance, *Around the World in Eighty Days.* As she made the journey in 72 days, 6 hours and 11 minutes, Pulitzer promoted her as a front-page heroine, personifying the independent American girl, the fascination of travel and the excitement of journalism.   One of the greatest publicity stunts of all time, the trip was rooted in theatrical — not journalistic — goals, making Nellie Bly a national celebrity with clothes, games and toys named for her. Most of the stories about her trip were written by other reporters, apparently because she was too busy traveling to file dispatches by the then-primitive cable, although on her final dash from California to New York by train she dictated notes of her adventures for publication.

Elizabeth Cochrane continued her career for five years, then married a wealthy industrialist, Robert L. Seaman, fifty years her senior. After his death in 1910, she lost her fortune through several business failures and returned to work as an obscure columnist on orphans for Hearst's *New York Journal.* She died in 1922.

Nellie Bly's first complete account of her trip around the world in 73 days appeared in the *New York World* on January 26, 1890, one day after she returned from her record-breaking journey. Headed "From Jersey Back to Jersey," it was prefaced with two paragraphs by the *World* noting that she had dictated the article on the train while "speeding from Chicago to New York at nearly fifty miles per hour," in the midst of being feted by well-wishers. Excerpts are reprinted here.

FROM JERSEY BACK TO JERSEY

M. Jules Verne said it could not be done. I have done it. He told me when he met me at Amiens that if the tour was made of the world in seventy-nine days he would applaud with both hands. It has been made in seventy-two days, and M. Verne may now applaud and two hands will not do; he must use four.

It was only sixty-eight days from the time I left American soil until I touched it again. During that time I was in many different climes. But only here, in God's own country, have I passed amid fruit and flowers in valley, and over mountain-tops amid snow and frost, all within the space of sixteen hours. In no country save America is the passage from orange groves to snow-crest mountains possible in the same space of time.

I have roasted and I have frozen since leaving home. I have dined on India curry, on Chinese chow and Japanese eel and rice. I have travelled on French and English trains, on English boats, on burros, in jinrickshas, in bullock carts, in catamarans, sampans, gherrys and half a dozen other conveyances peculiar to Eastern countries in my trip around the world.

Everybody knows that the idea was to make a tour of the world in seventy-five days. At many junctures since my departure have I been compelled to face what looked like failure. Did I ever give up hope of success? No, not exactly. Never having failed, I could not picture what failure meant, but I did tell the officers of the Oceanic, when success seemed very, very hazy, owing to the unexpectedly stormy weather, that I would rather go into New York successful and dead than alive and behind time.

When the whistle blew and the steamer Victoria moved off from the dock, then for the first time I regretted that I was leaving America. . . .

Miss Jusson, a niece of Carl Schurz, was the only lady besides myself travelling alone. She was going to Germany to her father. There were many bets made on the boat as to whether I would arrive in Southampton in time to catch the India Mail. I took all that were offered. When we failed to arrive at Southampton at the time the steamer was due I felt a little nervous, but still trusted to my never-failing luck.

LANDING IN ENGLAND

At 2:30 Friday morning, Nov. 22, we anchored off Southampton, but shortly afterwards the tug which lands passengers came alongside. A few people came on board, and I waited, with the rest of the passengers, trying to pick from the crowd *THE WORLD*'s London correspondent, who was to meet me. To show the interest passengers took in my welfare, one gentleman whom I had never met before leaving New York, said that if *THE WORLD*'s correspondent failed to meet me that he would leave the boat at Southampton and see me safely to London. This gentleman had his ticket purchased to Germany, and would have sacrificed all this to assure himself of my safety.

When the tug landed at the pier we had to face the Custom-house officials. *THE WORLD* correspondent marched boldly in with my little solitary bag in his hand: "Will you swear that you have no tobacco or tea?" "It is not his, it is mine," I said, at which he smiled and put a crossmark on the bag and allowed us to go free. There was some little delay about the train, the last regular one having left before our arrival, but arrangements were made, owing to the heavy mail, to run a special mail train to London that morning. This was not by any special arrangement of *THE WORLD*, but was my own usual good luck.

UP TO LONDON

I was hurried from the Custom-House out to where a dark train stood. A guard, as they call them there, came along, and with a key large enough for a policeman's club, opened a door and I stepped into an English coach. I must say that they leave much to be desired. First, I stumbled over something. Then I was bothered with the odor of the oil lamp. When I sat down I began to investigate the obstacle which had almost put me into the car headforemost. I found what looked to be a long piece of iron, but which I learned was a foot-warmer. They think this is comfortable travelling in England. My feet burned through the thin soles of my shoes while I froze about my shoulders.

In the morning they told me it was daylight or I would not have known it. I have a recollection of dim lights and a gray, dusty shade overhanging the city, and some fine buildings and people beginning to hurry when I reached London. As we glided over the beautifully paved streets I thought with shame of the streets of New York. *THE WORLD* correspondent asked, "What do you think of the streets compared with those of New York?" "They are not bad," I replied, patronizingly, determined in true American style not to hear one word against home. After getting my ticket and passport we went to the Victoria Street Station. We gave ourselves time for a light breakfast and started again on an English train. This was more uncomfortable, if anything, than the other, for here the footwarmer was cold. I was on my way now to Amiens to see M. Jules Verne, the author of "Around the World in Eighty Days." The boat on which we crossed the English Channel was a wretched thing. The people lounged about as if fearing seasickness, but at the same time drank and ate. I sat on deck and enjoyed the beautiful sky and water.

IN LA BELLE FRANCE

We landed at Bologne. Here, I think, my baggage was examined, but I did not see it done as one of the men in the boat with me took charge of it and also found us places in the train bound for Amiens. In the mean time we went into the restaurant on the edge of the pier and had something to eat. I found the waiters able to speak English and willing enough to take American money. The trip to Amiens was slow and tiresome, but I was fully repaid for the journey by meeting M. Jules Verne and his wife, who were waiting for me at the station in company with *THE WORLD*'s Paris correspondent.

* * *

THE ARRIVAL AT BRINDISI, ITALY

We were due at Brindisi at 12 o'clock, but when it came midnight and we were not yet there I began to get nervous. The train stopped at last and

there was a great rush and a good deal of yelling on the part of the men outside, mainly in broken English. The guard took charge of the fair girl and
her invalid father and myself. One omnibus was hired for the lot, with an
English-speaking driver. There was a little oil-lamp in the front which gave
out a weak glimmer and a strong odor. The glimmer at last went out, but
the odor remained. Two fat women had so many boxes that when they got
them all into the omnibus we had to sit as much on the seats as we could.
We drove first to the steamer bound for Bombay, where we bade farewell to
the Englishman and his sweet daughter. Then we drove back to the ship
that was to carry me to victory or to failure.

ON BOARD THE P. AND O. STEAMER.

The two fat women and their numerous bundles and boxes were
landed and carefully led up the gang-plank to the ship. Here we found a
crowd of men waiting to see the new arrivals. Some one pointed out the
purser's room and he looked at my ticket and told me where my cabin was.
The picture presented by the cabin interior was unique. Two bushy heads
were thrust out of two lower berths and two faces, with wide, inquiring
eyes, wore expressions of dismay when they saw that they were threatened
with another cabin-mate. Two mouths uttered shrieks of impatience. The
upper berth was filled with boxes and loose clothes and boots and such
things were scattered over the floor of the cabin. I returned to the purser
and handed him a letter from Mr. ——, asking him to give me every attention. Then the purser looked at his papers and told me to take cabin
104. There was but one girl to peep out here to see who was entering the
room. She proved afterwards to be the prettiest girl on board the ship.

SENDING A CABLE.

I put down my hand-bag and went out to the guard who was waiting
to take me to the telegraph office, where a cable might be sent to *THE
WORLD*. The purser said I had not much time, but it could be done. The
telegraph office was in a building down a dark street. The little room was
bare, and there was only a desk, one sheet of telegraph paper, a bottle without any ink in it and one pen. It had one small window, like a stamp-win-
dow in a post-office. But the office was closed, and there was nothing to do
except to wait and send a cable from Ismalia.

"The agent is taking a nap, but we'll get him up," said the guard hope-
fully as he rang a bell near the closed window. He rang it several times, and
then the window opened with a creak, as if long unused to business. A
dark, sleepy looking face appeared. The guard spoke in Italian and I finished it up in English, to which the man responded quite well. I wrote my
cable, after answering his inquiries as to what country New York was in and
paying the bill.

NEARLY MISSED THE BOAT TO INDIA.

Then we thought of the ship. "The man said we had but a moment,"
I cried breathlessly to the guard. I might possibly have missed my ship.

"Come," was all he said as his face paled and we started out of the door and down the narrow, dark street.

"Can you run?" he asked, quietly, and I, feeling the anxiety in his tones, felt myself tremble. "Come, I would not have you lose this boat for £50," he cried, and taking my hand without further words we tore madly through the dark streets and along the water's edge.

A whistle blew!

All power seemed to leave me. We stopped in the middle of the street and looked blankly and hopelessly into each other's faces.

"My boat!" I gasped, while my heart ceased beating. And again we started in a mad race which brought us by a sudden curve breathless at the foot of the plank. I uttered a prayer of thanks when I saw the Victoria still there. The boat bound for Bombay was gone, but I was saved.

SAFE ON BOARD

I hurried up the gang-plank, leaving the guard to bargain with the venders of chairs on shore, but I would not stay on land another second. I got my chair, testified my thanks to the guard, and went to bed tired but happy.

* * *

NOW FOR CHINA. . .

We arrived at the picturesque city of Singapore on the 18th of December, and having a few hours to spare there visited the gardens, the museums, the temples and other points of interest. Some people even here could speak English. I saw the first Chinaman and a Chinese funeral, which was very interesting. During the voyage from Singapore to Hong Kong we had the monsoon against us, but the Oriental, which was making its first trip to China and was trying to make a record, fought it bravely and reached Hong Kong two days ahead of my itinerary, Dec. 23. Here was another five days' wait before I could leave for Yokohama. European citizens were very good to me and the newspapers were most kind in mentioning my trip. Christmas Day I spent in Canton, China, eating my lunch in the Temple of the Dead, where there are hundreds of bodies, some of which have been lying in caskets for seventy-five years. While eating my dinner in company with two gentlemen and a Chinese guide, the priests were chanting masses in a room opposite for the repose of recently departed souls.

SIGHT-SEEING IN CHINA

I visited the leper city, saw the shops, the ivory carvers and many other things of interest. On the execution ground eleven people had been beheaded the day before. I returned to Hong Kong after nightfall, because there is no accommodation in Canton for English people. Even the foreign representatives are given a tract of land outside the city walls, which is guarded by soldiers and no Chinese are allowed to enter there, nor can foreigners come near the Chinese city after night has fallen. On Dec. 28 I started for Yokohama on the Occidental and Oriental steamship Oceanic.

New Year's Eve was celebrated on the boat. A quiet little crowd of Anglo-Americans sat up and welcomed in the New Year, those who could, and those who could not trying to sing "Auld Lang Syne."

YOKOHAMA AT LAST.

We had a stormy trip across to Yokohama, bad winds and rough seas, and reached that interesting Japanese town on the morning of Jan. 3. There was a delay here and I went to Tokio, where the Mikado lives, saw the famous Shiba Temple and everything else of interest. I also visited Kama Kura where the great god Diabutsu lives. When our vessel got into port I was waited upon by a representative of a Japanese paper. He presented me with copies of the paper containing a translation of *THE WORLD*'s story of my visit to Jules Verne, and also an account of my trip around the world. He interviewed me in a very amusing way, having all the questions written down on paper beforehand in English, which he read over and filled in as I replied. He was a Japanese but spoke English very well. He presented me with copies of the paper containing the interview, which I have brought home with me as a treasured souvenir.

JAPANESE DANCING-GIRLS.

The most interesting sight to me in Yokohama were the dancing-girls. I became so infatuated with their beauty and performance that I spent all of my evenings there enjoying and admiring their graceful dancing. The Consul-General's son being absent, his mother, Mrs. Greathouse, called upon me at the hotel. I also met Mrs. Seidmore, who is there with her son, the Assistant Consul. The United States Navy boat Omaha gave me a luncheon, and the day I started from Yokohama, Jan. 7, the band on the Omaha played for me "Home, Sweet Home," "Hail Columbia" and "The Girl I Left Behind Me." Everybody I met in Yokohama did their utmost to make my stay enjoyable.

ACROSS THE PACIFIC.

The trip across the Pacific was very tempestuous. In the first three days we were 110 miles ahead of the Oceanic's last record when she broke the record; but all this and more were lost when we struck the headwinds, which stayed with us the greater part of five days. I cannot say more of the crew than that they were perfect, from the captain down. They did everything for the comfort of the passengers, and, strange to say, with all the rough weather, only one or two suffered from seasickness. I could not have felt more grieved over getting into San Francisco one day later than they had expected than did the officers in charge of the Oceanic. How I landed in San Francisco and took *THE WORLD*'s special train at 9 A.M. Jan. 2, and was whirled across the continent, greeted with kindness and hearty welcomes at every point, has already been told in *THE WORLD*.

Nellie Bly.

CHAPTER 10

Ida M. Tarbell:
Investigative Journalism

As the twentieth century dawned, a group of mass circulation magazines began to expose political and financial corruption in American life.
Theodore Roosevelt, not totally in sympathy with the movement, dubbed it
muckraking, drawing an analogy with the "Man with the Muckrake" in *Pilgrim's Progress*, who refused to look up from the floor even though a heav-
enly crown awaited him. The movement, which lasted from 1902 to 1912,
was led by *McClure's Magazine*, whose staff included three of the most able
muckrakers, Lincoln Steffens, Ray Stannard Baker and Ida M. Tarbell.

In 1902 *McClure's* published a serialized version of Tarbell's *History
of the Standard Oil Company*, a factual and well-documented account of
the manipulations that had created the giant trust. At the time she received
the assignment, Tarbell already had established a reputation for careful research in connection with two successful series on the lives of Napoleon and
Lincoln.

She brought personal knowledge of the subject to her task of reporting on Standard Oil. As a girl she had lived in the booming oil town of
Titusville, Pennsylvania, where she had witnessed the sharp practices of the
company under John D. Rockefeller, whose ruthlessness had injured her
own father's business.

With a dedication to objectivity buttressed by a two-year study of
voluminous records and interviews with key oil industry figures, she wrote a
sober account of the company's unfair methods far more damaging than an
emotional outburst. Her articles, published in a book in 1904, caused a sen-
sation and brought her fame.

Her passion for accuracy stemmed in part from her education at Allegheny College in Meadville, Pennsylvania, where she studied science. Turning to journalism, however, she joined the staff of the *Chautauquan* maga-

zine for eight years before traveling to Paris to study women's participation
in the French Revolution. There she met S. S. McClure who urged her to
return to New York and join his magazine.

After the success of the *History of the Standard Oil Company*, Tarbell, along with Steffens and Baker, left *McClure's* and, with others, purchased the *American Magazine*, which they ran cooperatively until its sale
in 1915. Subsequently Tarbell lectured on the Chautauqua circuit on such
subjects as the social responsibility of business, disarmament and the League
of Nations (which she favored).

Although an ardent feminist in her youth, she did not favor woman
suffrage in later years, feeling that public life was incompatible with moth-
erhood. At 82, she published her autobiography, *All in the Day's Work*, five
years before her death in 1944.

In chapter 12 of *All in the Day's Work* (New York: Macmillan, 1939),
Tarbell described her impressions upon seeing John D. Rockefeller and also
described her distress at the muckraker label. Excerpts are reprinted here.

ALL IN THE DAY'S WORK

MUCKRAKER OR HISTORIAN?

By Ida Tarbell

Not a few of the personal experiences in gathering my materials left
me with unhappy impressions, more unhappy in retrospect perhaps than
they were at the moment. They were part of the day's work, sometimes
very exciting parts. There was the two hours I spent in studying Mr. John D.
Rockefeller. As the work had gone on, it became more and more clear to
me that the Standard Oil Company was his creation. "An institution is the
lengthened shadow of one man," says Emerson. I found it so.

Everybody in the office interested in the work began to say, "After
the book is done you must do a character sketch of Mr. Rockefeller." I
was not keen for it. It would have to be done like the books, from documents; that is, I had no inclination to use the extraordinary gossip which
came to me from many sources. If I were to do it I wanted only that of
which I felt I had sure proof, only those things which seemed to me to help
explain the public life of this powerful, patient, secretive, calculating man of
so peculiar and special a genius.

"You must at least look at Mr. Rockefeller," my associates insisted.

"But how?" Mr. Rogers himself had suggested that I see him. I had con-
sented. I had returned to the suggestion several times, but at last was made
to understand that it could not be done. I had dropped his name from my
list. It was John Siddall who then took the matter in hand.[1]

"You must see him," was Siddall's judgment.

To arrange it became almost an obsession. And then what seemed to
him like a providential opening came. It was announced that on a certain
Sunday of October 1903 Mr. Rockefeller before leaving Cleveland, where
he had spent his summer, for his home in New York would say good-bye in
a little talk to the Sunday school of his church — a rally, it was called. As
soon as Siddall learned of this he begged me to come on. "We can go to
Sunday School; we can stay to church. I will see that we have seats where
we will have a full view of the man. You will get him in action."

Of course I went, feeling a little mean about it too. He had not wanted to be seen apparently. It was taking him unaware.

Siddall's plan worked to perfection, worked so well from the start
that again and again he seemed ready to burst from excitement in the two
hours we spent in the church.

We had gone early to the Sunday-school room where the rally was to
open — a dismal room with a barbaric dark green paper with big gold designs,
cheap stained-glass windows, awkward gas fixtures. Comfortable, of course,
but so stupidly ugly. We were sitting meekly at one side when I was suddenly aware of a striking figure standing in the doorway. There was an awful
age in his face — the oldest man I had ever seen, I thought, but what power!
At the moment Siddall poked me violently in the ribs and hissed, "There
he is."

The impression of power deepened when Mr. Rockefeller took off his
coat and hat, put on a skullcap, and took a seat commanding the entire
room, his back to the wall. It was the head which riveted attention. It was
big, great breadth from back to front, high broad forehead, big bumps behind the ears, not a shiny head but with a wet look. The skin was as fresh as
that of any healthy man about us. The thin sharp nose was like a thorn.
There were no lips; the mouth looked as if the teeth were all shut hard.
Deep furrows ran down each side of the mouth from the nose. There were
puffs under the little colorless eyes with creases running from them.

Wonder over the head was almost at once diverted to wonder over the
man's uneasiness. His eyes were never quiet but darted from face to face,
even peering around the jog at the audience close to the wall.

----

[1]Henry H. Rogers was an old friend of the Tarbell family and a vice-
president of Standard Oil who met with Tarbell during preparations of her
series.

John H. Siddall was a journalist who helped Tarbell with some of the
research for her series. He later became editor of the *American Magazine.*

When he rose to speak, the impression of power that the first look at him had given increased, and the impression of age passed. I expected a quavering voice, but the voice was not even old, if a little fatigued, a little thin. It was clear and utterly sincere. He meant what he was saying. He was on his own ground talking about dividends, dividends of righteousness. "If you would take something out," he said, clenching the hand of his outstretched right arm, " you must put something in" — emphasizing "put something in" with a long outstretched forefinger.

The talk over, we slipped out to get a good seat in the gallery, a seat where we could look full on what we knew to be the Rockefeller pew.

Mr. Rockefeller came into the auditorium of the church as soon as Sunday school was out. He sat a little bent in his pew, pitifully uneasy, his head constantly turning the farthest right or left, his eyes searching the faces almost invariably turned towards him. It was plain that he, and not the minister, was the pivot on which that audience swung. Probably he knew practically everybody in the congregation; but now and then he lingered on a face, peering at it intently as if he were seeking what was in the mind behind it. He looked frequently at the gallery. Was it at Siddall and me?

The services over, he became the friendly patron saint of the flock. Coming down the aisle where people were passing out, he shook hands with everyone who stopped, saying, "A good sermon." "The Doctor gave us a good sermon." "It was a very good sermon, wasn't it?"

My two hours' study of Mr. Rockefeller aroused a feeling I had not expected, which time has intensified. I was sorry for him. I know no companion so terrible as fear. Mr. Rockefeller, for all the conscious power written in face and voice and figure, was afraid, I told myself, afraid of his own kind. My friend Lewis Emery, Jr., priding himself on being a victim, was free and happy. Not gold enough in the world to tempt him to exchange love of defiance for a power which carried with it a head as uneasy as that on Mr. Rockefeller's shoulders.

My unhappiness was increased as the months went by with the multiplying of tales of grievances coming from every direction. I made a practice of looking into them all, as far as I could; and while frequently I found solid reasons for the complaints, frequently I found the basic motives behind them — suspicion, hunger for notoriety, blackmail, revenge.

The most unhappy and most unnatural of these grievances came to me from literally the last person in the world to whom I should have looked for information — Frank Rockefeller — brother of John D. Rockefeller.

Frank Rockefeller sent word to me by a circuitous route that he had documents in a case which he thought ought to be made public, and that if I would secretly come to him in his office in Cleveland he would give them to me. I knew that there had been a quarrel over property between the two men. It made much noise at the time — 1893 — had gone to the courts, had caused bitterness inside the family itself; but because it was a family affair I had not felt that I wanted to touch it. But here it was laid on my desk.

So I went to Cleveland, where John Siddall had a grand opportunity to play the role of sleuth which he so enjoyed, his problem being to get me into Mr. Rockefeller's office without anybody suspecting my identity. He succeeded.

I found Mr. Rockefeller excited and vindictive. He accused his brother of robbing (his word) him and his partner James Corrigan of all their considerable holdings of stock in the Standard Oil Company. The bare facts were that Frank Rockefeller and James Corrigan had been interested in the early Standard Oil operations in Cleveland and had each acquired then a substantial block of stock. Later they had developed a shipping business on the Lakes, iron and steel furnaces in Cleveland. In the eighties they had borrowed money from John D. Rockefeller, putting up their Standard Oil stock as collateral. Then came the panic of '93, and they could not meet their obligations. In the middle of their distress John Rockefeller had foreclosed, taking over their stocks, leaving them, so they charged, no time in which to turn around although they felt certain that they would be able a little later, out of the substantial business they claimed they had built up, to pay their debt to him. Their future success proved they could have done so.

I could see John Rockefeller's point as I talked with his brother Frank. Frank Rockefeller was an open-handed, generous trader — more interested in the game than in the money to be made. He loved good horses — raised them, I believe on a farm out in Kansas; he liked gaiety, free spending. From his brother John's point of view he was not a safe man to handle money. He did not reverence it; he used it in frivolous ways of which his brother did not approve. So it was as a kind of obligation to the sacredness of money that John Rockefeller had foreclosed on his own brother and his early friend James Corrigan. He was strictly within his legal rights and within what I suppose he called his moral right.

But the transaction left a bitterness in Frank Rockefeller's heart and mind which was one of the ugliest things I have ever seen. "I have taken up my children from the Rockefeller family lot. (Or "shall take up" — I do not know now which it was.) They shall not lie in the same enclosure with John D. Rockefeller."

The documents in this case, which I later analyzed for the character sketch on which we had decided, present a fair example of what were popularly called "Standard Oil methods" as well as what they could do to the minds and hearts of victims.

The more intimately I went into my subject, the more hateful it became to me. No achievement on earth could justify those methods, I felt. I had a great desire to end my task, hear no more of it. No doubt part of my revulsion was due to a fagged brain. The work had turned out to be much longer and more laborious than I had had reason to expect. . . .

The book was published in the fall of 1904 — two fat volumes with generous appendices of what I considered essential documents. I was curious about the reception it would have from the Standard Oil Company. I had been told repeatedly they were preparing an answer to flatten me out; but if this was under way it was not with Mr. Rockefeller's consent, I imagined. To a mutual friend who had told him the articles should be answered Mr. Rockefeller was said to have replied: "Not a word. Not a word about that misguided woman." To another who asked him about my charges he was reported as answering: "All without foundation. The idea of the Standard forcing anyone to sell his refinery is absurd. The refineries wanted to sell to us, and nobody that has sold or worked with us but has made money, is glad he did so.

"I thought once of having an answer made to the McClure articles but you know it has always been the policy of the Standard to keep silent under attack and let their acts speak for themselves."

In the case of the Lloyd book[2] they had kept silent, but only because Mr. Rockefeller had been unable to carry out his plans for answering. What he had proposed was a jury of the most distinguished clergymen of the day to consider Mr. Lloyd's argument and charges. Certain clergymen invited refused unless there should be a respectable number of economists added to the jury. That, apparently, Mr. Rockefeller did not see his way to do, and the plan was abandoned. So far as I know Mr. Lloyd's book was never answered by the Standard Oil Company.

But I wanted an answer from Mr. Rockefeller. What I got was neither direct nor, from my point of view, serious. It consisted of wide and what must have been a rather expensive anonymous distribution of various critical comments. The first of these was a review of the book which appeared in the *Nation* soon after its publication. The writer — one of the *Nation*'s staff reviewers, I later learned — sneered at the idea that there was anything unusual in the competitive practices which I called illegal and immoral. "They are a necessary part of competition," he said. "The practices are odious it is true, competition is necessarily odious." Was it necessarily odious?

I did not think so. The practices I believed I had proved, I continued to consider much more dangerous to economic stability than airing them, even if I aired them in the excited and irrational fashion the review charged. As I saw it, the struggle was between Commercial Machiavellism and the Christian Code.

The most important of the indirect answers was an able book by Gilbert Holland Montague[3] It separated business and ethics in a way that must have been a comfort to 26 Broadway.

---

[2]Henry D. Lloyd was the author of a book hostile to the Standard Oil Company, *Wealth Against Commonwealth* (N.Y.: Harper, 1894).

[3]Gilbert Holland Montague, *The Rise and Progress of the Standard Oil Co.* (New York: Harper, 1904).

As soon as published, Mr. Montague's book became not exactly a best seller but certainly a best circulator — libraries, ministers, teachers, prominent citizens all over the land receiving copies with the compliments of the publisher. Numbers of them came back to me with irritated letters. "We have been buying books for years from this house," wrote one distinguished librarian, "and never before was one sent with their compliments. I understand that libraries all over the country are receiving them. Can it be that this is intended as an advertisement, or is it not more probable that the Standard Oil Company itself is paying for this widespread distribution?"

The general verdict seemed to be that the latter was the explanation.

Some time later there came from the entertaining Elbert Hubbard of the Roycroft Shop of East Aurora, New York, an essay on the Standard extolling the grand results from the centralization of the industry in their hands.

I have it from various interested sources that five million copies were ordered printed in pamphlet form by the Standard Oil Company and were distributed by Mr. Hubbard. They went to schoolteachers and journalists, preachers and "leaders" from the Atlantic to the Pacific. Hardly were they received in many cases before they were sent to me with angry or approving comments. For a couple of years my birthday and Christmas offerings were sure to include copies of one or the other of these documents with the compliments of some waggish member of the McClure group.

I had hoped that the book might be received as a legitimate historical study, but to my chagrin I found myself included in a new school, that of the muckrakers. Theodore Roosevelt, then President of the United States, had become uneasy at the effect on the public of the periodical press's increasing criticisms and investigations of business and political abuses. He was afraid that they were adding to the not inconsiderable revolutionary fever abroad, driving people into socialism. Something must be done, and in a typically violent speech he accused the school of being concerned only with the "vile and debasing." Its members were like the man in John Bunyan's "Pilgrim's Progress" who with eyes on the ground raked incessantly "the straws, the small sticks, and dust of the floor." They were muckrakers. The conservative public joyfully seized the name.

Roosevelt had of course misread his Bunyan. The man to whom the Interpreter called the attention of the Pilgrim was raking riches which the Interpreter contemptuously called "straws" and "sticks" and "dust." The President would have been nearer Bunyan's meaning if he had named the rich sinners of the times who in his effort to keep his political balance he called "malefactors of great wealth" — if he had called them "muckrakers of great wealth" and applied the word "malefactors" to the noisy and persistent writers who so disturbed him.

I once argued with Mr. Roosevelt that we on *McClure's* were concerned only with facts, not with stirring up revolt. "I don't object to the facts," he cried, "but you and Baker" — Baker at that time was carrying on an able series of articles on the manipulations of the railroads — "but you and Baker are not *practical*."

I felt at the time Mr. Roosevelt had a good deal of the usual conviction of the powerful man in public life that correction should be left to him, a little resentment that a profession outside his own should be stealing his thunder.

This classification of muckraker, which I did not like, helped fix my resolution to have done for good and all with the subject which had brought it on me. But events were stronger than I. All the radical reforming element, and I numbered many friends among them, were begging me to join their movements. I soon found that most of them wanted attacks. They had little interest in balanced findings. Now I was convinced that in the long run the public they were trying to stir would weary of vituperation, that if you were to secure permanent results the mind must be convinced.

One of the most heated movements at the moment was the effort to persuade the public to refuse all gifts which came from fortunes into the making of which it was known illegal and unfair practices had gone. "Do not touch tainted money," men thundered from pulpit and platform, among them so able a man as Dr. Washington Gladden. The Rockefeller fortune was singled out because about this time Mr. Rockefeller made some unusually large contributions to colleges and churches and general philanthropy. "It is done," cried the critics, "in order to silence criticism." Frequently some one said to me, "You have opened the Rockefeller purse." But I knew, and said in print rather to the disgust of my friends in the movement, that there was an unfairness to Mr. Rockefeller in this outcry. It did not take public criticism to open his purse. From boyhood he had been a steady giver in proportion to his income — 10 percent went to the Lord — and through all the harrowing early years in which he was trying to establish himself as a money-maker he never neglected to give the Lord the established proportion. As his fortune grew his gifts grew larger. He not only gave but saw the money given was wisely spent; and he trained his children, particularly the son who was to administer his estate, to as wise practice in public giving as we have ever had. That is, it did not take a public outcry such as came in the early years of this century against the methods of the Standard Oil Company to force Mr. Rockefeller to share his wealth. He was already sharing it. Indeed, in the fifteen years before 1904 he had given to one or another cause some thirty-five million dollars.

If his gifts were larger at this time than they had ever been before, his money-making was greater. If they were more spectacular than ever before, it may have been because he thought it was time to call the public's attention to what they were getting out of the Standard Oil fortune. At all events it seemed to me only fair that the point should be emphasized that it had not taken a public revolt against his methods to force him to share his profits.

CHAPTER 11

Rheta Childe Dorr: War Correspondence

During the Spanish-American War both Joseph Pulitzer of the *New York World* and his arch-rival, William Randolph Hearst of the *New York Journal*, carried stories written by women about the hostilities. These tended to focus on a "woman's angle" featuring care of the wounded and accounts of Cuban refugees in Florida. But Anna N. Benjamin, a reporter for *Leslie's Illustrated Newspaper*, refused to limit herself to behind-the-lines activity and resolved to follow American troops to Cuba in 1898.

"I know what you think," the 23-year-old woman was quoted as telling a British correspondent. "You think it ridiculous my being here, you are laughing at me wanting to go, that's the worst of being a woman. But just let me tell you, I'm going through to Cuba and not all the old generals in the army are going to stop me."

She won her goal and soon was scooping her competitors with news of American victories. The next year she covered the Philippine insurrection and in pursuit of news journeyed on to Japan, China and Russia. She died in Paris at the age of twenty-seven.

During World War I, experienced women journalists insisted on the right to be war correspondents. Peggy Hull, a *Cleveland Plain Dealer* reporter, was determined to go to France, but editors would not hire her. She finally persuaded Newspaper Enterprise Association, a news-feature syndicate, to send her abroad. Reporting on troop camps and accompanying the American expeditionary force to Siberia, she became the first woman correspondent officially accredited by the War Department.

Other World War I women correspondents included Alice Rohe, United Press representative in Rome, Bessie Beatty of the *San Francisco Bulletin* and Sigrid Schultz, who reported from Germany for the *Chicago Tribune* as the war ended. The best known, Rheta Childe Dorr, won distinction both as a journalist and as a feminist.

In 1917 Dorr announced to her editors at the *New York Mail* that she was going to Russia to cover the Revolution. They were not surprised. Then fifty years old and at the height of her career, she already had proven her ability to succeed at undertakings requiring exceptional courage.

Dorr, who had been a feminist from the age of twelve, decided in 1898 to leave an unsympathetic husband in Seattle, and, with her two-year-old son, moved to New York, determined to have a journalistic career. After a long struggle, she found a job on the *Evening Post*, where she began her career writing about industrial conditions of women workers.

During a 1906 trip to Europe (the first of nine), Dorr developed close ties with the suffrage movement in England and later became the first editor of *The Suffragist*, a militant publication in the United States, where she continued her reform efforts for women workers by laboring herself in laundries and factories. Through this work she gained first hand material for articles on sweatshop conditions.

Although a Socialist at one point, Dorr became disillusioned with the Bolshevik program when she went to Russia to cover the Revolution. She believed that the Communists were infiltrated by German spies eager to bring down the new republican government that had overturned the Czar. As a supporter of the republic, she accompanied the woman's Battalion of Death, a regiment commanded by Botchkareva, a formidable peasant woman, on its trip to the front lines. Its mission was to rally demoralized government troops by demonstrating the dedication of Russian women. Her articles ran on the front page of the *New York Mail* for weeks and were later collected in a book, *Inside the Russian Revolution.*

Dorr made several subsequent trips to Europe as a war correspondent but was refused permission to go to the front lines "because she was a woman."

Although injured in a motorcycle accident in Washington in 1919, Dorr continued to write books, including her autobiography, *A Woman of Fifty*. She died in 1948.

The selection reprinted here is from *Inside the Russian Revolution* (New York: Macmillan, 1917), describing her trip to the front lines with the woman's battalion.

TO THE FRONT WITH BOTCHKAREVA

Women of all ranks rushed to enlist in the Botchkareva battalion. There were many peasant women, factory workers, servants and also a number of women of education and social prominence. Six Red Cross nurses were among the number, one doctor, a lawyer, several clerks and stenographers and a few like Marie Skridlova who had never done any except war work. If the working women predominated, I believe it was because they were the stronger physically. Botchkareva would accept only the sturdiest, and her soldiers, even when they were slight of figure, were all fine physical specimens. The women were outfitted and equipped exactly like the men soldiers. They wore the same kind of khaki trousers, loose-belted blouse and high peaked cap. They wore the same high boots, carried the same arms and the same camp equipment, including gas masks, trench spades and other paraphernalia. In spite of their tightly shaved heads they presented a very attractive appearance, like nice, clean, upstanding boys. They were very strictly drilled and disciplined and there was no omission of saluting officers in that regiment.

The battalion left Petrograd for an unknown destination on July 6 in our calendar. In the afternoon the women marched to the Kazan Cathedral, where a touching ceremony of farewell and blessing took place. A cold, fine rain was falling, but the great half circle before the cathedral, as well as the long curved colonnades, were filled with people. Thousands of women were there carrying flowers, and nurses moved through the crowds collecting money for the regiment.

I passed a very uneasy day that July 6. I was afraid of what might happen to some of the women through the malignancy of the Bolsheviki, and I was mortally afraid that I was not going to be allowed to get on their troop train. I had made the usual application to the War Ministry to be allowed to visit the front, but I did not follow up the application with a personal visit, and therefore when I dropped in for a morning call I was dismayed to find the barrack in a turmoil, and to hear the exultant announcement, "We're going this evening at eight."

It was an unseasonal day of rain, and I spent reckless sums in droshky hire, rushing hither and yon in a fruitless effort to wring emergency permits from elusive officials who never in their lives had been called upon to do anything in a hurry, or even to keep conventional office hours. Needless to say, I found nobody at all on duty where he should have been that day. Even at the American Embassy, where, empty-handed and discouraged, I wound up late in the afternoon, I found the entire staff absent in attendance on a visiting commission from home. The one helpful person who happened to be at the Embassy was Arno Dosch-Fleurot of the New York *World*. "If I were you," he said, "I wouldn't worry about a permit. I'd just get on the train — if I could *get* on — and I'd stay until they put me off, or until I got where I wanted to go. Of course they may arrest you for a spy. In any other country they'd be pretty sure to. But in Russia you never can tell. Shepherd, of the United Press, once went all over the front with nothing to show but some worthless mining stock. Why not try it?"

I said I would, and before eight that evening I was at the Warsaw Station, unwillingly, participating in what might be called the regiment's first hostile engagement. For at least two thirds of the mob that filled the station were members of the Lenine faction of Bolsheviki, sent there to break up the orderly march of the women, and even if possible to prevent them from entraining at all. From the first these spy-led emissaries of the German Kaiser had sworn enmity to Botchkareva's battalion. Well knowing the moral effect of women taking the places of deserting soldiers in the trenches, the Lenineites had exhausted every effort to breed dissension in the ranks, and at the last moment they had stormed the station in the hope of creating an intolerable situation. In the absence of anything like a police force they did succeed in making things painful and even a little dangerous for the soldiers and for the tearful mothers and sisters who had gathered to bid them good-by. But the women kept perfect discipline through it all, and slowly fought their way through the mob to the train platform.

As for me, a mixture of indignation, healthy muscle and a rare good luck carried me through and landed me in a somewhat battered condition next to Adjutant Skridlova. "You got your permit," she exclaimed on seeing me. "I am so pleased. Stay close to me and I'll see you safely on."

Mendaciously perhaps, I answered nothing at all, but stayed, and every time a perspiring train official grabbed me by the arm and told me to stand back Skridlova rescued me and informed the man that I had permission to go. At the very last I had a bad moment, for one especially inquisitive official asked to see the permission. This time it was the Nachalnik, Botchkareva herself, who came to the rescue. Characteristically she wasted no words, but merely pushed the man aside, thrust me into her own compartment and ordered me to lock the door. Within a few minutes she joined me, the train began to move and we were off. That was the end of my troubles, for no one afterwards questioned my right to be there. At the Adjutant's suggestion I parted with my New York hat and early in the journey substituted the white linen coif of a Red Cross nurse. Thus attired, I was accepted by all concerned as a part of the camp equipment.

The troop train consisted of one second class and five fourth class carriages, the first one, except for one compartment reserved for officers, being practically filled with camp and hospital supplies. In the other carriages, primitive affairs furnished with three tiers of wooden bunks, the rank and file of the regiment traveled. I had a place in the second class compartment with the Nachalnik, the Adjutant and the standard bearer, a big, silent peasant girl called Orlova. Our luxury consisted of cushioned shelves without bedding or blankets, which served as seats by day and beds by night. We had, of course, a little more privacy than the others, but that was all. As for food, we all fared alike, and we fared well, friends of the regiment having loaded the train with bread, butter, fruit, canned things, cakes, chocolate and other delicacies. Tea-making materials we had also, and plenty of sugar. So filled was our compartment with food, flowers, banners, guns, tea kettles and miscellaneous stuff that we moved about with difficulty and were forever apologizing for walking on each other's feet.

For two nights and the better part of two days we traveled southward through fields of wheat, barley and potatoes, where women in bright red and blue smocks toiled among the ripening harvests. News of the train had gone down through the line, and the first stage of our journey, through the white night, was one continued ovation. At every station crowds had gathered to cheer the women and to demand a sight of Botchkareva. It was largely a masculine crowd soldiers mostly, goodnatured and laughing, but many women were there too, nurses, working girls, peasants. Occasionally one saw ladies in dinner gowns escorted by officer friends.

The farther we traveled from Petrograd, the point of contact in Russia with western civilization, the more apparent it grew that things were terribly wrong with the empire. More and more the changed character of the station crowds reminded us of the widespread disruption of the army. The men who met the train wore soldiers' uniforms but they had lost all of their upright, soldierly bearing. They slouched like convicts, they were dirty and unkempt, and their eyes were full of vacuous insolence. Absence of discipline and all restraint had robbed them of whatever manhood they had once possessed. The news of the women's battalion had drawn these men like a swarm of bees. They thrust their unshaven faces into the car windows, bawling the parrot phrases taught them by their German spy leaders. "Who fights for the damned capitalists? Who fights for English blood suckers? We don't fight."

And the women, scorn flashing from their eyes, flung back: "That is the reason why we do. Go home, you cowards, and let women fight for Russia."

Their last, flimsy thread of "peace" propaganda exhausted the men usually fell back on personal insults, but to these the women, following strict orders, made no reply. When the language became too coarse the women simply closed the windows. No actual violence was ever offered them. When they left the train for hot water or for tea, for more food or to buy newspapers, they walked so fearlessly into the crowds that the men withdrew, sneering and growling, but standing aside.

There was something indescribably strange about going on a journey to a destination absolutely unknown, except to the one in command of the expedition. Above all it was strange to feel that you were seeing women voluntarily giving up the last shred of protection and security supposed to be due them. They were going to meet death, death in battle against a foreign foe, the first women in the world to volunteer for such an end. Yet every one was happy, and the only fear expressed was lest the battalion should not be sent at once to the trenches.

CHAPTER 12

Ishbel Ross:
Front Page Reporters

After World War I the number of women entering journalism continued to increase although male editors rarely gave them the opportunity to handle the same kind of story as men reporters. In 1910 the U.S. census showed 4,000 women employed full-time as journalists, but by the end of the 1920's that number had tripled to about 12,000, representing one out every four journalists in the country. Many of these women, however, were still confined to the women's pages or to feature writing, stunt and "sob sister" reporting.

But occasionally a few managed to break into the masculine preserve of "hard" news — crime, politics, courts, government, general assignment — or gain a seat at the copy or city desks where decisions were made on news content. One who proved that she could hold her own with any man was Ishbel Ross, a talented woman from Scotland, who came to New York in 1919 as a reporter for the *Tribune* after working briefly in Canada.

During more than a decade with the *Tribune*, Ross "seemed to come closer than any of the others (newspaperwomen) to the man's idea of what a newspaperwoman should be," according to her city editor, Stanley Walker. Although Walker claimed many newspaperwomen were "slovenly, incompetent vixens," he gave her credit for "unflustered competence." He stated his views in a "Foreword" to *Ladies of the Press*, the first history of women reporters, written by Ross in 1936.

Ross researched the book shortly after she left reporting in 1933, following her successful coverage of some of the biggest stories of the day, including the kidnapping of the Lindbergh baby. While assigned to the celebrated Hall-Mills murder trial, she met Bruce Rae, a rival reporter for the *New York Times*, whom she later married. Her decision to give up journalism to write books came after the birth of a daughter.

For *Ladies of the Press: The Story of Women in Journalism by an In-sider* (New York: Harper, 1936), she interviewed scores of newspaperwom-en in different parts of the United States, making the book a valuable source today. It was among the first of her 16 published books, many of them bio-graphies of famous women, including Elizabeth Blackwell, Clara Barton and the wives of Presidents. She died in New York in 1975 at the age of 79.

Ladies of the Press sketched the careers of women in all phases of journalism from society pages to foreign correspondence. In the opening chapter, Ross told the exciting story of those few women who, weathering what she called "storms of prejudice," had been able to advance to covering top news stories. She titled the chapter "Front-page Girl." Excerpts follow.

FRONT-PAGE GIRL

Five years after the Civil War an eighteen-year-old girl named Sally Joy left the plush security of her home in Vermont and talked herself into a job on the Boston *Post*. It was only a matter of weeks until the men in the office were lining the floor with papers to keep her white satin ball gown from picking up the dust.

Sally did not need this newsprint carpet laid for her ambitious feet. It merely set the key for the befuddled dismay with which the normal news-paper man regards the unwelcome sight of a woman in the city room. Things have changed in the newspaper world since Sally's time. The type-writer has taken the place of the pen; the linotype has supplanted hand composition; there is little dust on the floor of the metropolitan city room; and the girl reporter rarely shows up during working hours in a white satin gown.

She must be free to leap nimbly through fire lines, dodge missiles at a strike, board a liner from a swaying ladder, write copy calmly in the heat of a Senate debate, or count the dead in a catastrophe. She never takes time to wonder why someone does not find her a chair, change the ribbon of her typewriter or hold smelling salts to her nose as she views a scene of horror.

"I want to be treated like a man," said Sally, who was a little ahead of her time. But she could not persuade her colleagues that she was anything but a helpless female. At first there was indignation about having "a woman on the sheet" and the youth assigned to escort her to all functions beginning after seven o'clock was the butt of the staff.

But the girl reporter hung on and got her reward. She was sent with-out masculine aid to cover a suffrage convention in Vermont, traveling with Lucy Stone and Julia Ward Howe. As the only woman at the press table, an admiring colleague chronicled her presence:

"Miss Sally Joy of Boston has a portfolio at the Reporters' table in the Convention for the *Post* of her native city. She is pretty, piquante, and dresses charmingly. She has a high regard for Mrs. Bloomer, although she diverges from that good lady on the science of clothes. Miss Joy has made a reputation as a newspaper correspondent and reporter of which any man might be proud. And this is saying a good deal for a woman. Miss Joy is as independent as she is self-supporting and she votes for Woman's Suffrage."

Sally was neither the first nor the best of the early women reporters. She was merely the symbol of a point of view that has changed surprisingly little in the last half century. She went from the Boston *Post* to the *Herald* to do a society column. She called herself Penelope Penfeather and sometimes wrote about fashions and the home. In due time she married and faded into the mists, but not until she had helped to found the General Federation of Women's Clubs and had served as the first president of the New England Women's Press Association.

Her demand to be treated as a man has echoed innumerable times in city rooms throughout the country. And all that she stood for is still regarded as a threat to the peace, honor and coziness of that sound haunt of masculinity — the city room, practically as sacred to men as a stag club or the pre-Volstead saloon.

To-day there are nearly twelve thousand women editors, feature writers and reporters in the country. They have found their way into all of the large newspaper offices and most of the small ones. They have invaded every branch of the business, but have not made much impression in the front-page field.

This does not mean that they have failed to make themselves felt in newspaper work; on the contrary, their success has been substantial. They hold executive posts. Two have dominant voices in important papers on the Eastern seaboard. Many of them edit small papers of their own. They run Sunday magazines and book supplements, write editorials, do politics, foreign correspondence, features, straight news, criticism, copy reading and sports writing, as well as the old standbys — the woman's page, clubs and social news.

They excel in the feature field and dominate the syndicates. They stop only at the political cartoon. They function in the advertising, business, art, promotion and mechanical departments, as well as in the editorial rooms. They have arrived, in a convincing way. But the fact remains that they have made surprisingly little progress on the front page, which is still the critical test. Not even a score of women take orders direct from the city desks in New York. The proportion is even less in other cities. They come singly or in pairs on a paper, rarely more. There are just as few on the general staff as there were at the turn of the century.

Whenever possible, they are steered into the quieter by-waters of the newspaper plant, away from the main current of life, news, excitement, curses and ticker machines. They are segregated where their voices will not be heard too audibly in the clatter. They get tucked away on the upper floors where the departments flourish. They lurk in the library, diligent girls wedded to the files.

Most of them would rather be where they are. The specialists increase in number and usefulness each year. They have better hours, fair pay, a more leisured existence. They get their own following. They don't have to beat the drums every day they live. They can make dinner engagements and keep them. They have time to buy their hats.

But out in the city room — where high-powered lights blaze on rows of desks, where copy readers bend like restless caterpillars over the reporter's work, where the city editor usually resembles a sedate professor rather than the Mad Hatter of the films, where phones jangle and tickers click — only two or three women can be found, working quietly at their typewriters in a fog of abstraction.

They are the front-page girls who somehow have weathered storms of prejudice — the odd creatures who have been pictured as doing things only slightly more impossible than they all have attempted at one time or another. They are on the inner newspaper track. They are there because they have felt the bewitchment of a compelling profession. There is little else they can do once they have tasted its elixir. Strange music sings in their ears. Visions haunt them as they walk the streets. They fall asleep with the sound of rumbling presses in their heads. They have seen too much and it hasn't been good for their health.

For the woman reporter goes beyond the news into the raw material from which it springs. She catches the rapt look of the genius and the furtive glance of the criminal. She detects the lies, the debauchery and the nobility of her fellow men. She watches the meek grow proud and the proud turn humble. She marvels only when people who have feared publicity get drunk with it, and strain for a place on the front page.

She walks unscathed through street riots, strikes, fires, catastrophes and revolution, her press card opening the way for her. She watches government in the making, sees Presidents inaugurated, Kings crowned, heroes acclaimed, champions launched on the world. She has a banquet seat with the mighty. She travels far and wide in search of news, and uses every vehicle known to man. She sees a murderer condemned to death and watches the raw agony of his wife while he dies.

Nine times out of ten her day's work takes her to the fringes of tragedy. News visits a home most often to annihilate it. The shadow of a reporter falling across the doorstep may presage the collapse of a lifetime of work. The woman reporter must face harsh facts without any qualms about her business. She must be ready for such hazards as may befall her. She must be calm and full of stamina. For she will savor strange bitters as well as alluring sweets; endure fatigue and disappointment beyond reason; withstand rebuffs that wither or exhilarate in turn; meet abuse with the equanimity born of self-control; and function with complete belief in what she is doing and loyalty to her paper.

She must have a sound sense of the values of life and great capacity to withstand the shocks of human emotion. She must see with clairvoyance, judgment or experience the salient points of any situation; be resourceful and good-natured; have initiative and enough perception to avoid being taken in. She must know how to get her facts, to weigh them with sagacity and, above all, how to write.

Where is this paragon to be found? No editor believes that she exists. She probably doesn't. And if she did, she would not have much chance to prove it, for although women have hit the sky in feature writing, they still have a long way to go to establish themselves as first-string news reporters.

* * *

Lorena Hickok repeatedly wrote the news leads on stories of national importance for the Associated Press, which has gone in heavily for women after years of indifference to their merits. Genevieve Forbes Herrick brought distinction to her craft by her work for the Chicago *Tribune*. She outmatched her competitors time and again, doing the major stories of the day with grace, speed and accuracy. Marjorie Driscoll, of the Los Angeles *Examiner*, is another example of the finest type of news writer.

Grace Robinson has starred so often in the role of front-page girl that she has no competitor in the number of big stories she has covered within a given period of time. She did the Hall-Mills and the Snyder-Gray trials for the New York *Daily News*, and scores of other assignments that any man might envy. Elenore Kellogg, who died in the summer of 1935, led the *World* repeatedly with brilliantly handled news stories, and had the satisfaction of seeing her work under banner heads. Ruth Finney, a Scripps-Howard star, tops the field for Washington. She has achieved spectacular success in the political field and ranks with the best men in the Press Gallery.

* * *

The most sensible usually make the best reporters. The women who have gone the farthest in journalism are not those who have yipped the most loudly about their rights. Unless aggressiveness is backed by real ability, as in Rheta Childe Dorr's case, it is only a boomerang. Nothing has done more to keep women reporters in the shade. Peace at any price is the city room philosophy.

It is absurd to maintain that a woman can do everything a man can do on a paper. She can't get into the Lotus Club in New York, or cross the Harvard Club threshold. She is denied the chummy Senator's room in Washington when he has no time to answer her questions except as he changes for dinner.

The rule does not work so conclusively the other way. The only obstacle the gentlemen of the press have encountered is Mrs. Roosevelt's Monday morning conferences. The youths who are picked for the pink tea assignments are welcomed with joy at the woman's meeting. It is a sad reflection for the woman reporter who swears by her sex that the most pampered

scribe at feminine gatherings is usually the man — and a man who would rather not be there.

But admitting that there are a few places from which women reporters
are debarred, this is scarcely an important argument against their usefulness.
It has no more significance than the inability of a man to write a good fashion story without expert aid. The functions of the city staff are always interchangeable. A woman may cover a subway wreck and a man do a fashion show on the same afternoon, with excellent results in both cases. A
good reporter can do telling work with almost any set of facts, short of rela-
tivity. He need not be a specialist. He need not even be initiated.

But the feeling is there and the seasoned newspaper woman has to recognize it. If she is wise she will go on her way, taking things in her stride.
She will not fuss over periods of quiet. She will mind her own business,
take the assignments handed out to her and never grouse unduly. She cannot always live in the new writer's seventh heaven. There are dull days with
nothing but obits to write. But be sure as she lives, news will stir again. She
will watch it rustle through the office. The city editor will come over to
her, hand her a bulletin, and from this cryptic note may spring the story of
the decade.

* * *

The doubts raised by editors about her are legion. Can she write?
Usually. Can she spell? At least as well as her masculine colleagues, often
better. Is she lacking in a sense of humor? Rarely. Reporting now is largely realistic, except for the occasional word orgies at a sensational trial, and
then it is an assumed frenzy, done with the tongue in the cheek. News writers have too much sense to beat their breasts in public now. Their editors
no longer expect it. The public would laugh.

But the most serious charge brought against the newspaper woman is
inaccuracy. This is the one real chink in her armor. Precision of thought is
the first requisite of good reporting. As far back as 1898 Arnold Bennett
seized on this weakness in the woman reporter. His criticism is much the
same as the city editor's to-day. No amount of careful work has served to
uproot it. Even the most unprejudiced editor shudders a little when a new
woman walks through the city room. Will her sentences parse? Will she get
the paper in a libel suit? Will she verify every fact? Will she know how to
round up a story? Will she cause trouble in the office? He values the wom-
en who happen to have succeeded in his own organization, but he thinks of
them always as the exceptions. He has not yet been able to accept the
species without reservation.

Therefore, the newspaper woman has to be twice as careful as the
newspaper man in order to make headway at all. The tradition of sloppy
work dies hard. She has every reason to worry when the copy boy brings
the wet paper fresh from the presses and lays it on her desk. There is something particularly appalling about the error in print. Her eye rushes to the
head the copy reader has given her story. It isn't vanity that makes her read

every line with care. She is desperately anxious to know if everything is right.

The layman who cherishes the foolish belief that only half of what he reads in a newspaper is true, never dreams of the conscientious work that lies behind the columns he hastily scans. No human being but a well-trained reporter would hunt through five books of reference to get a middle initial correct. No one else would find so many ways of checking a circumstance that the average person accepts at face value.

The reporter scourges himself to perfection. Yet the public still believes that he is slipshod, inaccurate, a deliberate falsifier. In actual fact, the conscientious news writer on a responsible paper is the most slavishly exact person in the world. He splits hairs and swears by books of reference. He has a passion for verification, an honest love for facts. The good woman reporter has the same exacting code. The crispness of her style, the keen viewpoint, the explicit phrase, the potent paragraph, are all nullified if she does not have the essential newspaper virtue of absolute accuracy.

Often her early training has a bearing on the exactitude of her mental processes. The newspaper women have arrived at their various goals by odd routes. They have taught and nursed and been stenographers. They have scrubbed floors and sold in shops and danced in the chorus. The present tendency is for them to break in fresh from college. Some have wandered into the profession by accident; others have battered their way in; a few have simply walked in the front door without knocking. But the same spirit of enterprise has propelled most of them into the exciting newspaper game.

* * *

On the whole, newspaper women make few demands on their city editors. They would gladly work for nothing, rather than be denied the city room. They scarcely ever fuss about their salaries, which range from $35 to $150 per week in the large cities, and from $7 to $50 in the smaller ones. They rarely ask for increases, or complain about their fare. They work hard and have a somewhat touching faith in what they are doing. They are seldom lazy. But the highest compliment to which the deluded creatures respond is the city editor's acknowledgment that their work is just like a man's. This automatically gives them a complacent glow, for they are all aware that no right-minded editor wants the so-called woman's touch in the news.

The fact remains that they never were thoroughly welcome in the city room and they are not quite welcome now. They are there on sufferance, although the departments could scarcely get along without them. But if the front-page girls were all to disappear tomorrow no searching party would go out looking for more, since it is the fixed conviction of nearly every newspaper executive that a man in the same spot would be exactly twice as good.

They may listen to smooth words and chivalrous sentiments, but what every city editor thinks in his black but honest heart is: 'Girls, we like you well enough but we don't altogether trust you."

CHAPTER 13

Margaret Bourke-White: Photography

World War II opened doors to women journalists. With men reporters in the armed forces, women moved into new jobs in the male-dominated city rooms and proved that they were able to cover "hard" news (stories written under deadline pressure) as well as "soft" (feature) assignments. Other women moved into radio jobs in programming, production and on-the-air spots.

For some the war brought opportunities as war correspondents. Among those reporting for wire services were Inez Robb of International News Service and Inez and Ruth Cowan of the Associated Press. Others who helped cover the war included Esther Van Wagoner Tufty, a Washington correspondent for Middle Western newspapers; Leah Burdette of *P.M.*; Marguerite Higgins of the *New York Herald Tribune*, who later won a Pulitzer Prize for her coverage of the Korean War; and Dickey Chapelle, a free-lance photojournalist who died while covering the Vietnam war in 1965.

In World War II — as well as the wars to come, Korea and Vietnam — women correspondents encountered varying degrees of prejudice. Higgins was once commanded to leave Korea because the Army claimed "there are no facilities for ladies at the front." She protested to General Douglas MacArthur, who rescinded the order. In Vietnam a major snapped at Gloria Emerson of the *New York Times*, "Vietnam is no place for a woman...Why, for Christ's sake, didn't they send a man out here?"

Perhaps more than anyone else it was Margaret Bourke-White, a photojournalist for *Life* magazine, who proved that competence as a war correspondent had no relationship to sex. One of the world's pre-eminent photographers, she pursued assignments ranging from Russia to India and the United States, moving from wars to riots and from floods to stories about world leaders.

Born in 1904, Bourke-White turned to photography when faced with the need to support herself after an early marriage failed. Beginning with a $20 second-hand camera with a cracked lens, she went on to earn a reputation as an industrial photographer in Cleveland. The perfection of her compositions, which transformed factories into "Gothic cathedrals" (according to one critic), caught the attention of Henry Luce, who hired her as a photographer for *Fortune* magazine. During the 1930's she and novelist Erskine Caldwell, who later became her husband, collaborated on a classic documentary of misery among Southern sharecroppers.

When *Life* magazine was launched in 1936, she became one of its original staff members, creating memorable pictures in the United States and Europe, including scenes of the Nazi attack on Moscow in 1941. When the United States entered World War II, she became the first woman correspondent accredited to the Army Air Force, and covered the fighting in North Africa and Italy. The Army used her as a model for its first set of uniforms for women correspondents, which included a pink dress for special occasions.

In spite of her fame, she met opposition from authorities when she sought permission to cover the war on the same basis as a man. To get to North Africa for the Allied invasion, she was forced to go by sea, instead of air, because flying was considered too dangerous for a woman. Her ship was torpedoed, but she escaped in a lifeboat, continuing to shoot pictures. She also had to plead for months before receiving permission to accompany bombing raids.

At the end of the war she took some of her best-known pictures, for example, photographs of the Nazi concentration camp at Buchenwald. Later she covered riots in India between Moslems and Hindus and journeyed to South Africa, where she descended 2,000 feet in a basket to photograph the interior of a gold mine.

During the Korean War, she concentrated chiefly on pictures of guerilla fighters. On her way back to the United States from Korea in 1952, she suffered the first symptoms of Parkinson's disease, a nerve disorder against which she waged a courageous but losing struggle for nearly two decades. She died in 1971 at the age of 67.

In the following excerpt from chapter two of *Purple Heart Valley: A Combat Chronicle of the War in Italy* (New York: Simon and Schuster, 1944), Bourke-White discussed her preparations to cover the Italian front.

I had come to Italy by air, flying by Clipper to ETOUSA and by troop transport plane to NATOUSA. ("They sound like aunts of Hiawatha," one of my friends wrote.) In the abbreviated vocabulary used by the Army, these stand respectively for European and North African Theaters of Operations, United States Army. After completing my work in NATOUSA, I was sent from MBS to PBS: from the Mediterranean Base Section to the Peninsular Base Section. As war correspondents, we go through the same formalities as Army personnel on transfers; although we may choose our spots, subject to Army approval, we obtain orders from the office of the commanding general. Our passage is free, but it must be authorized by the military authorities to whom we are responsible.

My travel orders — number-three priority — were headed cryptically in big red letters: U.S. CONFIDENTIAL EQUALS BRITISH SECRET. This sounded very hush-hush indeed. But it was less so than if they had been marked: U.S. SECRET EQUALS BRITISH MOST SECRET. Army legend has it that the ultimate in secret documents are classified: DESTROY WITHOUT READING.

My papers may not have been MOST SECRET, but they certainly were most impressive. They were supplied to me with six carbons, and they read:

SUBJECT: Travel orders
TO: All concerned
1. Following will proceed by first available transportation from North Africa to Italy, to such places within the Theater as may be necessary for the accomplishment of her mission.
2. Travel by military aircraft is authorized. Rations in kind will be provided.

Margaret Bourke-White, Photographer
By command of General EISENHOWER

Even traveling with all this CONFIDENTIAL EQUALS SECRET stuff, I still found myself resorting to what we correspondents call hitch-hiking. You hang around an airport until something is going your way and there is room for you on it. In my case, in addition to finding space for myself, I had to find room for one Speed Graphic, two Rolleiflexes, three Linhofs, a Graflex fitted for telephoto, a battery of interchangeable lenses, various filters, film packs, flash guns, flash bulbs, a bedroll, and a typewriter.

Several months before, when a torpedoing during the North African invasion had made almost a clean sweep of my photographic equipment except for a few small odds and ends I had managed to take with me in the lifeboat, I had resolved, while still bobbing around on the high seas, that if I ever reached shore I would replace my cameras with smaller sizes. It took a torpedoing to make me really appreciate a Rolleiflex, that admirable, compact, featherweight camera. I had to comb the entire United states to re-place the rest of the equipment, but I did it uniformly in 2¼ x 3¼ size. I am a fanatic about interchangeability of parts. Especially in a war zone, where it is so easy to break things and so impossible to replace them, I carry duplicate cameras so I can pull out a new one when the one I am using gets out of order, and I have all my accessories and lens mounts machined so that any item will fit into any camera. Each of the three Linhofs was fitted with a range finder and infinity stops, so it could be used either on a tripod or hand-held like a Speed Graphic. All lenses, including those on the Rollei-flexes, were fitted with synchronizers for flash-bulb equipment. This ar-rangement proved invaluable in Italy, for it rained so much that I would have lost many daylight pictures had it not been for synchronized flashes.

The paring of my film size from the 3¼ x 4¼ I had used on previous voyages to the 2¼ x 3¼ size used on this trip shaved two hundred pounds off the weight of my raw film stock and supplies. All told, my seven cam-eras with their thirty-odd lenses, their infinite repair parts and accessories, along with sufficient quantity of film and peanut flash bulbs to last half a year, weighed 250 pounds. This was an improvement over the 450 pounds I had carried to the wars the year before, and a great reduction from the 800 pounds with which I had flown across China into Russia at the outbreak of the war with Germany. To compress my equipment and supplies into 250 pounds I had figured down to the last ounce.

My clothes fitted into the fifty-five pounds allotted airplane travelers in war zones. This poundage was not easy to achieve either, as it had to in-clude both summer and winter uniforms, skirts for those occasions when even a war photographer has to wear a skirt, trousers to work in, heavy field clothes, boots, and woolen underwear.

What a war correspondent wears has been carefully laid down in the rule books by the War Department in Washington. A war correspondent wears officer's uniform but without officer's insignia. We have an insignia of our own which has made striking progress since the beginning of the war. First, it was a green armband (green signifies non-combatant) bearing the unfortunate letters WC. Many war correspondents were made happier when this was reduced simply to C for the reporters and P for the photographers. (Photographers in battle areas are classified as war correspondents.) Now we have replaced the wide green armbands, which were always clumsy and slipping out of place, with a neatly designed patch reading U.S. War Cor-respondent. In place of the usual shoulder bars worn by officers, we wear metal cutout insignia bearing the words War Correspondent, and on our caps and lapels we wear the army US. The purpose of our uniforms is not only to take on protective coloration among soldiers, but to save us from being shot as spies if we are captured. If we are taken prisoner we have another privilege in addition to staying alive. We receive pay, just as Army officers and soldiers do, under international law. Since we have no actual rank, we were given an arbitrary rank which at the beginning of the war was second lieutenant. Imagine my delight on my return to the battle zone last fall to find that we had been promoted. We are now theoretical captains. But we have to be captured before we start collecting that captain's pay, and we are always subject to certain Army regulations, and may be court-martialed.

Becoming a war correspondent is a matter of the most thorough investigation on the part of the War Department, as to background, patriotism, and reliability. By the time you are accredited you have no secrets from the War Department and neither do your ancestors; but it is right that this should be so because as a war correspondent you have access to many sources of vital military information. You are in a position of great trust.

I was a very proud girl indeed when I first received the Army credentials for which I had applied, as *Life* photographer, shortly after our country went into the war. The War Department had a new problem with me since I was a woman photographer. They had shown no discrimination, I am happy to say, because of my sex; the difficulty was in deciding what I should wear. They knew what the men should wear, because that had been laid down in the Army handbooks, but no one had ever had to dress a woman war correspondent accredited in America. I spent five days in Washington going over materials and details with the Army War College, and finally decided that I should wear just what the men war correspondents wear: the same type of blouse, coat, field cap, etc., as an officer wears, but with a skirt for "dress."

I had my uniform tailored to fit me, and I loved it. Then, during the torpedoing I have mentioned, all but the clothes on my back were sunk. The losses included some prized items: a fine pair of jodhpur boots which had been made for me in London, as only Bond Street can make them, and a neat little "battle jacket" such as pilots wear. These Air Force togs had been designed by General Eaker, and he had given the original jacket model to General Spaatz, who still wears it. Mine was made by London military tailors, during the time I was accredited to the Eighth Air Force, and it was the first that had ever been made for a woman.

I was almost as distressed by having these clothes sunk as by losing my camera. When I finally arrived like a drowned rat in Algiers, I was taken for a drying out by my Air Force pals to the gingerbread villa then occupied by General Spaatz. Inside the door the first person I ran into was General Eaker, who had flown down for a conference with "Tooey" Spaatz.

"I lost that wonderful jacket you designed," I blurted out, "and my beautiful jodhpurs."

So General Eaker, on his return to London, called up the shops, found they had my measurements on file, and a new pair of jodhpurs and a new battle jacket arrived in time for the Italian campaign.

After a torpedoing everybody helps you. General Doolittle had greeted me with the words, "Margaret, what do you need most?"

"I'd love to have another shirt to change into," I said. And then I hesitated.

"What else?" he asked.

"Well, of course I lost all my pajamas."

"Now I know why I've been carrying my sister-in-law's pajamas all these years," said kind General Jimmy. "She gave me green silk ones. I've never used them because I always sleep raw, but if you want them, they're yours."

The pajamas were wonderful, and the shirt with which he presented me had a history. After the bombing of Tokyo, when Jimmy Doolittle landed by parachute with his men in China, and finally made his way to the outside world, he arrived in Cairo with as meager a wardrobe as the one in which I had survived the torpedoing. Since he was to be given an official banquet that night, something had to be done. He found an Egyptian tailor who promised to make a uniform in a single day. By six in the evening a uniform of sorts was completed, but the blouse was so short, reported General Jimmy, that it reached up to his chest, and the shirt was so wide that it needed tucks. It was this shirt that he gave me, and I took it to an Arab tailor on the edge of the Sahara. The Arab spoke French, so to him the shirt was *la chemise du General*. Cut down to fit me, the Doolittle shirt did splendid service, although to the pilots with whom I worked it was always known as the General's chemise.

So in the fall of 1943, when I packed for North Africa and Italy, into my fifty-five pounds went the Doolittle shirt, my new jodhpur boots, and the new battle jacket designed by General Eaker. And at the bottom of my flight bag went one unwarlike item — an evening dress designed for me by Adrian in Hollywood. "I want something to dance in with soldiers," I had told him, adding, "if I get the chance. And it must pack up so small that it would fit in the palm of your hand."

Adrian had created just the right dress. It had a transparent white shirtwaist top and a cleverly draped black filmy skirt. Off, it was one of those little numbers that look prim on the hanger; on, there was nothing school-teacherish about it.

As on all trips, I carried cosmetics in a little pigskin-fitted case. I think I would have gone to the battlefield without rations before I would go without face cream. I remember once when this so fascinated a certain infantry major with whom I shared a dugout during a night at the front that he nicknamed me Crisco-puss. I also carried vitamins, but I might have spared those ounces of weight, for Army food is so well planned and substantial that never once did I feel the impulse to reach for a vitamin.

Each year, when I prepared for my trip to the war fronts, the selection of which spot I am to cover is the subject of much attempted crystalgazing among the editors of *Life* and myself. We get together and discuss how we think the news may develop and what places I am most interested in covering. The final choice is a mutual one. I always want to get to the spot where we think there will be the biggest news, and this is just where they want me to be to take photographs.

So far our guesses have been good ones, although none of us profess to be prophets. Much credit for the selections goes to Mr. Wilson Hicks, *Life*'s executive editor, formerly of AP, who seems to have an almost instinctive sense for how the news will unfold.

In the spring of 1941, both my executive editor and I believed that Russia would soon be big news. Only a month after I arrived there Germany invaded the Soviet Union, and I was fortunately on the spot to photograph the Russian war. In the summer of 1942, before a single Flying Fortress had flown over enemy territory, Mr. Hicks foresaw that the growth of our Bomber Command would be one of the great stories of the war. This was a happy choice, for I love airplanes. I became accredited to the Air Force, working with our heavy bombers during those early history-making flights from England, and following through with the North African campaign.

So in the summer of 1943, my editor and I again brought out the crystal ball and did our guessing about how we thought events might develop.

"I'd like to see the war on the ground," I said. "I'd like to photograph artillery. And see what the Engineers are doing. And there must be dozens of things that go on to make up a war that our American public doesn't know much about."

Just at this time an inquiry came for my services from the Army Service Forces in the War Department. Under General Brehon Somervell, the ASF was doing a gigantic job of supply about which our American people knew little. Sixty per cent of the war was a matter of supplying our troops with food, ammunition, medical and even spiritual services (the latter under chaplains). All this was the result of a chain-belt system which girdled the world — reached from our factories to the front lines, according to a process known to the Service Forces as "logistics." But to most American people "logistics," if they ever heard about it, was just a word. That was where I came in. From their headquarters in the Pentagon Building, the ASF issued a request that I go overseas with our Army to show how supplies are brought to our troops: to tell in photographs the great story of "logistics."

This logistics business suited everybody. It pleased *Life*, because they could show in pictures that "it's a big war," which was the title they subsequently gave to one series of pictures I turned out during my mission. It delighted me, because it gave me a chance to follow up many of the subjects in which I was most interested. Having always liked industrial photography, I was eager to portray the Engineers. ASF in addition to Engineers and Quartermaster, includes Medical Corps, Transportation, Signal Corps,

WAC's, Chaplains, and Ordnance. Through Ordnance I would reach Artillery. Through many of these diversified activities I would reach the soldier at the front and picture his activities from a new point of view. The focal point of all this gigantic system of service and supply was the front-line soldier, and that was the story that I wanted to tell in pictures.

I left by plane on Labor Day, 1943, and flew by way of England to North Africa. I carried in the pocket of my new summer uniform an informal note which brought me the world. It read:

WAR DEPARTMENT
Headquarters
Army Service Forces, Washington, D.C.

3 September 1943

Commanding General, NATOUSA
Army Services Forces

Dear Tom:

Margaret Bourke-White is coming to the North African theater to take pictures of Army Service Forces' operations; I have felt for a long time the need for such a service and was quite happy to accept her offer and that of her employer to do the job for us.

I am particularly anxious that Miss Bourke-White be given opportunity to photograph the complete supply and service story in the actual theater of war and will appreciate any assistance you and your staff can give to her.

Sincerely,

/s/ Bill
BREHON SOMERVELL
Lieutenant General
Commanding

That "in the actual theater of war" phrase was the most helpful one General Somervell could have written. It did much to overcome that natural reluctance in some quarters to allow a woman into the combat zone.

CHAPTER 14

Ruth Crane:
Early Days in Broadcasting

With the advent of commercial radio in the 1920's, women found their opportunities severely limited. Newscasting was reserved for men because station managers and advertisers held that men's voices alone carried authority and believability. Still, some women managed to find a place behind the microphone, although they were largely restricted to traditional women's fare — housekeeping hints and recipes interspersed with interview shows and public service programs.

When Mary Margaret McBride, a well-established magazine and newspaper reporter, began her radio career in 1934 in New York, she was told to pretend to be a wise old grandmother and dispense homey philosophy. In the midst of a sentence she finally burst out into the microphone, "Oh, what's the use? I can't do it! I'm not a grandmother! I'm not a mother. I'm not even married. Nothing about all this I'm saying sounds real to me and that's because it isn't. The truth is I'm a reporter and I would like to come here every day and tell you about places I go and people I meet. Write me if you'd like that. But I can't be a grandmother any more!"

Her listeners responded and she was launched on one of the most successful careers in radio history, earning the title First Lady of Radio for her daily interview program that continued on network radio until her retirement in 1960.

Other women entered off-the-air aspects of broadcasting. Judith Cary Waller was the first manager of WMAQ, a Chicago station that began broadcasting in 1922. She remained in broadcasting after the station was sold to NBC in 1931 although she was moved from station manager to public service director for the network's central division. She held the job until retirement from NBC in 1957.

During World War II, women were used on the airways to promote the war effort. But newscasting remained a field "for men only" well into the era of television that caught hold in the 1950's.

Yet, by virtue of hard work women began to be taken seriously as newscasters. In 1946 Pauline Frederick was hired by ABC even though she received regular news assignments only if men were not available.

"I had to make my own opportunity to cover real news," she recalled in a 1974 interview with a journalism student, Gioia Diliberto. "I was told by my editor that there was great objection to a woman being on the air for serious issues, and he had orders not to use me. But he said if by chance, I got an exclusive, he'd have to use me, adding 'though I'll slit your throat if you tell anyone I gave you this advice.'"

Frederick kept quiet but worked very hard to get exclusive stories at the United Nations. After covering a foreign ministers' conference, she asked her chief for regular news assignments. He turned her down, she told Diliberto, answering, "It isn't that you haven't proved yourself, but when listeners hear a woman's voice, they'll turn off their radios, because a woman's voice just doesn't carry authority."

Continuing to persevere in spite of prejudice, Frederick began television broadcasting in 1948 and became TV's first successful newswoman, covering the United Nations for NBC from 1953 until her retirement in 1972.

Difficulties encountered by women in early-day radio and television were discussed by Ruth Crane Schaefer, who spent 27 years in broadcasting in Detroit and Washington, D.C., in an interview conducted in 1975 as part of an oral history project of the American Women in Radio and Television. A somewhat shortened version is reprinted here.

Mower: My name is Pat Mower. I'm a member of the Washington, D.C. chapter of American Women in Radio and Television. The date is November 18, 1975, and I am in the home of Mrs. Ruth Crane Schaefer to interview her about her early days in radio and television — as a part of the AWRT Oral History Project on women pioneers in the broadcasting industry. Interviews will be placed on permanent record in the Library of The Broadcast Pioneers in Washington, D. C.

Mrs. Schaefer was born Ruth Franklin in Springfield, Missouri. She received her early schooling in Missouri. Then, special courses at Drury College, the University of Missouri — and later at Northwestern University and The Chicago Art Institute gave her a background in journalism, theatricals, salesmanship and literature which prepared her for a successful career in both radio and television.

Ruth, I know your broadcasting career began in the very early days of radio but just when, how and where did you get that first radio job?

Crane: Well, it was in 1929 and you remember that things were pretty bad then, or were getting bad — I mean financially. I was in Detroit and had to look for a job. I applied at two places — the J. L. Hudson Company as a fashion writer and WJR, the radio station — not knowing what I might be required or even able to do there. Oddly, I was accepted at both places and I guess I took the WJR job because it was within walking distance of where I lived. Of course, it turned out to be a lucky choice because the broadcasting business came through the depression better than many other businesses.

Mower: That's right. I remember those depression days and how difficult it was to get any kind of a job. What about your qualifications for a radio job, Ruth? I know your background. Was it helpful at all in fitting you for what you went into in radio?

Crane: I guess I was as much qualified, or maybe more so, than most people but I hadn't anything that exactly fitted the broadcasting business. No one else had either in those days.

Mower: There really weren't any college or university courses for radio, were there?

Crane: Not at that time. Of course, some came along later at the University of Michigan and I helped teach some classes there — but that was perhaps 10 years later. I had some dramatic experience and had written copy for some store magazines in Chicago — advertising copy — and had taught shorthand at night while attending Northwestern University. In Detroit I had done market research for an Advertising Agency and, of course, I could type and that was important.

Mower: That is an asset, isn't it?

Crane: I've tried to get so many younger people to understand that, but they don't always want to. Anyway, Leo Fitzpatrick, head of WJR, and later President of the National Association of Broadcasters, said, "Well, there isn't any job open, but we do need people and if you can make a job for yourself, O.K. — $30 a week to start."

Mower: Big money, too!

Crane: Well, in those days it was sufficient.

Mower: Right — it really was big money then.

Crane: So, I went to work — 9 to 5 or 6 or something of the sort — and I just helped out wherever I was needed. I soon observed that the time salesmen were coming into the studio with some commercial material scribbled on the back of an envelope and handing it to the announcer who, if he could read it at all, made little effort to put it together — and there was no record kept of what was actually said. We weren't making recordings in those days anyway. So, I decided that that procedure needed organizing and I did it — to everyone's relief. So, I became Commercial Editor, a job that I kept on with even during my tenure as Women's Editor.

Mower: Then did that develop into a permanent job or something else?

Crane: Yes, they had a woman on the air conducting a Foods Program but her family responsibilities and her health made it necessary for someone else to fill in for her frequently and so they called on me for that. This was a daily program called Mrs. Page's Household Economy and eventually I became the regular six days a week Mrs. Page.

Mower: You were on as Mrs. Page — not as Mrs. Crane?

Crane: Oh yes. You know in those days we always took a name other than our own on the air.

Mower: I know and I always wondered why.

Crane: Well, you know, I think possibly the station management felt that our ability to do a job might be questioned, if people knew exactly who we were, so we were given a pseudonym so we wouldn't be recognized. Oh, I was Alice Franklin — I think you mentioned that my maiden name was Franklin — and then Mrs. Page and I had several other names, I think. Eventually I became Ruth Schaefer after marriage but I continued on with the name Ruth Crane on radio and TV.

Mower: Really your — may I say your most "famous" name in the broadcasting business was Ruth Crane?

Crane: Well, yes. You see, I had established that in Detroit and when I came to WMAL in Washington it was necessary for me to carry on with it. Also Crane was a better radio name than Schaefer which has so many spellings.

Mower: At that time there weren't specific requirements made, were there, as to — oh, you know, ability to broadcast or type of voice or background. It was more being in the right place at the right time, wasn't it?

Crane: That's right. Mr. Fitzpatrick had said, "I want a regular Michigan mid-western type voice. I don't want anything southern. I don't want any broad A's. I want it down-to-earth." Well, I had enough dramatic experience to cover up what remained of my early Missouri twang — I guess I did — anyway, that was it. So, I started out giving cooking information on the air.

Mower: Oh, really! You mean cooking lessons?

Crane: Not exactly that, but it was a program directed to women covering all aspects of homemaking. We gave recipes, certainly, household hints and general news of interest to women. Remember radio was fairly new then — in 1929 — the depression was on and many women were more or less house-bound and they welcomed a friendly voice with knowledge of their daily problems and what appeared to be an effort to help them.

Everyone was fascinated with radio anyway, and the women's program was the only — with the possible exception of the Farm Program — the only radio vehicle that gave listeners an actual feeling of participating — of knowing the person on the air. What I mean is radio news, music and plays, you know, they didn't have the "you and me" relationship with the same problems — reading the letters, giving identity to the listeners, giving names, making the listener a part of it. A woman's program did that so listener mail was tremendous in those days, particularly on a 50,000 watt station covering three states and a large part of Canada.

Mower: Ruth, I was just thinking the other day — you know, now you hear credits given on radio and you see the credits given on television for all types of programs — so many writers, so many producers, so many assistant production people, and so forth — I know the answer myself, but I just want to ask you this — when you were doing all this programming, how much help did you have?

Crane: I didn't have any, of course — that's very simple. I was holding down two other jobs. I was on the sales staff, I was Commercial Editor and I was Women's Editor or Mrs. Page. Oh, I got a raise to $35 a week, too.

Mower: That was good.

Crane: Yes — well, you know, women broadcasters weren't very well paid in those days. I don't know how well they are paid now, but in 1944 when I left WJR in Detroit after 15 years there I think I was making $85 a week — that was all — and this covered all the jobs I had — the Women's Program Director, the Commercial Editor and the sales work that I did. Men on the air with far less responsibilities were paid much better, of course.

Mower: Ruth, were women broadcasters — that is women on the air in those days — did they all do just food and household hints?

Crane: Practically all, at that time. Each station usually had one woman personality on the air and at that time few of us had invaded the news or sports or other fields. You know, a man's voice was supposed to denote authority and knowledge and not very many of the women did interviews even. This, too, was a man's field. But, remember this, our sponsors were almost entirely foods and household items sold to women. Our bosses and sponsors wanted program material that fitted in with their products. We did our own commercials, of course, as you know. There weren't any transcribed commercials until later. And, so the transition was a very natural one from giving information about how to do something and the product to do it with. The familiar voice selling the product became more believable. I'm speaking of the early days, of course, perhaps up to the mid-forties. But early in the forties opportunities were expanded and women did take on the chores previously assumed to be a man's field. Just don't deprecate, though, the kind of job that the women did in the earlier years. It was listened to eagerly by housewives who felt their interests shared. It was helpful information that they could use in money saving ideas and they wanted a friend on the air.

Mower: And, Ruth, didn't you get a great deal of what was called fan mail from those very women?

Crane: Oh, yes, and very personal letters, commenting, asking questions and that sort of thing.

Mower: Questions about your own personal life and that sort of thing in addition to asking questions about the type of thing you'd had on the air?

Crane: Oh, yes, the fan mail was tremendous, especially on a 50,000 watt station covering three or four states.

I remember, speaking of the sort of broadcasting that we did during those early years, I remember later on I was irate when one of our own AWB* members who had gone on to news reporting, mentioned disdainfully women on the air telling how to revive a wilted lettuce leaf and such things. Believe me, I would gladly have passed on such information and I think it would have been happily received. I didn't think then, and still don't, that the only really proud function of women on the air is to deliver what the newcomers at that time and perhaps still do call hard news. There is a lot of other information, as is well known and practiced, that women find interesting and beneficial when expounded by an expert. Of course, the whole situation is expanding now.

Mower: Well, Ruth, as I recall, the woman broadcaster didn't just do a fifteen-minute or thirty-minute program on the air as sometimes they do today. She usually had many other duties around the station in addition to the time she was on the air. In most cases they were also designated as a Director of Women's Programs or Director of Women's Activities —

Crane: Yes, that was giving us a nice high-flown title. Actually, it covered almost anything. I had to go out and make talks to women's groups and — well, for awhile I did auditions, too — I remember that — that is, audition appointments — I didn't always listen to the auditions. And there were just countless duties that one was called on to do. I mean there was no time requirement. You worked from 9 o'clock or 8:30 in the morning until 5, 6, or midnight — whenever you were through.

Mower: You were a combination public relations and promotional director in a way, too, because many of the stations didn't have much personnel at that time, did they?

Crane: Yes, that was a job that I assumed on my own, more or less, a sort of PR job and publicity job. Oh, one of the newscasters was supposed to be the publicity man but did very little about it, and I did that. Of course, there was no objection on the part of the station management as to how many jobs I held or what I did as long as I didn't ask to be paid for it.

Mower: Doing all of these things probably set the woman up as a very important personality around the station. Was she attributed a great deal of respect by other members of the staff?

Crane: That's the funniest question I've heard yet. No — and I've checked this with many other women who were in radio and TV too. I think a phenomenon of the early days of both radio and TV — and, for all I know it still exists — is that the Women's Director who had her own shows

*Association of Women Broadcasters.

was inescapably considered a character by her station associates. Oh, of course, some were — I've known some who really were, and I'm sure you have, too. But, oddly, the lowest branch on the organization tree was usually that of the woman who did foods, children's programs, women's activities and so on, no matter how well sponsored and notwithstanding this woman in almost all cases was also her own complete staff — writer, program director, producer, public relations, innovator, outside speaker, often saleswoman for her own sponsors, radio or TV and sometimes both. But a character nevertheless she was expected to be and they all made jokes about it and all that. You were really not supposed to know anything about food or household or any of the subjects you were broadcasting on. Our efforts were not taken very seriously by our associates even though the announcers and technicians were often the veritable beginners on the staff. And the jokes directed at her were not always innocent. Later on in TV it became almost the practice, according to several of the early women broadcasters who told me about it — and it was in my case as well — for the floorman, the cameraman and others to make away ahead of time with the food she had prepared in advance for use on her show. You know — she opens the oven door or the refrigerator door and ha-ha nothing is inside.

Mower: Great big joke, hunh?

Crane: Oh, yes, of course. We tried putting locks on the refrigerator and all, but they'd break it open. And the management didn't do anything about it. Or, in the case of a complicated commercial requiring what was called an "idiot sheet" it was considered uproariously funny to turn it backwards or turn it so fast that it couldn't be read correctly. Strangely, as I say, the management of the station did nothing or at least too little to correct these occurrences. And, I've heard this from other broadcasters as well. I don't understand it.

Mower: Ruth, television must have been quite a departure from the type of programs you had been doing on radio. When did you actually start your television program?

Crane: That was in '46.

Mower: That was here?

Crane: Yes, that was in addition to the radio I was doing here. By then, by the way, I had acquired a secretary.

Mower: Oh, good for you! How did you get into TV? I know WMAL had a TV station but did you go to the boss and have a completed script and that kind of thing and say, "I'd like to be on television"?

Crane: I got into TV simply by being there — that's all. And, naturally, they wanted to use the same people as long as they could. They didn't want to put on another staff to operate TV — we all doubled up. And so, there I was. I had been warned some time previously that I would be expected to go on TV eventually, and I, at that time, was President of the National Assocation of Women Broadcasters and was pretty busy with that and my radio job and making speeches and heaven knows what all. And one day Ben Baylor, who was the sales manager, called me into his office and said, "Now, look, you're to start your TV program a week from Tuesday." It was to be an evening program because they were not on during the daylight hours then. I said, "Well, all right, I guess so, what do you plan to have me do?" He said, "What do I plan to have you do? That's your job. You put on a program — that's all I'm requiring — you put on a program." So, I had a week to plan it. Well, Christmas was approaching and I decided to do a sort of burlesque on Christmas shoppers. I borrowed the materials from a department store and it was real good, actually, for a first program. As a matter of fact, I look back on it now when I come across the script and think, that wasn't bad.

Mower: But you had it all to yourself as far as the preparation and getting the people and the whole thing set up — writing the script?

Crane: Oh, yes, of course. All through my TV career I had that all to do with the help I had, which was sometimes one and sometimes one and a half persons to help me, but theirs were strictly clerical duties. There was the planning, the writing, the preparation, the rehearsing — but we rarely rehearsed on TV — we didn't have time. We just went on. I think that's almost as well, really. I didn't regret that particularly.

Mower: You had a program called "The Modern Woman" program, I remember, that ran for several years.

Crane: Yes, it was "The Modern Woman" on radio and "The Modern Woman" on TV, and that ran for, oh goodness, I'd have to — well, we started in '46 and that ran for about 9 years, I believe. In addition to that, I did other TV programs.

Mower: I remember you had a shopping program of some kind.

Crane: It was a very interesting development in TV. It had national publicity — national recognition. Many people attempted to copy the program, but for various reasons none of the others happened to be as successful as our own. "Shop by Television" was sponsored by the Hecht Company on TV. It was on in the evening. We took orders directly over the telephone. That is, we had telephones installed on the set and we had operators there. We frequently did about $6000 worth of sales directly on the phone. We demonstrated — Jackson Weaver and I demonstrated the materials, and sometimes very funny things happened on the program. It was a very popular listening, looking or viewing program even by people who didn't care to order anything because most anything could happen — such as the time I was displaying plastic dinnerware and said, "Now this is unbreakable and you can put it in your dishwasher," and so on and threw it on the floor to display its unbreakability. Well, you know what happened.

Mower: It broke, I suppose.

Crane: Naturally. A lot of things happened like that, but we always made a joke about it. We didn't take it seriously, and I think people enjoyed that.

Mower: So you really combined a little entertainment with the shopping service.

Crane: That's what we tried to do, and I think we succeeded, really. As I say, that program was a departure from the usual thing. Actually, the National Association of Broadcasters put out a brochure on it for the benefit of other stations.

Well, there were a lot of things in those days because TV was new, and no one knew what to do any more than I did programwise. We were allowed to do whatever we wanted to do. There was no set format, and it gave us the opportunity for innovations and experiment.

Let's see — on my daily afternoon show in order to encourage interest in TV and bolster TV set sales, I devoted one hour a week to demonstrate the activities and personalities of important women's clubs, selecting only the larger organizations. One hundred fifty members of each one, including the officers and members were invited to the studio to take part. Now, that doesn't sound unusual, of course, but it was in those days. It wouldn't sound unusual now. However, members who could not be invited by the space limitation in the studio, were required to hold TV teas for 20 members or more in each home. The program consisted of introducing the officers and members and demonstrating and telling about the work of the organization. This required a stage and many props, of course, and then when the program ended samples of all my sponsors' products — mostly foods, of course, and other products, too — were handed out, and we then served tea in the studio to the company — and foods prepared from the sponsors' products. Fortunately, I had an Angel Food cake mix, potato chips and coffee among my sponsors. And, fortunately, too, as I said, by that time I had an assistant. Thus, in order to see the work and the personnel of the organization on TV — that was excitingly new, if you can imagine that. Many of the members, you see, had to buy TV sets for their own families to see them on TV, as, of course, did the members who were asked to give the teas for the members in their homes. Well, of course, that was just one thing.

Mower: I suppose you always had some funny or peculiar things happen on this type of a TV program which was put on — I guess we could say "informally." That's what it amounted to in comparison to the way they do television today?

Crane: Oh, heavens yes, not rehearsed. For example, the man who came to demonstrate the proper way to open a bottle of champagne couldn't open the bottle of champagne. Things were always happening like that. I think that's one of the reasons why people watched the program.

CHAPTER 15

Women's Magazines: Nora Magid

In 1963, Betty Friedan, in *The Feminine Mystique*, confessed to pangs of guilt over "the picture of the modern American housewife that I myself was helping to create, writing for the women's magazines." She saw herself and her colleagues as unwitting conspirators in a massive deception of readers of American women's magazines.

The longevity and high circulation of women's magazines enabled their editors to write one of the most striking success stories of the magazine industry. Women's magazines have enjoyed large, faithful audiences since the early 19th century when *Ladies' Magazine*, the first of its kind, began publishing.

Six of the top ten magazines in the United States are women's magazines: *Women's Day, Family Circle, Better Homes & Gardens, McCall's, Ladies Home Journal*, and *Good Housekeeping*, in that order. Together they enjoy a circulation of more than 46 million. Add pass-along readership to that, and it can be expected that half the American population reads these magazines.

The "deception" about which Friedan and later, others, worried, was deepened by the very formula that had made this genre of magazines so successful: the pursuit of home, happiness and husband, almost as if it were a Constitutional right. In the opinion of some women, this required a reader to take flight from herself. But according to the magazines, competence in the home and as a guardian of one's family represented the best way for a woman to secure her own fulfillment.

A number of women's magazines began as clothing pattern books. They survived the First World War and the Depression, literally by sticking together — imitating one another with an abundance of prescriptive advice about fashion, homemaking, health and family care. By the mid-1930's the women's magazines were in a rut — there were too many of them, and they were too much alike. The solution for some was changing the balance of editorial content to include other topics, such as careers, a broader range of fiction, articles on social issues of the day, and observations of famous people. For others, the solution was to specialize, tailor the product to a more specific audience with its own needs and preferences. This last solution gave birth to some new magazines — *Mademoiselle, Parents' Magazine, Glamour* — and caused a revamping of some older ones — *Cosmopolitan* and *Redbook.*

McCall's, Ladies Home Journal and *Good Housekeeping* have an entertainment/fashion/service format, although they have made space for emerging social themes and "coping" pieces geared for the woman with a changing lifestyle. *Vogue* and *Harper's Bazaar* cater to readers interested in high fashion and jet-set activity. Helen Woodward, in *The Lady Persuaders*, said, "Both magazines were known in the trade as the 'rags,' indicating the cynical attitude toward high-priced clothes within the trade. In their contents they were the acme of snobbishness."

The "shelter" magazines also are popular among women, although their editors say they serve a "dual" readership composed of men as well as women. A top seller is *Better Homes & Gardens*, which, along with *American Home*, provides hints on interior decorating, remodeling, crafts, food and family projects. *House & Garden* and *House Beautiful* are the *Vogues* of the shelter magazines. They are the "dreamhouse" books, concentrating more on ornamentation than "how-to" advice.

The circulation leaders among the women's magazines are *Woman's Day* and *Family Circle*. These "handbooks for homemakers" are sold in an environment which invites high sales — the supermarket. Located right at the site of purchase — the cash register — the homemaker is being told that the magazine is as vital a purchase as the food in her grocery cart.

But feminists say an increasing number of American women are not adequately served by periodicals edited for "the middle-class American housewife." In 1970 the first "alternative" magazine for mass distribution hit the newsstands — *Essence*, directed to the young, urban, black female market. Four years later *Essence*'s circulation was growing faster than that of any other woman's magazine. A year after *Essence*'s debut, a group of feminist journalists — many of whom had been editors of and contributors to traditional women's magazines — started *Ms.* magazine after a preview issue of *Ms.*, packaged as an insert in *New York* magazine, sold out in a matter of days.

Tennis star Billie Jean King and her husband Larry began publishing *womenSports* in 1974. Ms. King, who was instrumental in securing larger purses for women playing professional tennis, was unhappy with sports magazines' coverage (or lack of it) of women athletes, and thought a women's sport magazine might be the answer.

In the following excerpts from her article, "The Heart, the Mind, the Pickled Okra: Women's Magazines in the Sixties" (*North American Review*, Winter 1970), Nora Magid describes the idyllic landscape painted by traditional women's magazines. There are no tennis courts, feminist collectives or minority women in the painting, because her article antedates *women-Sports, Ms.,* and *Essence.* The decade of upheaval which paved the way for more specialized magazines for women − the Sixties − was portrayed by traditional magazines in pastel colors with soft edges. Magid's pungent analysis strips away the colors and bares the canvas.

WOMEN'S MAGAZINES IN THE SIXTIES

By Nora Magid

"Jackie Kennedy was like a sister to me, and neither time nor distance can erase the memories of the years we shared together. I wish her happiness and all good things. I cannot express how much she has enriched my life by letting me put one foot in Camelot."

The lady's other foot is parked firmly in her mouth. Jacqueline Kennedy, having refused to perpetuate her own myth − she did, in effect, run off with Eddie Fisher − has become fair game, and Mary Barelli Gallagher, one of an army of former employees with a yen to spill the beans, explodes with secrets: "I'll never forget the first time she wanted me to make an appointment for her with New York hairdresser, Kenneth, for a hair straightening, shampoo and set. The 'hair-straightening' part took me by surprise. Jackie, I had always thought, had a lovely, natural line to her hair. Why would she want to have it straightened? Yet the receptionist at Kenneth's confirmed that Jackie was, indeed, going to have her hair straightened! Beauty was important to Jackie. She had the little dark hairs on her arms bleached. She used Sardo bath oil and a medicinal-type liquid cleanser, Phiso-hex."

Many of the titillating revelations are second-hand, and Provi, the maid, is the unwitting source: (1) "Mees Kennedee like nice, fresh sheets"; (2) "Oh yes, Mees Gallaga, Mees Kennedee likes to find her stockings in nice, neat pile in her closet"; and (3) after the J. F. Kennedy funeral, the punchline, "Oh, Mees Gallaga, that's Onassee, the millionaire."

Mrs. Gallagher says that Jackie's mother said that when Jackie bent over, you could see her garters at the top of her hose. And Jack said that

Jackie was extravagant, and Jackie said, "Gosh, I guess Jack was real-l-y upset, wasn't he?" to which Mrs. Gallagher said, " 'Well, Jackie, I don't mind so much his being upset. It's just that I'm always in the middle.' She apologized." And when Jackie and Mrs. G. have a squabble, Mrs. G. says, " 'And Jackie, the one thing I'd like to ask now is that you never speak to me that way again. I was never more hurt or humiliated.' She apologized again, asking that we just forget the whole thing." Good old Walter Mitty.

Now the Sixty-Four Dollar Question is who wanted to read such trash? The answer is everybody. We all live two lives, our own and that of the Kennedys, and the above, good for plenty of mileage in every newspaper in the country, was also presumably good for business — for *Ladies' Home Journal* business, that is. Given the insatiable appetite of the public for Kennedy material, the saga had run a predictable course even before calamity befell Teddy. The media created the Kennedys; and up to a point the media collaborate just as cheerfully in their destruction. Over the past ten years, there has hardly been an issue of a woman's magazine without one story and sometimes two on the family; and each periodical has to some extent defined them in its own terms. The *Journal* (mass circulation) capitalizes on that fascination with an animosity toward the rich and powerful that is inherent in Americans. *Vogue*, on the other hand, wealthy and snobbish, once unblushingly captioned a portrait of Mrs. Kennedy, "J.B.K. . . . . the American Woman, a creature possessed of thoughtful responsibility, a healthy predilection for the good and the beautiful and the expensive. . . "

Besides the cult of personality, what are women's magazines selling? The answer—again—is everything. The service area is a tricky one. It resembles the old one-room schoolhouse, in which the instructor had simultaneously to manage many learners at many stages. Some housekeepers are beginners, some have been at it for years. For each, different instructions need to be devised; and for all, convenience foods and new designs must be pushed. You may have a toaster, or even — heaven forfend — make toast in the oven; but suddenly daisies are in. "These peppy petals are spreading cheer over kitchen tools, ice buckets, pitchers, and even a toaster (by Toastmaster)." You certainly must buy a blender, an electric can opener, an outdoor carpet. Since there are just so many ways to do a bird (and for some classic recipes like cream puffs there is just one method), the effort to achieve novelty, particularly at holidays, which have a way of recurring, may border on hysteria. "To make ye roast goose, as it's served at ye John Peel Inn, follow ye recipe below, plus ye spiced plums and plum sauce. Bet ye'll think it's dandy."

Or, in wishful reminder that ordinary people tend to lead ordinary lives, "What's it like to feast like a star in the finest restaurants, the most glamorous hotels, with others bringing you such out-of-the-world food as chicken baked with green grapes, or lighting a flame beneath a fragrant, bubbling supper dish? How would you like to feed your children the same amusing frankfurter dishes the boys in *Oliver!* go for?" (The franks they go for are dipped in cheese-beer goo.)

* * *

A columnist bleats, "Recently, I asked a visitor from abroad what were his impressions of America. 'I see a busy, active people,' he replied. 'Busy not merely with earning a living, but with enjoying living.' Then he added, 'Your huge volume of advertising has played a tremendous part in bringing all this about.'"

Promotion is then the primary business of the woman's magazines, and like the networks they are first of all self-congratulatory. Every issue carries its built-in praise. They then praise all gadgets, cosmetics, detergents and tires as well as whatever politics occupy the White House. Now many appliances are irrelevant, many mixes are filled with chemicals, many cosmetics and detergents prove harmful, and obviously vary in quality and in effect. Many pharmaceutical developments, inadequately tested, turn out to be premature and/or dangerous. Crackpot diets are regularly endorsed (Joseph Alsop, for instance, raved about the efficacy of the Air Force Diet; it was four years before *McCall's* mentioned in an article by an expert on nutrition that it was unbalanced and hazardous.) The Pill was widely heralded as "effective and perfectly safe." It is only recently after irresponsible hard-sell tactics that it is intimated that, well, there just might be side effects.

The medical columns, a feature of all women's magazines, are like nothing under the sun. There are usually some straight-forward simpleminded questions, and the answer to these is usually run, do not walk, to the nearest psychiatrist. Occasionally there is a real block-buster: the external genitalia of our baby appear different from those of our other children. In fact there seems to be a mixture of male and female organs. "At birth, the female organ was dominant. Now my husband and I are puzzled and worried because the male organ seems to be growing longer. Should we let things go and let nature take its course, or is there anything that could be done medically?" (For answer, see *McCall's*, January, 1964.)

Women's worries are ticked off, and they are manifold: How to save your marriage if you are an over-solicitous mother, are cheating your creative talent, have trouble-making neighbors, collect injustices; if your husband is impotent, jealous, rude, stingy, a perfectionist, a gambler, a drunk. What to do if you outgrow one another. How to define femininity, how to define masculinity. "Appreciation of artistic experiences is in no way the sole province of the female. By the same token, enjoyment of sports is not necessarily indicative of a man's masculinity."

There are horoscopes for weight-watching, spring cleaning, job-hunting, budget-keeping. Readers can also learn vicariously what it is like to be a widow, or have cancer or whatever the disease-of-the-month is. And if they persist in telling their troubles at the beauty parlor, *McCall's* psychiatrist-in-residence is permissive. He hopes "that informal care-givers, like hairdressers and bartenders, would read columns like this and increase their understanding of common life predicaments in other ways, so that their counsel would be more consistently sensible."

Fashion is, of course, another commodity. Here the aim is to make everyone look alike, and there are complicated tie-ins with tourism bureaus, resorts, airlines, name brands and anyone's fame. In one layout, to indicate how much lovelier she could be, a bouffant hairdo, colorless makeup and mini skirt are superimposed on a photograph of Queen Elizabeth. She looks ridiculous. In another, a literary touch is lent by Harper Lee, who has a snippety text on the discovery of America by two small foreign children. They take her tour, show off their brand name clothes, and end up in various sets of American arms, those of Hubert Humphrey, Lynda Bird, the Nelson Rockefellers, George Murphy, Casey Stengel, and Colonel John H. Glenn, Jr.

These itty bitty paragraphs have always been popular. Harlan Miller used to whip up regular batches for *The Journal*. Once he said, "If a wife can manage to look cute or winsome while needling her husband, she can look cute saying anything!" A while later he said, "My Dream Girl thinks there is a cute way to needle a husband — by sitting on his lap to do it." Then there were Chanel's thoughts on the order of "Between madness and poetry there is a thin piece of paper." And now there is Lyn Tornabene using the format to tell how much the astronauts' houses cost ($61,000), which wives dress like Mrs. Nixon, Mrs. Onassis and Mrs. Edward Kennedy, and which moon person "wears Brut and can be sniffed before seen." The advent of NASA has also brought a spate of new layout gimmicks — space foods and space clothes. Kicky culottes give you "a chance to soar off into a new fashion orbit, wearing the kinds of clothes that make you feel as free and weightless as a spacewalker."

*   *   *

Women's magazines are expensive to put out. In the chatty section at the beginning of the issue, the editors are likely not only to romanticize themselves (we feel like Liza Elliot, the heroine of *Lady in the Dark*; obviously we don't feel like Liza Elliott, girl editor, or we would resign in favor of a man), but also to boast of their expenditures. Models are flown all over the world to be photographed against exotic backdrops. And for a clutch of pieces that might have been assembled from clips — to show that Prince Charles' investiture would be a "smash hit" — "our editors, authors, reporters and emissaries covered thousands of miles, clocked scores of air hours and consumed uncounted dramamine pills." Authors are also well paid, and it is a truism that an excellent article may be prepared for an academic or professional journal for nothing, while something worthless in the popular press may command thousands, even hundreds of thousands of dollars.

The point should be made, however, that not all women's magazine prose is terrible. (The poetry is about crowded closets and thinning hair and is terrible.) Jean Kerr and Peg Bracken are funny women; and such disparate writers as Jessica Mitford, Jean Stafford, and Harvey Cox have written well and astringently in this medium. Michael Field for a while had an amusing and vitriolic column in *McCall's*, in which he dissected famous restaurants, taking them to task for tacky art, ludicrous hauteur, contemptuous service and terrible food. Part of the general problem is visual. When John W. Gardner writes on the abused child, the piece is sandwiched between a story about a clever lady who thinks that marriage is obsolete, and a Treasury of French Cooking. The layout tyrannizes the copy and it is difficult for material to sound serious when it does not look it, when on all sides, it is hemmed in by ruffles, and, in this particular case, ads for corn remover, hemmorhoid pain reliever and skin bleach. This problem defeats not only the writer, but also the New York reader, who must plough her way through the many alphabetized regions insert pages. Just trying to trace a story to its conclusion may be an exhausting and irritating exercise.

* * *

Anyone who has ever been a literary editor knows that a lot of good fiction is circulated that never gets to see the light of publication. It is right only for women's magazines, and women's magazines do not print it. For fiction, *McCall's* has a large staff. Since all of *McCall's* fiction is by Barbara Robinson, one wonders what the fiction staff does. In the past few years, Miss Robinson has had at least eighteen short stories here, and has also made guest appearances elsewhere. The titles speak for themselves: Three to Make a Marriage, Something Very Much in Common, Someone to Love, Beyond this Moment. . . .

"Almost any Friday" (*McCall's*, June, 1969), a typical story, is prefaced by a teaser to entice the skimmer: "Rob was in love, his parents supposed, but his plans were suspiciously vague. Did he really want to get married? For that matter does any young man?"

The fiction not written by Barbara Robinson sounds as if it had been written by Barbara Robinson. In *McCall's* for August, 1969, is Evan Hunter's "Wilt Thou Have This Woman?" — "From the big new novel, *Sons*, by one of America's most popular authors: A tender story about a young man back from war, and the home-town girl he had always thought he loved." Same basic situation. Same story. Same ending. Bittersweet happy.

CHAPTER 16

Action for Change:
The Sit-In

By 1968 the women's movement was getting some coverage in the mass media. Television, newspapers, and newsmagazines gave space to the movement when the movement, in the opinion of these media, was "news." However, most feminists felt the media had a predilection for sensationalism and didn't take the movement seriously enough to get at the reasons behind feminist demonstrations and protests. Women's liberation groups felt that the mass media, because of their own biases, were lumping movement activists into a comic category of "bra-burners" (a form of protest invented by the media, not used by feminists).

But the feminists' dissatisfaction with communication about the movement did not stop with *Time, Newsweek*, the networks, or the metropolitan daily newspapers. Their ire was directed towards the publications whose snub of women's liberation was the most damaging — the women's magazines. These publications had an audience of millions of women that the feminists also wanted to reach. The question was: how could the editors of women's magazines be persuaded to open up their pages to new themes about women?

The answer was: go and talk to them.

Helen Gurley Brown, editor of *Cosmopolitan*, received a visit in 1970 from a group of feminists who hoped to get Brown to reduce the *Cosmo* reader's anxiety about herself by encouraging the reader to develop her own talents and energies rather than over-instructing her on how to be the type of woman she might not be at all. *Cosmopolitan* did run excerpts from Kate Millett's *Sexual Politics* that year.

The more famous of the visits was paid to John Mack Carter, then editor-in-chief of the *Ladies Home Journal*. On March 19, 1970, about 150 feminists arrived at the Lexington Avenue offices of Downe Communications, owner of the *Journal*, for a heart-to-heart talk with the *Journal*'s managing editors. The group presented Carter and his associates with a dummy of an alternative *Journal*, which included articles on abortion, career vs. family, and prostitution. The cover showed a pregnant woman carrying a sign which said "Unpaid Labor." Obviously not receptive to such a sudden departure from his editorial policy, Carter and the feminists sat down for what was to be an 11-hour face-off.

At the end of the negotiations, Carter promised the feminists an eight-page section in the August 1970 issue. Written collectively (everyone critiqued everyone else's contributions, and rewrote them if necessary) by 30 women who did not sign their contributions, the insert appeared on schedule. It presented the authors' frank opinions on education for women, childbirth, homemaking, marriage, love and sex.

The group who invaded Carter's office was composed of members of the National Organization for Women, Media Women (a group of women who worked in media), Redstockings, and New York Radical Feminists. Also in their midst was Vivien Leone, a member of Older Women's Liberation, who wrote the account that follows here.

It was an active week in New York. Four days before the sit-in at the *Journal*, 46 women at *Newsweek* announced that they had filed a Complaint with the Equal Employment Opportunity Commission charging *Newsweek* with discrimination against women on the editorial staff. Their announcement was timed to coincide with *Newsweek*'s "Women's Liberation" issue. The cover story for that issue had been commissioned to a woman writer who *did not* work for *Newsweek*. (An agreement between *Newsweek* and the women subsequently settled the EEOC Complaint.)

And two days after the sit-in, 50 young women marched down Fifth Avenue to protest the passing of the miniskirt. Known as GAMS (Girls Against More Skirt), the marchers won about the same amount of space in the *New York Times* (a 15-inch story with photo) as the women at the *Journal*. The following week *Time* magazine described the *Journal* protesters as "mod- and trouser-clad feminists." After jotting down their demands, reporters were still careful to note what the protesters were wearing.

Vivien Leone is a writer who collects women's poetry and is involved in the arts. Her article "Occupying the Ladies Home Journal" appeared in the *Manhattan Tribune*, March 28, 1970. It begins on the next page.

OCCUPYING THE LADIES HOME JOURNAL:
MY FIRST HURRAH

By Vivien Leone

I was seven minutes late for the feminist invasion of the *Ladies Home Journal* on Wednesday morning, March 19, because I couldn't bear to leave the house without eye make-up.

Already full of self-castigation, I compounded it by taking a cab (a cab! Shouldn't the aggrieved inch arduously toward redress?), and passed the ride to 54th and Lexington fighting queasiness.

Could I, a 40-year-old fledgling feminist enroute to my debut demonstration, hope to cope? What a cinch it would be to sour-grape me out on my ear, I thought, as I ticked off my misfitness: overtall, overweight, overage, unmarried, unfamous, unemployed, dreamer, dilettante, divorcee; manless, jobless, childless; physically comfortable, financially fixed, but: aspirationally starved. For what? For choices. For dignity, grace, productiveness and sisterhood. For the vision of an unlimited number of new ways to be a woman.

At 9:07, in front of St. Peter's, the contact point, I picked up a fact sheet and list of demands from a pair of unobtrusive lieutenants and joined the workadailies swarming into 641 Lexington with my eyes peeled.

In case of interrogation, it had been suggested we aim for Avon on the eighth floor and walk down three flights, but I felt hopeless about being able to pass for one of their door-to-doorsters. Since I have seen them only through TV lenses, nobody of my acquaintance ever having been called on (dingaling!) by Avon, it is hard to identify with them in the flesh, which is pretty much the trouble with the women we come to know on glass, paper and celluloid. We spend our lives trying to pass for phantoms of whom nobody has ever actually had any real carnal knowledge.

Luckily, that test did not have to be passed. It was clear that alarm had yet to grip the lobby, and the self-service trip to the fifth floor passed without incident.

Only two of us stepped out. A somber-faced sentinel pointed the way. We went through several doors into what looked like the cheerless corridor of a military hospital ship. Now and then the efficient character of the abandoned cubicles would be broken by some spur of personality — I recall particularly an adoring display of the Many Faces of Paul Newman — but for the most part the atmosphere was colorless, windowless, labyrinthine. Now and then it was necessary to skirt an earnest tri- or quadripartite conversation between Them and Us.

"Why did you pick us?" one of Them asked plaintively. "We're allowed to wear pants suits here." As if liberation were a matter of fashion.

"Not an attractive one in the bunch," sneered an especially doll-like Them-er, to which a tiny Us-er with vividly un-madeup Picasso eyes replied,

"That's what flesh-and-blood women look like . . . if you hadn't been taught from the cradle to hate your own real looks, you'd see how beautiful they are."

At last the overflowing captain's quarters came in view. Experienced head-counters placed their estimates at over 100, but it was still possible to squeeze through. I cleared myself a corner position and decided that we were indeed beautiful. Every fat, thin, hairy, cropped, tall, short, fancy, plain, young, old, straight, wild one of us. Behind the executive desk we were all facing sat Editor and Publisher John Mack Carter, a cool character if ever there was one.

Despite the context of the occasion, my idiot reflexes, relentlessly moulded by all the Carters of this world, churned out the following: "good looking, might be old enough, but much too short."

Standing behind him was one of his two male managing editors (there are three, and one is female), Dick Kaplan, far from cool, and on the other side, the sole, semi-powerful distaffer, Lenore Hershey, her bewilderment crowned by a Shrafft's-Lady hat. Beside her a faintly beige woman, who was rumored to have been summoned to the foreground as soon as management got wind of our concern over lack of representation for its 1.2 million black readers, stared at us out of scared green eyes.

Against this proscenium of calm, anger, puzzlement and fear, demands were being enumerated by a rotating group of vanguardians. There is much painful grappling going on just now with the conflict between self-assertion and anonymity in a heart-rending pursuit of the ideal of the collective. The opposition wants Names, responds, in fact, only to Names, and the Names themselves are afraid to betray the nameless by making it off the movement. This ever-impending accusation accounts for a debilitating amount of modesty, but no alternative is currently thinkable.

Media Women did most of the spokeswomanship because as the more irascible hecklers were continually being reminded, their group begot the action, although maternity might well be traced to the newspaper *Rat*. Jargon did not get out of hand. There were a comforting minimum of "Right On's," and pig-press was alluded to only twice.

Getting Carter to respond to the demand was like pulling teeth from a rooster. The single most-repeated retort of the entire action was "ridiculous," but at last the ridicule was being felt to be on the other Wedgie. When your 7 million readers are about to find you yourself have been gleefully calling your book the *Ladies' Bungalow Journal*, who's to laugh last.

The least tractable demands — in a short-term sense anyway — were those having to do with the sexic and ethnic composition of the editorial and advertising staffs. Nobody had really expected Carter to turn his chair over to Hershey, although at mid-point she actually did sit in it, and by the finale her point of view had undergone such a startling transformation that many of us would have been glad to see her get it. I remember finding myself moved in the course of this transformation to place my hand on her arm and tell her she was a peach. It happens all the time. The woman thing. Once layers of suspicion and competition crack, we start really digging one another and a new kind of bonding begins.

Draperies were now parted and blinds upped so that a pair of banners announcing the action could be dropped out the windows. And although they blew illegibly in the wind and rain, our sense of reality was somehow enhanced by the dingy light of day.

Carter wound up sitting atop the glass-covered desk, a fashionable executive stance that aggravated the demonstration's only dangerous split. Fortunately, the danger was short-lived, and even proved useful in the last analysis. A small faction of separatists, led by the famous (I don't think she has any problems about being famous) Ti-Grace Atkinson, had phoned Media Women the previous night to ask if they might participate.

Their tether was short. When one of them said she had not come there to talk, but to Destroy, it took an hour of honey-coated filibustering to get things back into focus, during which Destroyer leapt on the desk, intent on Carter's forcible eviction. "We can do it," she urged, "he's small."

That did it. That combination of physical and psychological violence — the same combination that has been so successfully used to keep women down — was the last trick many of us were about to use to pry ourselves out from under. I lent my own hands to the several pair that evicted the potential evictress from the table-top.

It was then that Ti-Grace (a short form of peTIte-Grace, a name that sticks to her out of a Louisiana childhood, although there is nothing dainty about her) displayed why she is such a widely feared and respected force in the struggle. The woman has a mind as rich, gleaning, intricate and cold as an ice palace. She added it up very neatly for Carter. "If you don't deal with them," she reminded him, "you get us."

I began to appreciate how important it is to have her group, the Feminists, at one pole and, say, the Pussycats, at the other. It provides lots of stretching-room for all of us in between. I suspect there isn't a single woman who considers herself part of the movement who doesn't wish she could be a little more radical than she now is. In the meantime, it's good to have Grace out there — a way, out there.

Throughout this period it kept getting harder to distinguish between the press (print, tape, tube & film), the oppressed (many of us were making our own tapes, films & candids), and the oppressors (one knot of staff-dollies suddenly formed a pyramid outside the door with the top-dolly calling out, "We love you, John!").

Pants suits were no sure indication of allegiances. Pia Lindstrom of Channel 2 was overheard to say she not only did not identify with women's liberation, she didn't even identify with American women! Marlene Sanders of Channel 7, of course, was a filly of another color. She did her job swiftly and feelingly and got out without bumping into anybody.

Not so for the males, the only ones whose high-visibility presence was continually open to challenge. Fellows from such highly unlikely magazines as *Media Marketing* and *Holiday,* insisting they had been invited, were not too hard to expel. Telephone invitations requesting female coverage had been extended shortly after the first wave arrived. WINS and *Women's Wear Daily* were among the many who said they had no woman reporter available, and Dorothy Schiff's *Post* sent a lad who had hardly outgrown his Sigma Chi Blazer.

The reporter from EVO burst in at one point to say she had been manhandled by a staffer who claimed it was her father's fault she'd grown up wrong, that her father should have taught her her place at an early age. Carter's Kentucky-gentleman's code seemed visibly shaken by her tale.

By far the largest segment of time — about three hours — was consumed in setting up the mechanics of negotiation. The shape of the table was the only subject not at issue. Our nonladylike disregard for private property and winning ways was mystifying to them. When it became clear that we would not settle for a future appointment, the emphasis was placed on getting us to adjourn to a second-floor conference room. Orders were even issued to clear the conference room for our hoped-for displacement. "It's four times bigger than this office," Carter explained, "so we can all be seated comfortably and proceed in a democratic manner."

Why we should fail to be lured by the promise of comfort and democracy seemed an utter mystery to him. The lure of coffee and pastry was, however, too strong for us. A collection was taken and $27 worth of nourishment was distributed at about 2 p.m.

Finally, Carter had to be told we might have some cause to suspect that once he got us all onto another floor he could just cut out and retreat to his emptied-out bastion.

The next hurdle was the size of negotiating teams. On this point we made our first concession by agreeing to allow about 14 demonstrators to do the talking. There followed another split between those who wanted to remain — silently — in the room for the talks, and those who agreed to retire to the anteroom. At this juncture I elected to leave with the majority, confident my interests would be superbly represented by Madelon X from my own group.

It's a new group, formed only since the beginning of the year, called Older Women's Liberation (OWL) — and if that isn't laying it on the line, I don't know what is. I believe we were the first group to form on the basis of age, although there is now also a split-off from the Radical Feminists called Over 35, and we each have lists of dozens of candidates clamoring for entry. As products of a much more intensive dose of sexism, we feel we'll be in a position to develop ways of dealing with many of the forces that lie in wait for the activists now in their 20's, forces we have already been shaped and shaken by. We've just been obliged to close ranks at 17 members, and five of us took part in this action. Not bad for a three-month-old group.

It seemed to me that most of us did clear out of Carter's office and into the adjoining waiting room, but a substantial number of not-very-silent majorityites refused to budge. Out in the anteroom, we continued picking at and sharing each other's brains and mixing with whatever staff would confront us, between agonizingly infrequent and mostly useless bulletins, such as, Carter's gone to the bathroom. Somebody noticed that a lamp had been placed plunk in the center of the anteroom coffee table, although there was no plug to be found. This struck us as fittingly hilarious at the *Journal.*

Reports from the outside trickled in. Seems a pair of us had gone down in the elevator with a policeman (nobody is clear who called the police). "I don't see why I should hang around," he remarked, "nothing dangerous is happening. I'm going home." When they told him he would probably read about how violent it had been he smiled and shrugged, "I wouldn't be surprised." New breed of philosopher-cops a-borning.

The pair went for coffee at the Mayflower on 57th Street and compared notes at the counter. Before long the woman on their left began to ask questions, the one on the right, chimed in. Next the waitress, then another waitress, soon the whole counter. Then customers began getting up from tables to join in, and in no time the place looked like a Marx Sisters movie set. Addresses were collected, our emissaries promised to send literature and left on a wave of elation.

Meanwhile, back at the negotiations, the notion of a women's liberation supplement in an upcoming issue was taking shape. The longest stalemate had to do with offensive advertising, until a compromise was worked out whereby the ads could remain intact as long as the liberationists could review them and do a piece explaining which ones were insulting, and why.

Around 4:45, I was acutely thinking about one of our proposed article ideas, "How Psychiatrists Oppress Women," because I had a 5:15 appointment with my Counter-Shrink. I couldn't let him down. He really depends on me to enlighten him about what this woman wants — what, dear God, she really wants. Is this any way to run a healing partnership? You bet it is!

You see, it's the movement that finally is making it possible for me to achieve partnership status. At last I've found the thing I, too, can be an expert on.

Before leaving I copied the number from a convenient phone. That way I could check about coming back if talks were still in progress later on. Neither drizzle nor snow flurries brought me down or stayed me from the swift completion of my appointed 45 minutes of enlightenment-giving on the Upper West Side. The C.S. was so enthusiastic he even suggested I use his office telephone to check out the possibilities of returning to the front.

"Candybars!" my contact gasped, "please come back loaded with candybars."

At 6:30 I carried a large shopping-bag stuffed with dextrose, apples, and grape juice into the lobby, was questioned about my destination by the captain, levelled with him and was turned down. Seems he had explicit orders, etc. As I began to try the elevators, he made a signal to turn the power off. Just for me.

I spent the next half hour moping about trying to look both sad and harmless, which should be a natural for me, since I'm half Russian and half Italian, but it didn't seem to be getting across. I tried to spread out my apples to prove they weren't ticking. Nothing doing. I tried slipping in with an authenticated Milquetoast hireling. I even offered him a candybar, but he kept whispering, "I don't want to get involved." As he disappeared in a special manually-operated car, I called after him, "but you already are involved!"

It finally occurred to me to phone from the lobby, and when managing editor Dick Kaplan himself walked down the stairway to accompany me back up, I knew the tide had turned.

From then on it was Milky Ways (not to mention Lenore Hershey bars), unfermented wine and the original fruit of Eve all the way.

The cast had dwindled to a manageable, totally exhausted 30. The talk was of eight pages as soon as possible, and a probable monthly column, to be created by movement members without bylines. Amazing, when you consider the diminishing demands had been 1) an entire issue (considered virtually unattainable); 2) a column (attainable, but unlikely); and 3) one article on the why of the action (that minimum we were determined to hold out for). The outcome was therefore a partial victory on all three counts — that is, a lot more victory than was strictly needed to get rid of us.

There was little doubt the idea of a takeover issue must have appealed to Carter's business instincts. It's no accident he entered college at 16, was a newsman at 17 and assistant editor of *Better Homes and Gardens* at 21. But the Sulzberger syndrome held back; after all, if you tolerate disrespect for lawful process, what cherished institution will crumble next? Only your postman knows for sure.

There was a spidery first-strand of trust floating shakily in the room. A man who agrees to set up an appointment between someone in his legal department and one of our people who specializes in advising management on the creation of daycare facilities can't be half bad. A man who contemplates setting up an editorial training program so that women will have a chance to advance from clerk-typistry can't be 100 per cent plastic, especially when he makes this startling confession, "You know, I haven't really talked to my staff in about two years."

It was an authentic mind-altering discovery the guy was making, and he was making it out loud. We believed it, at least I did.

After 11 extraordinary hours, nobody wanted to face the long-lingering press. It was one of those moments of such fragile accord that the press can so easily knock out of whack. We pulled ourselves together and casually chose the four most likely representatives. After urging them to report first (Thank you, Carla X and Madelon X and Sally X and Susan X — in alphabetical order), Carter said "See you 2:30 on Monday."

"To work out the details?"

"No, to start working on the issue!"

So. My kind of movement is moving me at last.

I remember how I used to think, in the early 60's, what a great time to be black. It simplifies your life. You can wake up in the morning knowing what's important, and where you fit in, because you're a natural-born expert on the subject.

At long last I'm an Activist.

Right now I really go for the idea of active feminism, but pretty soon I bet I'm going to enjoy some of that newly liberated womanliness.

I think I can work it out now. With a lot of help from my friends.

The Journalism of
Women's Liberation

The women's movement that surfaced in the 1960's had communication problems from the beginning. Many people, knowing only what the mass media told them about it, were without sufficient information to judge its extent or its significance. What they thought of the movement was generally a reflection of what they had read or heard or were shown about it.

The feminists, both radicals and moderates, were eager to tell their story. But many were hesitant to share it with the mass media. Some of the movement organizers were veterans of "New Left" politics or civil rights campaigns which they felt had been hampered by the mass media's faulty analysis and coverage of events in which they participated. Yet, they understood the potential of the mass media for education, good as well as bad, because of the vast numbers of the public these media reached.

The experience of feminists whose participation in women's liberation received coverage by the mass media was uneven. Some women reported positive and enlightening experiences. Others had read or viewed what they regarded as appalling reporting about themselves and their activities. A number of these simply would not cooperate with establishment media at all, regardless of the sex of the reporter on the story. They felt that the media's, particularly television and radio's, need to condense inevitably results in oversimplification and distortion of feminist news. They also didn't believe that the media's majority of male editors would permit accurate reporting of women's issues or the women's movement, or that they and these "gatekeepers" would even agree on what women's issues *are*.

The underground newspapers that had given so much strength and focus to the peace and student movements of the same decade provided little comfort to the feminists. Women on their staffs complained that male reporters and editors' liberal politics did not extend to female-male relationships, either in the newsroom or in the newspaper's columns. Female staff members of the underground paper *Rat* became so fed up with the sexual exploitation of women and double standard of the paper in 1970 that they ousted the male editors and took over the publication themselves.

All this, and the recognition that sharing of information is the life-blood of any social movement, led feminists to take typewriter in hand and create their own instruments of communication.

Most of these first publications were issued by women's liberation groups. Carol Lease, a feminist writer, recalled that "These underground newspapers tended to be heavy on rhetoric and personal experience, to give women facts they couldn't find elsewhere, and were published irregularly on shoestring budgets. They gave us a sense of community, of mutual support, a means of venting anger, and a vision of sisterhood."

The number of women's movement publications grew to 560 in the early 1970's, according to Anne Mather's "A History of Feminist Periodicals," but the figure fluctuated from year to year, depending on funds, staff, and the stability of the organizations from which the publications originate.

In the next three chapters, women who have edited feminist periodicals discuss their place in the mainstream of women's liberation and their relationship to the mass media.

CHAPTER 17

Voice of the women's liberation movement

In 1968 a number of women's liberation groups were formed around the country. The National Organization for Women had been organized in 1966 but had not yet developed the extensive national network it later came to have. For the most part, women's liberation was composed of disparate groups with different agendas. Often they were not aware of sister groups or activities by women in other cities which paralleled their own.

The major problem all of them faced was how to bring women in touch with one another and how to provide an amplifier for their opinions, concerns and theories so that the public could learn about the movement directly from its source.

Communication between new organizations of feminists was sporadic. The few women's liberation centers then in existence were staffed by volunteers; lack of money hindered their outreach. Chapters of NOW were small and isolated from each other as well as from a national office which was still trying to establish its focus and goals. Some women's groups were components of larger organizations, such as anti-war groups, which maintained regular lines of communication with each other but not with other women's groups.

A coalition of Chicago women's groups started a newsletter in March 1968 under the editorship of Joreen, a radical feminist who instituted a "revolving editorship" for the publication. The *Voice of women's liberation* carried articles on political theory, Third World women, and parodied advice columns and advertisements. It featured a feminist comic strip. In the Spring of 1969 the collective which published *Vwlm* announced that they were giving up their journalistic efforts to concentrate on building up the women's movement in the Chicago area. By then, other feminists around the country had begun publishing about the movement.

Joreen is Jo Freeman. She teaches American politics, public policy
and social movements at the State University of New York College at Purchase. Her recollections of the founding of the *Voice of women's liberation*
and the reactions of feminists to media coverage of the movement, excerpted from her book, *The Politics of Women's Liberation*, follow.

FROM *THE POLITICS OF WOMEN'S LIBERATION*

The advocates of "women's liberation" liked the term not so much
because of its implied identification with Third World and black liberation
movements but because they wanted to define the terms of debate in what
they saw as a potentially significant movement. They had been educated by
the misunderstandings created by the referent "the Negro problem" which
inevitably structured people's thinking in terms of "the problem with Negroes" rather than racism and what to do about it. They were also aware of
the historical "women question" and "Jewish question" which led to the
same mistake. The problem, they felt, was not one of women, but of wom-
en's liberation and the best way to get people to think of the problem in
those terms was to label it such from the very beginning.[1]
These were the people who first conceived the idea of starting a national newsletter for the miniscule movement, and one of them was the first
editor. The first issue came out in March 1968 as three mimeographed
sheets of paper with no name. Its tag line labeled it "the voice of the wom-
en's liberation movement." By the second issue, three months later, it had
grown to four sheets offset, and the new editor had elevated the tag line to
the name. Under a different editor each issue, the *Voice of the women's
liberation movement* served as the main vehicle of communication for the
growing movement for the next sixteen months. It represented the national
movement to most women receiving it and from it they picked up and used
the name. "Women's liberation" became more and more frequent an appel-
lation and "radical women" receded into the background.
Initially, the term "women's liberation" applied only to the younger
branch of the movement. Organizations such as NOW considered themselves
a part of a women's movement, but not a women's liberation movement.
Gradually, however, more and more NOW people and other women associated with one of the small groups adopted the name until today it has a generic meaning. Some feminists still do not like to be thought of as part of
women's liberation and some of the latter do not like the term feminist, but
for most, the two are synonymous. This dual use of the term women's
liberation has created some confusion as most of the small groups have no

[1]Unfortunately, they did not anticipate that "liberation" would be
caricatured as "lib," "libbie," and "libbest" and contribute to the women's
movement, like women, not being taken seriously.

specific names. It occasionally is difficult to tell whether "women's liberation" refers to the whole movement or just to its younger branch.

The original newsletter ceased publication in June 1969, but during its short life it was one of the most useful organizational tools of the movement. Adopting an expansionist policy, its revolving editors gave most issues away to anyone indicating any interest whatsoever in the women's movement and placed many on bookstore shelves. It was financed by donations, some subscriptions, unpaid labor, and the sale of women's liberation literature at exorbitant prices.[2] Its purpose was to reach any potential sympathizer in order to let her know that there were others who thought as she did and that she was not isolated or crazy. It also functioned to put women in contact with other like-minded women in the same area and thus stimulated the formation of new groups. To do this, all mail had to be answered whether it was simply requests for literature, contacts, or for advice on organizing, as well as news and articles solicited for subsequent issues. This grew to be a herculean task. The *Vwlm* grew from 200 copies the first issue to 2,000 the seventh and last; from 6 pages to 25. It was finally killed because the work of keeping it up had grown too big to handle and because the then editors thought no "national newsletter could do justice to the role of 'voice' at the present time."[3]

At the time of its death there were no other major movement publications apart from an occasional local journal. Three months later, the first women's liberation newspaper, *off our backs*, was published in Washington, D.C. The number of feminist papers and journals increased rapidly thereafter. To date there are over 150, and many more were started but did not survive.[4] None of the papers is national in scope though they borrow from one another freely. Magazines range from scholarly to popular to propagandistic, with the majority being literary in nature. Some have a policy of printing literally everything they receive, in the belief that all women have something to say and should be given the opportunity to see their work in print. Some are as exclusive as any professional journal.

Media Hostility

In part this multitude of publications was started out of disillusionment with the commercial press and in the belief that only movement publi-

[2]One of the early clashes of women's liberation with the radical movement occurred when the New England Free Press decided to publish women's liberation pamphlets at very low prices. While this made these materials available to a greater public, it undercut the financial base of the newsletter, which was not highly appreciated.

[3]*Voice of the women's liberation movement* (*Vwlm*), June 1969, p. 25.

[4]*New Women's Survival Catalog* (New York: Coward, McCann and Geohegan, 1973) lists 163 feminist publications.

cations would give the movement fair coverage. Young feminists had been hostile to the press from the beginning — significantly more so than other social movements. Some of this fear was traceable to inexperience as even those women with a political background had not done press work before. Much more derived from watching how inaccurately the press had reported the social movements and student protests in which they had previously been active. Unlike blacks, for example, young white women had grown up believing that the press was as objective as it liked to portray itself. When their political experiences made them conscious of the gross discrepancies between what they saw at a particular demonstration and what was reported, they withdrew from any press contact in disgust. Blacks, on the other hand, had never had any illusions about who controlled the press, and saw the media as a tool to be used. Women had wanted to relate to reporters honestly; when the results were not what they expected, they chose not to relate at all.

Most of the media compounded this problem by treating early women's liberation activities with a mixture of humor, ridicule, and disbelief. Some of these early activities did seem funny on the surface. Yippies had utilized zap actions and guerilla theater as a respite from the boring ineffectiveness of mass marches. Women's liberation picked up on this idea as a way of making a political point in an unusual, eye-catching manner. The first major public action, at the 1968 Miss America contest, featured a "freedom trash can" into which bras, girdles, false eyelashes, and other instruments of female oppression were tossed, and a live sheep was crowned Miss America. This impulse was furthered by the spread of WITCH covens (Women's International Terrorist Conspiracy from Hell) to hex objects of local ire after the first incantation on Wall Street in the fall of 1968 was followed by a five-point drop in the stock market.

Some reporters looked at the serious side of these actions, but most only laughed. Whereas reporters had examined the political message underneath the Yippie spoofs, they just glanced at the surface of the women's actions and used them to illustrate how silly women were.[5] The press treated women's liberation much as society treats women — as entertainment not to be taken seriously.

If they thought it would be funnier, newspapers even made up their own actions, of which the "bra-burning" episode is the most notable. There has yet to be a woman in women's liberation to burn a single bra publicly,

[5]This was not true in all countries. When the Dolleminas of Holland whistled at men on the streets and held other similar actions, their local press was much more sympathetic; but there was a firmer tradition behind these acts. The Provos there had developed the idea of *ludik* actions to a fine art. These actions were intended to make people laugh, but always carried a political message. The press became accustomed to looking for the politics and carried this over to reporting *ludik* actions by women.

but this mythical act was widely reported in the press.[6] "Bra" stories and related nonincidents usually got front page coverage, while serious stories on employment discrimination were always on the women's page. Photographers inevitably depicted feminists with unattractive poses or facial expressions. Reporters commented on interviewees' femininity, marital status, or style of dress more than their views. Editors ordered production to "get the Karate up front" and writers to "find an authority who'll say this is all a crock of shit."[7] Underground and New Left papers were often the worst of the lot, frequently running women's liberation stories illustrated by naked women and exaggerated genitalia.[8]

Women's liberation dealt with the conflict between desire for coverage and dislike of misrepresentation by refusing to speak to male reporters. First established at the Miss America contest, this practice soon became an informal rule everywhere, and has only partially broken down. There were two main reasons behind this policy, but it had even more unexpected benefits. The first was to compel the media to hire more women reporters and to give others opportunities to do news reporting usually denied to women. The second was to get better coverage. Young feminists had discovered that even sympathetic men were often incapable of understanding what they were talking about because men simply had not had the same experiences as most women. They did not, for example, understand women's anger at being sex objects. With women reporters feminists could communicate their concerns through discussion of experiences common to women that were incomprehensible to men. And in these early stages anecdotes on such experiences were the main means of articulating women's grievances; the ideas had not yet been refined into specific issues.

Even women reporters covered the early movement only with difficulty. Most young activists would not talk to them at all as they saw no value in distorted coverage in the commercial press. Those who would consent to be interviewed often required anonymity and frequently demanded the right to edit the final copy (which was of course denied). Reporters were tossed out of women's liberation meetings when discovered, hung up

---

[6]For details of how this myth developed, see Joanna Foley Martin, "Confessions of a Non Bra-Burner," *Chicago Journalism Review* 4 (July 1971): 11. It should be remembered that draft-card burning was much in the news those days and many other things were going up in smoke.

[7]Sandie North, "Reporting the Movement," *Atlantic Monthly*, March 1970, p. 105.

[8]Sometimes women retaliated. In 1969, Berkeley women held hostage an editor of a new underground newspaper, *Dock of the Bay,* until he agreed to stop publication of a special "sextra" issue planned to raise money for the new paper.

on when they phoned; saw their notes grabbed from their hands and destroyed at rallies; had their microphones smashed, their cameras threatened, and their films stolen.[9] They also found some sympathetic feminists who would talk to them at length, give them reams of material to read, arrange interviews and group discussions for their benefit, and direct them to good sources of information.

The immediate results of these policies were seen not so much in the quality of the news stories as in their numbers. There was something intriguing about the very difficulty of covering the new movement. Further, the idea that *men* were being excluded from something, especially male *reporters*, generated much more interest than women normally get. People were *curious* why *men* were excluded; and if the stories ridiculed feminists for discriminating, many women read between the lines and flocked to join. Female reporters joined also. Initially skeptical, they often found themselves much more involved in the ideas of the movement than they intended. What many thought would be an ordinary story turned out to be a revelation.

In the fall of 1969 the major news media simultaneously began to do stories on women's liberation, and they appeared steadily for the next six months. Quickly discovering that only women could cover the movement, they tried to pick reporters known for their objectivity and unfeminist views. It made no difference. Virtually all the initial stories in *Time, Life, Newsweek*, etc., are personal conversion stories. These stories had as much effect on the media as they did on the movement. Women writers, researchers, and even secretaries became conscious of their secondary role on their publications and began protesting for better conditions and forming their own small groups.[10]

Male Exclusion

The exclusion of male reporters was in conformity with the general policy of excluding men from all movement activities. Initially, this was one of the most controversial aspects of the movement to the outside world,

---

[9]North, "Reporting the Movement."

[10]*Newsweek* in particular illustrated all these phenomena. The original person assigned to the story was a young writer being "given her chance." Her piece was criticized for unobjectivity, rewritten by a male writer, and finally dropped. In her place a free-lancer who happened to be the wife of one of *Newsweek*'s senior editors was hired. She was paid in advance, specified no undue editing, and wrote the most personal report of all. Despite the fact that it was quite different from *Newsweek*'s usual style, it was printed. In the meantime, women staffers had watched these developments with great interest and made plans of their own to commemorate the occasion. They chose the day of the special issue's publication to announce their complaint of discrimination filed with the EEOC.

but it was and is one of the most uncontroversial within the movement itself. There was virtually no debate on this policy in any city at any time. Originally the idea of exclusiveness was borrowed from the Black Power movement, much in the public consciousness when the women's liberation movement began. It was reinforced by the unremitting hostility of most of the New Left men. Even when this hostility was not present, women in virtually every group in the United States and Canada soon discovered that the traditional sex roles reasserted themselves in groups regardless of the good intentions of the participants. Men inevitably dominated the discussions, and usually would talk only about how women's liberation related to men, or how men were oppressed by the sex roles. In segregated groups women found the discussions to be more open, honest and extensive. They could learn to relate to other women and not just to men.

Women continued the policy of male exclusion because they felt men were largely irrelevant to the development of the movement. They wanted to reach women, and found it both frustrating and a waste of time to talk to men. Of course many did talk to men, usually on an individual basis, and many men eventually formed their own groups around the problem of the male sex role. Initially, women's liberation discovered that there was a tactical value in male exclusion. As with the exclusion of male reporters, their activities were taken much more seriously when they insisted they wanted to speak only with women. The tactic had shock value. A good example, followed many times more, was the organization of a women's discussion group at the August 1968 National Student Association convention at the University of Kansas. To arouse interest in the meeting women stood in the cafeteria lines passing out leaflets to women only. When the man in a couple unthinkingly reached for one, they made a deliberate point of giving it to the woman. When a man took the leaflet from the woman with him, it was taken from him and returned to the woman. The men were indignant, the women curious, and of course everyone wanted to know what the leaflet said. The real purpose of this technique was not to keep men from reading the innocuous leaflet but to catch people's attention and make them think. This it succeeded in doing. It also solved the litter problem; no leaflets were left laying on the floor.

A variation on this theme was used by the sellers of *Notes from the First Year*, a mimeographed magazine of early feminist thought. It sold for $.50 to women and $1.00 to men. One reason for this was that the authors wanted to reach women, thus preferring to keep the price low, but felt men ought to be charged for the privilege of reading the magazine if they insisted on it. They fully realized that a man could get a woman to buy a copy for him at the lower price. That was the second purpose. It was a form of political education to demonstrate to men and women the discomforts of having to go through someone else to fulfill one's desires or needs. It illustrated the true nature of the female role by reverse example. . . .

CHAPTER 18

Off our backs

Less than a year after the *Voice of the women's liberation movement* ceased publication, Marilyn Webb, a feminist writer, and some of her friends founded *off our backs* in Washington, D.C.   *Off our backs*, a tabloid, is described by its staff as a "news journal." According to a 1974 survey of feminist editors, it is one of the best-produced publications of the women's movement, and it is one of its few newspapers.

Off our backs is a monthly whose estimated readership has grown to 15,000 since its first issue was published in January 1970. It covers breaking news about women and is devoted primarily to analyses of feminism and sexism. *Oob* has a sense of humor; it often parodies contemporary issues, such as nude centerfolds, comic book romances, and advertising about women. It is vigilant in its coverage of women's rights and problems, and devotes a great deal of space to interviews with or essays by women of different backgrounds. One memorable essay was penned by a woman who had gone underground to avoid prosecution for alleged destruction of draft records. *Oob* also reviews books, films, plays and keeps a sharp eye on the news media.

An editor for *oob* (a collective where everyone is an editor) said that "*oob* never felt that the establishment was going to deal honestly with sexism and classism. We believe in an independent women's movement and try to be a feminist news journal that helps the women's liberation movement achieve its goals."

Off our backs' statement of purpose from its March 1970 issue is reprinted here, beginning on the next page.

STATEMENT OF PURPOSE
off our backs

By Nancy Ferro, Coletta Reid Holcomb, and Marilyn Saltzman-Webb

The women's movement can no longer afford to be naive about the nature and function of the mass media in this society. Every major magazine, newspaper and television network has done a story on us and most are clamoring for interviews, permission to do documentaries, and any special coverage they can get. We no longer need to use the mass media to tell people we exist. We now need to develop a practical critique which we can use to guide our future actions and determine how our communication needs can best be met.

Relying on our own experiences, we can see the ways in which the mass media work to serve interests directly opposed to our own. For example, we are attempting to build, within our movement, non-exploitative ways of relating to one another based on trust and concern rather than political expediency. We have serious personal/political intentions in breaking down hierarchical and elitist structures, and for experimenting with leaderless groups and collective decision-making. In dealing with the media these revolutionary principles and practices are destroyed. The media work to create leaders, they know of no way of relating to us on our own terms. Being interviewed and presented as a leader is a real ego trip — the media brings out the most counter-revolutionary traits in people. Elitism, dissension and division are the ultimate results.

Creating leaders also increases the power of the mass media to define our movement for us. What the media-created leader says becomes a standard, usually very restrictive, for the whole movement. Then the press discredits the entire movement by discrediting the leader through attacking her personal life rather than dealing with her politics.

A major misconception is the belief that the media will deal with us seriously and present a truthful picture of who we are. There is no reason to assume that the mass media are free of the sexism pervasive in all other American institutions. The mass media are primarily interested in lining their own pockets and assuring themselves of the continuance of their powerful position in society by kowtowing to the interests of the ruling class. Agnew's attacks are really too high praise. In the end the mass media will capitulate rather than fight for the truth, for to meet the needs of the people and the demands of objective journalism would mean the end of the mass media in its present form.

The mass media serve our society as a reality-definer. By presenting what is news the media define what exists; by interpreting the news the media determine what people should think about what exists. Almost all events and significant communications between individuals and groups of people are mediated by the Establishment press and thus transformed into the reality the media wish to project. Women's liberation does not fit into that reality. Demands for free medical care and public transportation, an end to sexual exploitation and discrimination, the dismantling of an economic system based on profits rather than human needs, make no sense in the nonsensical society in which we live. From the perspective of the mass media *we* are abnormal and absurd. Women who join the movement must be able to see themselves in the liberated woman, she must become "the girl next door." But the media-created liberated woman is not merely unusual and exceptional, but a total weirdo — a bra-burner, man-hater, lesbian, sickie!

In this outrageous society, the mass media have become a prime anesthetizer. They cannot deal with issues in their complexity, but only in a public-relations, simplistic way. Every superficial story threatens overexposure, making it easy for people to ignore the substance of what we are doing. Building a movement demands confronting people directly in an active process; no one is radicalized by passively watching TV. Using the mass media may look like the easy way to reach many women, but it is ultimately impotent and self-destructive.

Any group of people fighting for liberation must recognize as their enemy an institution whose very survival depends upon the perpetuation of the evils they are struggling against. The mass media are our enemy: no matter how seriously they may approach, no matter how enlightened they may seem, women's liberation threatens the power base of the mass media. Each time we respond to them we legitimatize them and the reality they are defending, and we risk sacrificing all that we are working for.

It is time to call a halt to all dealings with the mass media — no more interviews, no more documentaries, no more special coverage. We don't need them and we don't want them. In the interests of self-defense and honest communication we have begun to create our own papers and our own magazines. Our energies must turn now to the strengthening and expansion of our own media.

CHAPTER 19

Ms. Magazine

Most of the women who were attracted to the women's movement of the late 60's were well-educated and came from a middle-class background. Their relationships with women's liberation varied from sympathy to an activist commitment. What they shared was a desire for change. Some women wanted to change their old style of life; others wanted to be available to women to help them make such changes.

Both types of women combined to form the audience and the editorial board of *Ms.* magazine. Although a number of regional newsletters or magazines and national feminist journals devoted to scholarship and the arts had been developed by 1971, there still was no national feminist publication that could claim a large share of readers from all over the nation. At this time *Ladies Home Journal* and *McCall's*, the neck-and-neck leaders of the women's magazine trade, had close to seven million readers each. It seemed like the time to place a feminist competitor on the corner newsstand. *Ms.* was created.

The founders of *Ms.* originally thought of entering the newsletter market, but felt that they couldn't reach the women they wanted to through that format. So they began to talk about the possibility of starting a magazine. Their idea was pooh-poohed wherever they sought backers. They were reminded that some of the giants of the industry — *Saturday Evening Post* and *Look* — had succumbed to rising costs and postal rate increases. It was nearly impossible to project the size of the market they could anticipate. No one knew how many women would be interested in a magazine about and for feminists, which would include articles on women's issues, profiles of women, excerpts from novels, poetry, book reviews — everything the traditional women's magazines had, but from a feminist point of view — and without the food emphasis.

In 1971, *New York* magazine offered the *Ms.* group an opportunity to produce a "Preview" issue as a pull-out insert in its end-of-the-year "double issue." The group accepted.

The 40-page *New York* insert contained articles on "Sisterhood" by Gloria Steinem; "Why Women Fear Success" by Vivian Gornick; "The Housewife's Moment of Truth" by Jane O'Reilly; "My Mother, the Dentist" by Nicholas von Hoffman; "How to Write Your Own Marriage Contract" by Susan Edmiston; and "Rating the Candidates: Feminists Vote the Rascals In or Out" by Brenda Feigen Fasteau and Bonnie Lobel, a study of the 1972 Presidential candidates' positions on women's issues.

The issue set a newsstand sales record for *New York*, and in July 1972 the first regular issue of the new *Ms.* magazine appeared. Despite the predictions of failure, it succeeded. *Ms.* now has a circulation of more than 400,000 and has established the Ms. Foundation, which sponsors research and projects on women, including several in other media, such as books, records, and television.

An inside account of *Ms.*'s beginnings, from its Vol. I, No. 1 issue, July 1972, is reprinted on the following pages.

A PERSONAL REPORT FROM MS.

First, there were some women writers and editors who started asking questions. Why was our work so unconnected to our lives? Why were the media, including women's magazines, so rarely or so superficially interested in the big changes happening to women? Why were we always playing the game by somebody else's (the publisher's, the advertiser's) rules?

Then, there were questions from activists, women who were trying to raise money for an information service and self-help projects, particularly for poor or isolated women, and having very little luck. Mightn't a publication — say, a newsletter — serve to link up women, and to generate income as well?

The two groups met several times early in 1971, and agreed that we all wanted a publication that was owned by and honest about women. Then we did some hard financial figuring. Newsletters that made decent profits seem confined to giving stock-market tips, or servicing big corporations. Some small but valuable ones for women were already struggling along. Besides, newsletters were a fine service for people already interested, but weren't really meant to reach out in a populist way.

So the idea of a full-fledged national magazine came up; a publication created and controlled by women that could be as serious, outrageous, satisfying, sad, funky, intimate, global, compassionate, and full of change as women's lives really are.

Of course, we knew that many national magazines were folding, or doing poorly. Rocketing production and mailing costs, plus competition from television for both advertising and subject matter, had discouraged some of the people who loved magazines most. Even those magazines still flourishing were unresponsive to the silenced majority. Women just weren't getting serious or honest coverage, and we doubted that we were the only people who felt the need for change. Besides, the Women's Movement had raised our hopes; it had given us courage.

So we had many more meetings, and we made big plans: long lists of article ideas, a mock-up of illustration and design, proposed budgets, everything. Then we spent many months making appointments, looking for backing from groups that invest in new ventures — and just as many months getting turned down. Flat.

Why? Well, we usually heard one or several reasons like these from potential investors:

. . . all around us, magazines are failing; why spend money to buck the tide?

. . . even though local or "special interest" magazines are making money (curiously, anything directed at the female 53 percent of the population is regarded as "special interest"), they are bad investments compared to, say, apartment buildings, computer hardware, and the like;

. . . the more we insisted on retaining at least 51 percent of the stock, the more everyone told us that investors don't give money without getting control; who ever heard of a national magazine controlled by its staff?

. . . setting aside some of the profits (supposing there were any) to go back to the Women's Movement is so unbusinesslike as to be downright crazy — even black magazines or other publications attached to movements haven't managed that;

. . . and, finally, the investors said, there are probably only ten or twenty thousand women in the country interested in changing women's status anyway; certainly not enough to support a nationwide magazine.

We got discouraged. Some of us thought we would either have to jettison a requirement or two, or give up. But there was support: friendly magazine people who thought we should try to find "public-spirited" money; women in advertising who were themselves trying to create ads that were a service to women; feminist speakers who have been traveling around the country and knew that a mass audience was there.

Most of all, there were the several women writers and editors, one businesswoman, and some all-purpose feminist volunteers who were willing to contribute their talents and time in return for very little except hope. "It's very simple," said one of the writers. "We all want to work for a magazine we read."

Then, two concrete things happened to bolster our hopes. First,

Katharine Graham, one of the few women publishers in the country, was willing to pretend that a few shares of stock in a nonexistent magazine were worth buying, a fiction that allowed us some money for out-of-pocket expenses. (She preferred to be generous in anonymity, but her help — a matter of corporate record anyway — was noted in a newspaper report, so we include her name as an inadequate way of saying thank you for helping women in hard times.) Second and even more unusual was an offer from Clay Felker, editor and publisher of *New York*, a weekly metropolitan magazine. He had thought up an ingenious way of helping *Ms.* produce the thing it needed most: a nationwide test; a sample issue to prove that we could create a new kind of magazine, and that women would buy it.

The plan was this. *New York* needed something special for its year-end double issue, and also wanted practice in producing national "one-shot" magazines (single issues devoted to a particular area or subject). *Ms.* needed the money and editorial freedom to produce a sample issue. Therefore, *New York* offered to bear the full risk of the $125,000 necessary to pay printers, binders, engravers, paper mills, distributors, writers, artists, and all the other elements vital to turning out 300,000 copies of our Preview Issue. (Plus supplying the great asset of *New York*'s staff, without which the expenses would have been much higher.) In return, some of the *Ms.* articles and features would appear first as an insert in that year-end issue of *New York*, half of the newsstand profits (if any) of our own Preview Issue would go to *New York*, and so would all of the advertising proceeds. (We had editorial autonomy but no say about advertising; all but two of the ads were the same as those in *New York*'s issue anyway.)

It was an odd way of introducing a magazine, but a generous and unusual offer — the first time, as far as we know, that one magazine would give birth to another without the *quid pro quo* of editorial control, or some permanent financial interest. Clay Felker made a few gruff noises about how it was strictly a business deal. After all, didn't *New York* stand to make a profit if *Ms.* did very well? (This last was generally said in earshot of his Board of Directors, who might otherwise think he was as crazy as we were.)

Several of us were regular writers for *New York*, however and we had a different idea. Over the years, we must have convinced him, or at least worn him down. Clay had begun to believe, like us, that something deep, irresistible, and possibly historic, was happening to women.

The Preview Issue

In a small office, with four people working full time and the rest of us helping when we could get away from our jobs, the Spring Preview Issue was put together, start to finish, in two months. There were a lot of close calls and emergencies: cherished article ideas that didn't get finished on time, authors whose other commitments made them drop out at the last minute, indecision about the cover which resulted in doing four of them, and an eleventh-hour discovery that we had one week and eight pages less than we thought.

But the work got done, and the decisions got made. They happened communally. We never had time to sit down and discuss our intellectual aversion to the hierarchy of most offices, where decisions and orders float down from above. We just chose not to do anything with which one of us strongly disagreed. And we didn't expect our more junior members to get coffee, or order lunch, or do all the typing, or hold some subordinate title. We each did as much of our own phone-answering and manuscript typing as deadlines and common sense would allow. On the masthead, we listed ourselves alphabetically, divided only by area of expertise and full- or part-time work.

Feminist philosophies often point out that a hierarchy, military or otherwise, is an imitation of patriarchy, and that there are many other ways of getting work done. We didn't approach the idea so intellectually, but we did arrive at the same conclusion from gut experience. As women, we had been on the bottom of hierarchies for too long. We knew how wasteful they really were.

The crowded *Ms.* office had an atmosphere of camaraderie, of people doing what they cared about. But there was apprehension, too. Could there possibly be even 100,000 women in the country who wanted this unconventional magazine? We had been listening to doomsayers for so long that we ourselves began to doubt it.

When the insert from our Preview Issue appeared as part of *New York* in December, the issue set a newsstand sales record, more than *New York* had ever sold. Of course, said the doomsayers, women in a metropolitan area might be interested. But would we appeal to the women of Ohio or Arizona?

When the full-length Spring Preview Issue of *Ms.* was distributed nationally in January, we packed off all available authors and staff to talk to women's groups around the country, and to appear on any radio or television shows that reached women (thus changing the lives of several of us, who had never spoken in public before).

The Preview Issue was designed to stay on the newsstands for at least two months (which is why it was dated "Spring"), and we wanted to make sure women knew about it. But we got to our various assigned towns only to be met with phone calls: "Where is *Ms.*?" "We can't find a copy." "What newsstands are selling it?"

Worriedly, we called the distributor, and the truth finally dawned on us. The 300,000 copies supposed to last for at least eight weeks had virtually disappeared in eight days. *Ms.* had sold out.

We celebrated. We breathed sighs of relief. And only in that moment did we realize how worried we had been — worried that we would make the

Women's Movement seem less far-reaching and strong than it was by creating a feminist magazine that did poorly, worried about *New York Magazine*'s risk, and all the friends who had helped us, worried about letting down ourselves, and other women.

But the most gratifying experience was still to come. Letters came pouring into our crowded office, more than 20,000 long, literate, simple, disparate, funny, tragic and very personal letters from women all over the country, including Ohio and Arizona. They wrote about their experiences and problems. They supported or criticized, told us what they needed, what they thought should be included or excluded, and generally spoke of *Ms.* as "our" magazine. (We've reprinted a few of them in this issue, and we will continue to make more use of readers' letters than most magazines do. After all, using only women who happen to be writers is itself a kind of discrimination, and misrepresents the lives that women lead.)

We were feeling inundated by all the mail, but didn't realize how unusual it was until we asked the editor of another women's magazine — with a circulation of 7 million, compared to our 300,000 — how much editorial response each issue got. "About 2,000 letters," she said, "and a lot of them not very worthwhile. Four thousand letters of any kind would be considered quite extraordinary."

Obviously, the need for and interest in a nonestablishment magazine were greater and deeper than even we had thought. More out of instinct than skill, the women of *Ms.* had tapped an emerging and deep cultural change that was happening to us, and happening to our sisters.

When all the returns were in, *New York* breathed a sigh of relief, too. Their share of the newsstand sales was $20,000. And so was ours. We felt very rich indeed, until we figured out that our check wouldn't pay even half the postage for one national mailing of a letter inviting people to subscribe. In fact, if we had paid ourselves salaries, we would have just about broken even. We were learning the terrible truth of how much it costs to start a magazine, even one that readers want.

So we set off again to look for financial backers, but this time we had that magic thing known as a track record. And we also had more than 50,000 subscription orders, each one a potential asset, but each one a promise to keep.

*   *   *

Where We Are Now

After the Preview Issue, we spent another three months looking for investors who believed in the magazine, and who would therefore give us the backing we needed without taking financial and editorial control.

In spite of all the looking, we can't take credit for finding Warner Communications. They found us. We are grateful to them for exploring many kinds of new media. And we are especially impressed that they took the unusual position of becoming the major investor, but minority stockholder in *Ms*. It's a step forward for free women, and free journalism.

We still must reach the break-even point with a third of the money, and in a third of the time, that most magazines require. (The average seems to be $3 million and three years before a national publication begins to show profit.) But thanks to the head start from *New York* and our subscribers, plus the opportunity given us by Warner Communications, we have a fighting chance.

If we do make it, we will own ourselves. We will also be able to give a healthy percentage of our profits back to the Women's Movement; to programs and projects that can help change women's lives.

In addition to financial struggles, the past few months have been spent gathering a staff. Our full-time members now number twenty instead of four, and a few more of us are helping part-time. Soon, there will be more names added to the masthead, mostly in advertising and circulation.

At the moment, we vary in age from 17 to 45, from no college at all to a Ph.D., and from experience as the editor of one of the country's biggest magazines to experience as a taxi driver. We are white Southerners, black Midwesterners, Latin American-born New Yorkers, homesick country-lovers and urbanites who never miss fresh air. One of us, an assistant art director, is male. (Since he was already working for our woman art director, he feels right at home. And so do we.) One of us is a radical Catholic, several are Jewish, and many are garden-variety WASP. We got more or less educated at Malcolm X College, Darien High School, Vassar, Smith, the University of Delhi, Millsaps College, Columbia, Radcliffe, Willamette University, the Sorbonne, the University of Wisconsin, and VISTA. We are married, never-been-married, and divorced. Some of us have children; some don't. Some of us have turned our friends into family, and some have done just the reverse.

All together, we're not a bad composite of the changing American woman.

If you asked us our philosophy for ourselves and for the magazine, each of us would give an individual answer. But we agree on one thing. We want a world in which no one is born into a subordinate role because of visible difference, whether that difference is of race or of sex. That's an assumption we make personally and editorially, with all the social changes it implies. After that, we cherish our differences. We want *Ms*. to be a forum for many views.

Most of all, we are joyfully discovering ourselves, and a world set free from old patterns, old thoughts. We hope *Ms*. will help you — and us — to explore this new world. There are few guidelines in history, or our own past. We must learn from each other.

So keep writing. *Ms*. belongs to us all.

CHAPTER 20

Challenging Broadcast Licenses: WABC-TV

Broadcasting is the only component of the mass media that is regulated by the Federal Government. The First Amendment to the Constitution guarantees freedom of the press, but the finite amount of space on the airwaves necessitates supervision by an official body to insure that broadcast licensees truly serve the market in which they are located. If the Federal Communications Commission finds that a licensee has been abusing the "public trust" that its license symbolizes, the FCC can revoke it.

But proving that a radio or television station has not served the public interest is very difficult to do. Licenses are granted for three-year periods. In the last year of the period, the licensee must apply for renewal. At that time the renewal application can be challenged by "legitimate representatives" of groups in the licensee's market, who can file a petition with the FCC opposing renewal of that broadcaster's license. A petition to deny a broadcaster's license must document abuses in great detail, or else the Commission can throw out a petition for "lack of specificity." A group or an individual unhappy with a station's performance usually must retain legal counsel to prepare a petition that will pass muster with the FCC.

This type of grievance procedure for listeners and viewers has only been in practice since 1966. Up until that time, the FCC was disposed to hearing complaints only from citizens who had experienced electrical interference or economic injury from the licensee. But in *United Church of Christ* vs. *FCC*, the U.S. Court of Appeals told the Commission it must grant "standing" to a citizen group which argued that a station in Jackson, Mississippi, was guilty of racism in its programming. The Court said that "public participation in FCC action was not meant to be limited to writing letters to the Commission, to inspection of records, to the Commission's grace in considering listener claims, or to mere nonparticipating appearance at hearings." This opened the door to citizens who wanted to register their complaints with the FCC, which feared that it would be flooded with capricious complaints from viewers and listeners with axes to grind.

So it was with six years of precedent that the National Organization for Women filed a petition to deny the license of WABC-TV, New York City, on May 1, 1972. The NOW petition attacked the station for deficiencies in three key areas: ascertainment of women on their opinions about community issues, news and programming about women's issues, and employment of women at the station. These three key points provided the model for petitions that have been drawn up by women's groups in many other markets since that time.

Ascertainment is a procedure the FCC requires of broadcast licensees. The licensee must show that it has polled community leaders to determine what constitutes "important community issues" which it should cover in its news and public affairs programs. The FCC requires only "a good faith attempt" on the part of the licensee, not a pure random sample or statistically reliable findings. NOW claimed that too few women were polled by WABC, and that women were ignored "as a group," particularly those women involved in the women's movement.

NOW also complained about the way women were depicted in entertainment programs, and said women's issues were ignored or treated with condescension on news and public affairs programs. NOW said this was a violation of the Fairness Doctrine, which requires a station to show "overall balance" in its programming.

NOW also criticized the balance of responsibility among WABC-TV's employees. In 1970 the FCC added "sex" to its equal opportunity requirements for licensees, but NOW said adherence to this provision was not in evidence in WABC's employment data. Very few women held professional or managerial positions; most of the women at the station were employed in clerical jobs.

WABC and NOW sparred, with the FCC as referee, for several years. On March 21, 1975, the Commission finally handed down a decision, rejecting NOW's petition to deny the license against WABC. At this same time, it also rejected a petition to deny the license of WRC-TV, Washington, D.C., filed by NOW and a host of other women's groups in that area — even though the Equal Employment Opportunity Commission had said it had "reasonable cause" to believe WRC-TV had discriminated against women in hiring and promotion.

In reference to all three points on which NOW built its case, the FCC said that in most cases it would defer to the "discretion" of the licensee.

Ascertainment was a vague requirement for which the FCC had not designed rules or procedures. *Programming* content was to be left up to the licensee, barring an infringement of the Fairness Doctrine, in which case the FCC would direct the station to air opposing viewpoints. NOW tried to show that sexist depictions of females were a violation of the Fairness Doctrine. The FCC replied that *mere depiction* will not invoke the Fairness Doctrine; the person depicted must herself be *discussing* a "controversial issue of public importance" before fairness comes into play. And *discrimination* in employment must in the end be dealt with by the Equal Employment Opportunity Commission, not the FCC, it said.

Excerpts from NOW's petition to the FCC to deny WABC-TV's license begin below.

PETITION TO DENY WABC-TV LICENSE RENEWAL

1. *WABC-TV wilfully failed to meet FCC requirements that it ascertain the needs, problems and interests of women in the community to provide suitable programming.*

Letters from individual members of the New York Chapter of NOW (petitioner herein), explaining the nature of their complaints, were first sent to WABC-TV in August, 1970. As a result of those letters, a meeting was held in September 1970, between representatives of NOW and WABC-TV. While this meeting, attended by both Mr. Kenneth H. MacQueen, General Manager, and Mr. Al Primo, News Director, evidenced no serious effort on the part of WABC-TV to ascertain or seriously consult with members of the feminist community as to their needs and interests, it did make WABC-TV aware that a segment of the women's community was concerned about its programming service to the community. Petitioner contends that this initial meeting, over a year and a half ago, put WABC-TV *on notice* that a segment of the women's community was ready and available to meet with WABC-TV for the purposes of ascertainment. WABC-TV has not attempted to follow up with NOW for ascertainment purposes.

Subsequent contact between NOW and WABC-TV has only resulted from the dogged, affirmative efforts of NOW alone. Prior to the second "Women's Strike for Equality" in August 1971, Ann Cavallero, Chairwoman of the NOW Image Committee, wrote to Mr. Goldenson, President of WABC-TV, criticizing WABC-TV for failing to give full and fair coverage to the Women's Movement; requesting a camera crew for the Women's March, and offering to serve as a guide for the crew. This letter was never acknowledged. As a result of WABC-TV's failure to respond to this request, members of NOW went to the office of WABC-TV to insist on a meeting with Mr. Goldenson. Frustrated by WABC-TV's total failure to respond, Ms. Cavallero called Mr. McCarthy in November, for the purpose of setting up another meeting with the station and finally arranged for a meeting. This meeting, held on November 23, 1971, was equally unproductive. Members of the station's staff manifested no serious interest in petitioner's grievances and refused to acknowledge its responsibility as a public broadcaster to listen to or respond to such complaints. Again there was no follow-up from this meeting.

On January 23, 1972, Ms. Dorothy Crouch, President of the New York Chapter of NOW, wrote to Mr. Elton H. Rule, President of ABC, Inc., complaining once again of the station's neglect of women's issues in program content as well as in news and public affairs programming. This letter asked specifically that the licensee devote a substantial portion of its programming to the Equal Rights Amendment, including daytime programming, prime time and editorial time, and to present live coverage of the Equal Rights Amendment hearings. On February 1, Ms. Crouch received a response from Mr. K. H. MacQueen, Vice-President and General Manager of WABC-TV, in which he stated that WABC's programming executives would review NOW's request for coverage of a meeting with members of NOW to discuss covering women's rights issues more fully. No further word was heard and no meeting was set up. The Equal Rights Amendment received minimal and demeaning coverage by the station.

* * *

When a community group, such as NOW, attempts to inform the licensee of its special needs and interests and to consult with the station on a continuing basis, WABC-TV's failure to consult with the group on a continuing basis constitutes a failure to meet its public obligation and constitutes a fatal defect in the applicant's ascertainment.

Finally, the deliberate omission by WABC-TV of any mention of the meetings already held with NOW and its failure to respond to the individual letters from women who were critical of WABC-TV's programming is in violation of its stated policy of handling complaints and suggestions and can only reflect a deliberate refusal to recognize women as a significant group and meet the needs of this group. This is a violation of FCC requirements for renewal applicants. The withholding of this information from the FCC clearly brings into question the station's entire ascertainment procedure. Unless the FCC has the community ascertainment information, there is no way for the Commission to evaluate whether the station is in fact responding to community needs. Certainly, this factor alone raises substantial issues of fact to warrant a hearing, if not to deny the applicant's license outright.

2. *WABC-TV violated the Fairness Doctrine by failing to develop programming which accurately reflects women.*

First, the station has wilfully and deliberately excluded issues of concern to women from the list of community needs that they intend to meet. Secondly, WABC-TV's news and public affairs programming is woefully lacking in coverage of issues of particular concern to women. Further, no women host or control any of these programs. Finally, daytime programming which is almost exclusively directed to a female audience, is totally devoid of any meaningful content. . . .

The most dramatic evidence of the station's blatant refusal to meet the needs of women is demonstrated by the lack of any substantial programming or news coverage dealing with the Equal Rights Amendment (ERA). After fifty years of struggle by women and women's groups, both Houses of Congress have finally passed an amendment to the Constitution which, when ratified by the states, will guarantee equal rights to women.

An amendment to the Constitution is the single most fundamental legal and moral statement this government can make. It is of historic importance. The ERA, because of its long and torturous route, has taken on even greater significance. With the rebirth of the feminist movement in the United States, it has once again become an issue of importance and significance.

Petitioner has made every affirmative effort to communicate its concerns to afford adequate television coverage of the ERA prior to the passage of the Amendment. On January 31, 1972, a letter from Ms. Dorothy Crouch, President of the New York City Chapter of NOW, was sent to Mr. Elton H. Rule, President of WABC-TV, requesting future coverage of the ERA. On February 15, Ms. Crouch received a response from Mr. R. H. MacQueen, Vice President and General Manager of WABC-TV, in which he stated that WABC-TV's programming executives would review NOW's request for coverage and arrange a meeting with members of NOW to discuss fuller coverage of women's rights issues. No meeting was ever arranged, as had been promised, and no further communication was received from the station. . . .

This discriminatory treatment of women's groups is shown by the station's lack of news coverage concerning final passage of the ERA on March 22, 1972. Neither local news show, Eyewitness News (6:00 P.M. to 7:00 P.M.), nor the Eleven P.M. Evening News (11:00 P.M. to 11:30 P.M.) even reported this momentous event. In a blatant mocking of the seriousness of women's issues, that same night WABC-TV did feature an extensive story about *Cosmopolitan* Magazine's centerfold picture of a male nude.

WABC-TV network News at 7:00 P.M. minimally covered the passage of the ERA. The story was not placed on the news board as a major item, and less than ten seconds were devoted to a news flash announcement. Three minutes were given to a mini-documentary on Singapore although there was no "hard" news in that story.

* * *

General News.

WABC-TV's minimal news coverage of serious issues affecting women is reflective of the station's deficient ascertainment and indicative of the applicant's belief that these issues are insignificant.

Two monitoring studies were conducted by petitioner in 1971 and 1972. They carefully analyzed and compared the total coverage given to all news stories concerning women and stories about women. The category of "women's topics" is all-inclusive and covers vital issues such as abortion to women's fashions, and coverage of stories of women when treated as sex objects, i.e., the Miss America Contest.

Our studies revealed that, despite the broadness of the category, as delineated above, news concerning or about women accounted for only 14.5% of all news stories reported during the 1971 monitoring period, and dropped to 14.2% during the second monitoring period.

Interestingly, when considered in terms of news time accorded, the time for the above stories diminished to 13.5% and 12.7% of total air time, respectively. But, even more significantly, in 1971, only a mere 1.3% of actual air time was devoted to women's issues of significance, such as abortion, jobs, and equal opportunities. In 1972, this coverage increased to 1.9% of total news time.

A second serious women's issue, women in politics, was also given minimal treatment. The 1971 study revealed that WABC-TV devoted only 2.6% of total air time to this subject. This percentage decreased to 1.2% of news air time in 1972.

In contrast, stories about women in fashion represented 2.1% of news air time in 1971, and dramatically increased to 3.6% of air time in 1972. Coverage of women as "sex object" represented 1.4% and 1.7% of air time in 1971 and 1972, respectively.

WABC-TV's coverage of women's sports stories exemplifies the stations's deliberate distortion of news as it relates to women. In the 1972 Winter Olympics, American women won seven of the eight United States medals — four of those being Gold Medals. However, when called upon to report this extraordinary performance of American women, WABC-TV gave only ten seconds in one program, and thirty seconds on the following day. In addition the names of the women were never mentioned. During the same monitoring period, as part of the sports news, two minutes and fifteen seconds were devoted to a women's pancake-eating contest (6:00 P.M. Eyewitness News, February 15, 1972), and two minutes and thirty seconds given to women cheerleaders at Notre Dame (11:00 P.M. Eyewitness News, February 17, 1972). No doubt, we would have been shocked if, while Jesse Owens was walking away with the 1936 Olympic prizes, the news coverage was devoted to a watermelon eating contest for Blacks. Yet, such lack of coverage of women's achievements is so pervasive that it had previously passed *without review by the FCC.*

Finally, there is only one female reporter on the air out of a total of eleven reporters. During the 1971 period she covered 4.9% of all news. This dropped to 2.3% in 1972.

Public Affairs Programs.

WABC-TV states that it recognizes that public affairs programming is important "to stimulate discussion of and provoke interest in major problems and issues of concern to the public. . ." Here, too, WABC-TV's stubborn refusal to acknowledge the growing demands for equality made by women is reflected in a lack of programming on significant issues of public concern.

Interestingly, in the area of public affairs, the applicant has exhibited some sensitivity to the real needs of ethnic and racial minorities and has programmed specifically to reflect the needs of a broad segment of the Black and Puerto Rican communities. For example, "Like It Is" is a weekly program devoted entirely to the problems of racial minorities in the United States. Not only does WABC-TV recognize the public significance of programming on these issues, but further recognizes that if the program is to truly reflect community needs, it must be staffed and produced by minority group employees. "Like It Is" makes it clear that when ascertainment is properly conducted, WABC-TV is capable of developing programming to meet the community needs.

In contrast, there is no public affairs program specifically directed by and for women. WABC-TV has not even seen fit to devote any of its infrequent special public affairs programs to women's issues. As illustrative of the station's "policy of presenting (public affairs) programming to meet public needs and interests whether or not commercial sponsorship is available," WABC-TV's renewal application lists 21 programs in addition to specials on space flights and Presidential addresses. Not one of these specials focuses on women's issues. Of forty programs listed illustrating WABC-TV's "application of its policy" of pre-empting regular time to broadcast special public affairs and instructional programs — none dealt with women's issues.

The most prestigious of WABC-TV's public affairs programs, "Issues and Answers," presented only one woman, the Prime Minister of Israel, Golda Meir, among a list of twenty-five representative guests. None of the guests addressed herself/himself to problems and issues concerning women's status in our society. Further, Eyewitness News Conference, the locally produced interview program, is geared specifically to "probe, in greater detail, into issues and problems of concern in the community." Among the twenty-nine representative guests, two were women, Eleanor Holmes Norton and Bella Abzug. But only Ms. Norton directed her attention to women in politics and government. WABC-TV's plans for the future of the News Conference follows this pattern — no women's issues are scheduled.

Interestingly, while WABC-TV finds an insufficient community need to warrant public affairs specials on issues such as day care or the Equal Rights Amendment, they do find a need for programs devoted exclusively to the study of American wildlife. On March 19, 1971, *one hour of prime time was pre-empted* for a documentary focused on the American Bald

Eagle; five months later, *another hour of prime time was pre-empted* to study the cycle of the American Bald Eagle (November 26, 1971). Prime time was also pre-empted to feature six programs studying underwater life. Only two of the special programs pre-empting the regular schedule featured women at all; one was "A Visit With The First Lady," and the other was "White House Wedding."

Certainly, we do not contend that it is poor programming to expose residents of a metropolitan area such as New York to the study of wildlife that exists totally outside of their normal range of daily experience. However, it is questionable that there existed great clamor by the community for this programming, or any community expression that the extinction of the Bald Eagle was a significant community problem. Such discriminatory weighing of programming raises a substantial question about the nature of WABC-TV's evaluation of community concerns.

* * *

The ratings indicate that over 80% of the television viewing audience in the New York metropolitan area, between 9:30 A.M. and 6:00 P.M., is made up of women. Despite this fact, WABC-TV neither offers nor proposes to offer any local programming responding to the community needs of women. Daytime programming begins with a two-hour movie (usually a rerun), and proceeds through another six and one-half hours of network-produced game shows, situation comedies, and culminates in an afternoon of soap opera. Even more insulting, all but the soap operas are programs repeated or reruns originally produced for prime time viewing.

WABC-TV clearly believes that women viewers are a sub-class, lacking the need or interest for decent, informative local programming. During the daytime hours, 9:30 A.M. to 6:00 P.M., there are *no* news programs, *no* editorials, *no* public affairs programs, *no* documentaries. There are not even new and original entertainment shows. . . .

WABC-TV's refusal to present balanced daytime programming, reflecting a wide range of local programming, is clearly violative of FCC policies in two important ways: First, women are equally entitled to information on public issues which affect them as citizens. Second, they, like other viewers, have a right to "balanced" programming — including news and public affairs that licensees are obligated to provide under FCC Rules. The fact that all daytime television, from 9:30 A.M. to 6:00 P.M., is network-produced, is clear evidence that WABC-TV has wilfully determined not to equally service the daytime audience — women. Evidently, when WABC-TV, in its application committed itself to "continue to present a balanced schedule of locally produced and locally oriented programs," they had no intention of applying this standard when the audience was primarily female.

* * *

Petitioners would note that media stereotypes about minority groups have largely disappeared. WABC-TV, like other stations, has abandoned the "Amos 'n Andy" image. It would never call Black leaders, "boy" or snicker about the civil rights movement. Nor would it portray Black men exclusively as porters, waiters and song-and-dance men. Women should be accorded similar unbiased treatment.

In sum, the stereotypes described above would be intolerable if WABC-TV presented them about Blacks or any other minority group. They are no less damaging about women. Women are working hard to overcome the barriers against them in employment and other areas. By programming as it does, WABC-TV reinforces those barriers, perpetuates invidious sex-based discrimination, and does a major disservice to its broadcast community as a whole.

ABC News Commentary on the Women's Movement.

Bias against the women's movement is even more overt when WABC-TV discusses the issue directly. Since November 1971, the station has presented no fewer than five full-scale network-produced editorials on "women's liberation" and the role of women, four of them negative, and the fifth one neutral at best.

On November 8, 1971, in "Commentary," ABC News correspondent Harry Reasoner argued that putting women into leadership positions won't solve any of the world's problems; we should "deal with people and politics as they are" and solve the problems of war and peace and strife between nations without calling on women to save us."

On December 9, 1971, Mr. Reasoner reported in another issue of "Commentary" that fashion writer Ann Hencken "reports that the torso is coming back in next spring's fashions. She also says the spring fashions encourage women to be ladylike and to behave themselves." In Mr. Reasoner's view, "that's all to the good."

On December 21, in yet a third issue of "Commentary," Mr. Reasoner attacked *Ms.*, the new women's rights magazine edited by Gloria Steinem. In what must surely be one of the most vicious and irrational series of remarks ever made about the women's movement or its members, Mr. Reasoner compared *Ms.* to *Eros* (whose publisher was convicted for obscenity) and *Fact* (whose publisher was successfully sued for defamation). He noted that the magazine could be successful if it were run by an H. L. Mencken, but that "there is no sign in *Ms.*, or indeed in the whole women's movement, of an H. L. Mencken." *Ms.* is "just another in the great but irrelevant tradition of American shock magazines," he concluded, "and its speedy demise is certain."

On December 22, 1971, only a day after the editorial on *Ms.*, ABC News Commentator Howard K. Smith delivered yet another attack on the women's movement. "Among the multitude of causes in this cause-ridden age," he began, "one that has not — to me, at least, made its case is Women's Lib." Discrimination against women is like "prejudice against every class of human," he said, too inconsequential to "make a federal case out of."

Thus, within a six-week period WABC-TV had presented no fewer than four prime-time editorials opposing the women's movement, its leaders or its views. Even a subsequent editorial, on January 13, 1972, in which Mr. Reasoner professed to agree with women's protests against advertising, said as much about demeaning stereotypes against men as it did about those against women. The editorial was especially ironic since WABC-TV has not exercised its duty to eliminate those commercials which contain such stereotypes. Clearly, the weight of opinion on ABC's "Commentary" is against the women's movement and everything it stands for. By promoting that view without airing the feminist position as well, WABC-TV violates the most elementary requirements of fairness.

General News Coverage.

In other kinds of news coverage, WABC-TV is equally biased. Either the station treats the women's movement as a joke or it ignores women's issues altogether.

On August 26, 1970, thousands of women in New York and throughout the country marched to observe the 50th anniversary of the 19th Amendment. The purpose of this demonstration was to protest sex-based discrimination, yet Eyewitness News reporter Roger Grimsby directed his comments to film footage of women in mini-skirts and sneering comments such as, "Women shouldn't complain when they're being supported by men." In addition, Mr. Grimsby interviewed one participant by asking her "How do you and the other girls at the strike office feel about the march today?" When she answered, "I'd like to ask you to refer to me and the other women who worked on the strike as women," Grimsby smirked and said, "Well, is 'female' all right?" By comparison, it is difficult to imagine Roger Grimsby asking a Black male demonstrator at a civil rights march: "How do you *boys* feel about today's march?"

More importantly, the WABC-TV news staff seems determined to ridicule women's efforts to remove sex-based barriers in the job market. In January 1972, the Eyewitness News team did a story on the woman who, after considerable effort, had won the right to be a baseball umpire. Commenting on this important breakthrough in employment, newscaster Jim Bouton remarked, "The most important thing about an umpire is eyes; I've seen her eyes; they're beautiful." Similarly, on January 31, 1972, WABC-TV broadcast a story about a new barbershop which trains women to shave male customers. The reporter asked one woman, "If you had a fight with your husband, do you think your hand would slip?" Certainly, other more important aspects of this event could have been discussed. Or coverage might have included an in-depth documentary on women's economic plight in this country and the importance of sex-segregated jobs in maintaining women in an inferior economic position. But WABC-TV saw only a joke.

Besides treating women's achievements as trivial wherever possible,

WABC-TV reporters also ignore many important women's news stories altogether. For example, the station provides far less than fair coverage of women's sports. As already noted, although women won seven out of eight U.S. medals in the Winter Olympic Games, only two WABC-TV news programs even mentioned their victories. The women were not mentioned by name, and only forty seconds of air time was given to the issue.

3. *WABC-TV's discriminatory employment practices are violative of FCC rules and regulations.*
Section 73.125(a) of the Commission's Rules and Regulations provides that each licensee shall afford equal opportunity in employment and that no licensee shall discriminate on the basis of sex. Section 73.125(b) of the Rules requires each licensee to establish and carry out a continuing positive program to assure equal opportunity in every phase of employment policy and practice.

The Commission has made it clear that compliance with these Rules is of the highest priority since discrimination on the part of a licensee has a direct and profound bearing on its qualifications to be a Commission licensee. Violation of these regulations reflects on a licensee's attitude toward its community and hampers efforts to serve the public interest since employment discrimination is a violation of federal statutes and policies.

In adopting its employment regulations, the Commission discussed fully the implications of imposing employment standards on its licensees. It is clear from the documents issued by the Commission that its intention was to impose upon the broadcaster a duty in conjunction with its public interest duty to follow federal policy and insure equal employment opportunity. The Commission found numerous reasons to consider these rules to be in the public interest. First, the Commission observed that violation of the equal opportunity rules by a licensee in its internal employment was a clear violation of state and federal laws, particularly Title VII of the Civil Rights Act of 1964. Therefore, violation of these laws by the Commission licensee clearly raises questions as to its qualifications to operate a broadcast license in the public interest.

Second, the Commission pointed to a national policy going beyond specific laws against sex-based discrimination, as embodied in the Presidential Executive Orders, the Civil Rights Act, the Equal Pay Act, the formation of the Equal Employment Opportunity Commission, various Department of Labor pronouncements, as well as numerous other sources. Many commissions have been formed to focus national attention on the problem of employment discrimination, and many federal agencies have directed their attention to this problem.

Third, a broadcaster operates on the basis of a federal license and, by accepting part of the public domain, the broadcaster becomes subject to enforceable public obligations. Given the national policy against discrimination, a broadcaster who acts in violation of this policy by discriminating in its employment on the basis of sex, abuses its federal license and it therefore should be withdrawn.

Lastly, and perhaps most important under the public interest standard, the Commission noted a correlation between programming and employment practices. Discrimination in employment by the station will inhibit the broadcaster in its effort to serve the needs and interests of the community. Each applicant for renewal of license is required to ascertain the community's needs and interests in order to plan programming to meet these needs and interests on an equitable basis. The Commission stated that if a broadcaster pursues a policy of discrimination, serious questions are raised as to whether the broadcaster is serving the *entire* public and whether the applicant is consulting with each significant group to determine its needs and interests.

Nowhere is the correlation between employment discrimination and failure to serve the public interest more evident than in the present case. WABC-TV, as will be shown herein, has failed to comply with the letter and the spirit of the FCC's rules and policies against job discrimination based on sex. Petitioner alleges that the station's failure to employ or promote any significant number of women is reflected in its failure to recognize the needs of women and provide programming to meet them.

* * *

The FCC has recognized that the law surrounding sex discrimination, as developed in legislative enactments and case law, has focused on the overall employment practices of an employer that, when taken as a whole, show a total pattern of discriminatory behavior. Since unlawful sex discrimination in employment is generally the result of institutionalized practices rather than isolated acts, the Commission has called for the gathering of statistical information from its licensees to indicate areas of non-compliance with its rules, as well as point out to each licensee its own problem areas.

* * *

The 1971 Annual Employment Report, Form 395, dated May 26, 1971, shows the following breakdown of men and women in each job category.

Job Category	Men		Women	
Officials and Managers	25	92%	2	8%
Professional	45	88%	6	12%
Technicians	30	100%	None	0%
Sales Workers	13	100%	None	0%
Office and Clerical	14	28%	36	72%
Craftsmen	16	100%	None	0%
Operatives	2	100%	None	0%

Out of a total employment of 189 persons, only 44, or 23.3%, are women. In contrast, the New York State Department of Labor Study shows that women comprise 40.3% of the total work force in metropolitan New York. More importantly, women comprise 66.0% of the total number of employees in the field of communications in the New York SMSA [Area].

CHAPTER 21

Filing Federal Complaints: *Washington Post*

Title VII of the 1964 Civil Rights Act prohibited sex discrimination in employment. In the years that have passed since President Lyndon B. Johnson signed the Act into law, many complaints have been filed with the Equal Employment Opportunity Commission, the agency responsible for determining whether discrimination has occurred. Human Rights Commissions in many states also have fielded complaints. Many grievances have been resolved under threat of an EEOC complaint by employees, just the way many citizen group/licensee agreements have been negotiated under threat of a challenge of a broadcaster's license. The concessions typically made by the defendants in such cases are promises to implement affirmative action programs, in-house training for women, integration of sex-typed positions such as research and clerical jobs, equitable salary schedules, and the promotion of qualified women into managerial positions.

In a frank article in the 1972 volume of *Once A Year*, the Milwaukee Press Club's annual magazine, Dorothy Austin of the *Milwaukee Sentinel* and Jean Otto of the *Milwaukee Journal,* observed that "The woman who was editor of her college paper can never expect to have the same title again, unless she inherits her father's paper or outlives a husband who owns one. Chances are, if she's lucky to be hired at all, the woman journalist will find herself somewhere on the fringe of the action that drew her to the career. While the male journalist covers campaigns, she'll tag along with the candidate's wife and attend luncheons. She'll go to meeting after meeting, reporting the wise words of men who talk to ladies. She'll run into the same women reporters again and again and come to recognize that the haunted looks on their faces reflect the one on her own.

"Though she might not trade her job for any other profession, she knows she's been cheated," Otto and Austin said. "Like women in practically every other profession, she recognizes that in journalism, a skirt is a hair shirt."

Breaking down the prevailing attitudes in the newsroom has been difficult. Women reporters say male editors have been reluctant to send female reporters into "combat zones" during riots, or to assign them to meaty political beats or crime stories. Women have swelled the ranks of feature writers and women's page staffs, but have been less visible on city or national assignments.

Women at the *Washington Post*, through the Newspaper Guild which represented reporters at the paper, filed a sex discrimination complaint with the EEOC, which decided in June 1974 that the *Post* needed to improve its record in hiring and promotion of women. An account of the EEOC's findings appears here.

EEOC FINDINGS OF SEX DISCRIMINATION

Charging parties allege, *inter alia*, that females because of their sex are discriminated against with respect to hiring, compensation and other terms and conditions of employment. Specifically, Charging Parties allege that females, because of their sex, receive lower salaries than male employees who benefit from over-scale wage payments; that they are not promoted to higher paying or more responsible positions such as managerial positions; that they occupy the majority of low-salaried positions in many departments; and, that they are neither recruited nor trained by Respondent to reduce the negative impact of the above described discriminatory practices.

* * *

Of the 46 females in the higher paying news classifications 39% are paid at rates of $400 per week or more while 67% of the 245 males earn salaries at $400 or more per week. Records further show that of these higher salaried newsroom employees 27 males and one female earn weekly salaries of $500 or more.

* * *

Of those 46 females in the news department, over 50% are assigned to the Style or Suburban/City units. The highest concentration of total employees in the news units is in the city unit where among 15 editors and assistant editors there are no females, but where 6 of the 32 reporters are female. The evidence further demonstrates that of 16 news units with 3 or more persons, 3 units employ no females in the higher paying jobs and 4 units, all with an excess of 10 employees, employ only one female.

* * *

With respect to terms and conditions of employment, certain Charging Parties state, and witnesses support, that females assigned to the metropolitan desk, shown on the computer printout as the city and suburban desks, do not receive the same consideration and opportunity for story assignments made by the assigning editors. They specifically cite instances where experienced female reporters have been given assignments typically associated with new and inexperienced reporters, such as night and weekend duty and the writing of obituaries, and denied assignments which would enhance their promotion and career potential.

* * *

The Commission has no interest in attempting to regulate Respondent's editorial policies or functions nor in attempting to dictate who should be assigned what stories. Job assignments, however, are clearly a condition of employment and this Commission is authorized to investigate allegations regarding disparate job assignments based on sex. If the investigation supports a conclusion that females are indeed denied equal terms and conditions of employment with respect to story assignments, we would insist as a remedy that female reporters be given equal consideration for story assignments with male reporters. Such a remedy in no way interferes with Respondent's right to carry out its editorial functions as it sees fit.

With respect to the composition of the editorial staffs or the suburban and city desks, Respondent's records indicate that on the suburban desk, there are two male and no female editors and five male and two female assistant editors. One of the female assistant editors stated during the investigation that she is actually a copy editor and is not involved in assigning stories. The other female assistant editor has left Respondent's employ, according to a witness' statement. On the city desk, Respondent's records indicate that there are 4 male and no female editors and 11 male and no female assistant editors. Thus, the evidence demonstrates that all of the editorial staffs on the city and suburban desks, who presumably are responsible for story assignments, are exclusively male.

* * *

With respect to promotions, Respondent's records indicate that in the commercial and news departments the employee initiates the request for consideration for promotion whereas when there are vacancies in managerial positions, the department head/manager recommends those employees believed to be the most qualified for the position. The Respondent provided a listing of all employees pormoted between June 1, 1972 and May, 1973. This shows the following breakdown by salary ranges of the jobs into which the employees were promoted.

Weekly Salary Ranges	Male	Female
$100-200	27	20
201-300	11	6
301-400	10	2
401-500	10	0
Total	58	28

In addition there were 3 male and 3 female employees promoted but who have hourly wages. There were also 3 males and 1 female promoted but whose salaries were not given.

Thus, of the 58 males promoted, over 50% were promoted into jobs with a weekly salary over $200 while 71% of those females promoted were still in jobs whose salaries were between $100-200 per week. Of all promotions into positions with weekly salaries above $200, 79% are males.

We have previously concluded in Section I above that Respondent restricts the opportunities of female employees to occupy its higher paying positions. Respondent's promotion statistics indicate that, while female employees are not denied promotions as such, they do not receive promotions into higher paying positions on a similar basis with male employees. We therefore conclude that female employees are denied equal promotional opportunities with male employees as part of Respondent's pattern of restricting and limiting females from its higher paying positions.

Charging Parties further allege that Respondent discriminates against females by considering the marital or family status of females and not males in hiring, assignments and promotions into higher paying jobs. . . .

Charging Parties contend that married females, especially those with young children, experience greater difficulty in getting hired or promoted into higher paying positions than single females and that such considerations do not affect the opportunities of male employees. One Charging Party specifically stated that she was informed by Respondent that one of the reasons for its denial of a correspondent job for her was that she had a child and the job required travelling. Another Charging Party stated that she was harassed and denied assignments commensurate with her experience and competence after Respondent became aware of her plans to marry another employee.

* * *

Statistical evidence presented coupled with witness testimony raises the inference that Respondent prefers single rather than married females for its higher level jobs in the news departments and that it applies no such preference to male employees. To maintain one employment standard for women and another for men is an unlawful employment practice within the meaning of the Act, absent a showing by Respondent that the narrow BFOQ* exception of 703(e) is applicable. We hold that, as a matter of law, the BFOQ exception is not applicable here. Accordingly, we conclude that Respondent's preference for single females, but not males, discriminates against females as a class, in violation of Title VII.

---

*Bona fide occupational qualification.

CHAPTER 22

Negotiating Agreements: KNBC-TV

The threat of license challenges and the spreading interest in monitoring news, entertainment, and commercial content in radio and television, brought broadcasters into closer contact with women's groups. Out of conferences between the women and station managers who wished to avoid the expense and length of a license challenge at renewal time, came a new form of commitment: the community women's group/licensee agreement.

The first agreement between a broadcaster and a citizen's group was negotiated in 1969 between KTAL-TV and the Texarkana (Texas) Junior Chamber of Commerce and 12 other associations in that market. The citizen group did not complain about the omission of viewpoints of one sex, but of one race — Blacks — and about management's inaccessibility to viewers. After the agreement was signed, the citizen group withdrew its petition to deny renewal of KTAL-TV's license. The station had agreed to hire two Black reporters; to implement a toll-free telephone line to service the public information needs of its far-flung subscribers; to make no nonessential reference to the race of a person; to meet monthly with an advisory council to discuss KTAL-TV's programming; and to present a monthly magazine-type program seeking participation from the entire service area.

The Federal Communications Commission gave its blessing to the resolution of differences between KTAL-TV and its audience, but it warned that it would not sanction agreements that deprived the licensee of its discretion in programing.

Since the KTAL-TV and the Texarkana group signed their agreement, other groups have been successful in ironing out their differences with broadcasters. In 1973 KTTV-TV, Los Angeles, signed an agreement with the National Association for Better Broadcasting in which the station agreed to remove certain violent cartoon programs from the air.

Women have negotiated notable agreements in Pennsylvania, Colorado, New York, Tennessee, California, and other states. In California, the Los Angeles Women's Coalition for Better Broadcasting, made up of seven women's organizations in the Los Angeles area, was formed specifically to work toward the goal of obtaining improvements in the broadcast media through negotiated agreements with all licensees in the area. Coalition members monitored radio and television programs, obtained affidavits from women at the stations to document employment conditions, and studied the stations' ascertainment procedures.

In some cases the process involved taking legal action. In 1976 the Coalition went to court seeking to obtain an FCC hearing, which the Commission had refused to grant them, on their petition to deny the license renewals of KNXT-TV, CBS's Los Angeles station, and KTTV-TV, the Metromedia station.

In other cases, agreements have been reached. In 1974, the Los Angeles Women's Coalition for Better Broadcasting signed agreements, basically similar, with Los Angeles stations KNBC-TV and KABC-TV, the NBC- and ABC-owned stations in that city.

The agreement negotiated with KNBC-TV was signed by Raymond J. Timothy, Vice President and General Manager for KNBC-TV, and stated in a letter of understanding dated October 29, 1974 addressed by him to the Coalition members. Excerpts are reprinted here.

LOS ANGELES WOMEN'S COALITION FOR BETTER BROADCASTING AGREEMENT WITH KNBC-TV

After a series of meetings with members of your organization in which we discussed a proposed agreement submitted by your organization to KNBC on September 27, 1974, KNBC is prepared to effectuate the following relating thereto. This letter will be filed with the Federal Communications Commission and will become part of the station's application for renewal of its license. In view of these undertakings, the Coalition affirms its determination to take no action in respect to KNBC's license renewal application.

* * *

(1) ASCERTAINMENT OF COMMUNITY NEEDS

(a) KNBC will welcome the establishment of a women's Advisory Council ("WAC") by the Coalition and will meet at least quarterly, at mutually convenient places and hours, with WAC to discuss the problems, needs, and interests of women in the Los Angeles community as well as all other topics encompassed in this letter.

(b) KNBC will establish and maintain a women's resource bank to which the station will refer in seeking qualified female spokespeople to appear on its locally produced programming and news when, in the exercise of KNBC's good faith judgment, such spokespeople are needed.

(c) KNBC will consider for broadcast in the exercise of its good faith news judgments, information submitted by the Coalition or any women's news sources regarding possible news stories and events. All such information should be directed to the assignment editors at KNBC News. . . .

(2) NEWS REPORTING

In the area of news reporting, KNBC is cognizant of the Coalition's concern with respect to the use of certain prefixes, pronouns, stereotypical language, and other descriptive terms and phrases, and certain interviewing methods, which the Coalition believes are unnecessary, if not demeaning. Accordingly, KNBC is prepared to consider the institution of a series of sensitivity sessions for management level employees and employees with programming and news responsibilities as referred to elsewhere in this letter and will endeavor to continue to avoid the use of such terms and phrases and interviewing methods.

(3) PROGRAMMING

(a) As a matter of policy, KNBC has not and will not accept any program the purpose of which, in the opinion of KNBC, is to ridicule, attack or otherwise misrepresent any individual or group on the basis of race, creed, color, national origin or sex. . . .

KNBC will discuss any Coalition allegation of derisive programming at the above described meetings with WAC, and KNBC will advise appropriate NBC personnel of any such allegations directed to network programming or programs supplied by outside packagers, KNBC will, as KNBC deems it necessary, endeavor to arrange meetings between the WAC and appropriate network personnel or program packagers.

(b) KNBC has not and will not broadcast any commercial message which, in its good faith opinion, is demeaning to any individual or group. KNBC will discuss any Coalition allegation that a commercial is derogatory or demeaning at the above-described meetings with WAC and KNBC will advise appropriate advertisers or advertising agencies in the case of local commercials or appropriate NBC personnel with regard to network commercials. In addition, with respect to such allegations, KNBC will, as KNBC deems it necessary, endeavor to arrange meetings between the WAC and advertisers or advertising agencies.

(c) Public Service Announcements. KNBC will consider for broadcast any public service announcements related to the women's movement for equality and women's role in American society provided such announcements are informational rather than controversial in nature and otherwise comply with KNBC policies and broadcast standards.

(d) Public Affairs Programming. With respect to public affairs programming, KNBC broadcast 'The Quiet Revolution of Mrs. Harris,' 'Working Women and Your Organization,' 'To Be a Woman,' 'Momma,' 'Gloria Steinem,' 'Women in Law,' 'August 26 Feminist Celebration' and other programs dealing with aspects of the feminist movement and women's roles in American society.

As a result of input received in response to its ascertainment efforts, KNBC will broadcast during prime time three (3) 30-minute public affairs programs of a similar nature by the end of the 1975-76 broadcast season.

In addition, KNBC will consider in good faith increasing its coverage of issues of concern to women in other programs broadcast during prime time and other periods of the broadcasting spectrum. Furthermore, if the results of its on-going ascertainment efforts conducted during the 1975-76 and 1976-77 broadcast seasons warrant, KNBC will broadcast during the 6:00 PM to 11:00 PM prime time period three (3) 30-minute public affairs programs, or an equivalent amount of other such prime time programming, during each of these broadcast seasons.

However, KNBC firmly believes that any additional specific commitment of program hours to such programs would be contrary to the spirit of the ascertainment concept and a deviation from programming flexibility which, according to the Federal Communications Commission, KNBC is required to maintain.

(e) Editorials. KNBC has and will continue to present editorials and replies in opposition thereto in accordance with the dictates of the Fairness Doctrine and the results of its ascertainment efforts.

KNBC welcomes comments on editorial opinions and is willing to broadcast responsible opposing viewpoints. Thus, KNBC circulates copies of each editorial and editorial responses to numerous community leaders and organizations within its coverage area, and will add the Coalition, as well as each of its constituent groups, to its mailing list.

(f) Instructional Programs. KNBC will consider in good faith a wide range of female role models in all instructional programs.

(4) EMPLOYMENT

(a) KNBC has adopted an Affirmative Action Program for the employment of minorities and women at KNBC. KNBC has established three-year objectives, which the station will in good faith endeavor to achieve, for the employment of women, with particular emphasis on the employment of women in the top four categories of Officials and Managers, Professionals, Sales Workers (which includes Account Executives) and Technicians (Skilled). As of December 31, 1973, twenty-six (26) women were employed at KNBC in the top four categories. Consistent with the spirit of its Affirmative Action Program, KNBC will increase the number of women in the top four categories combined by at least nine (9) additional women during a period beginning January 1, 1974, and ending December 1, 1977, subject to the following:

    1.   No decrease in the turnover rate during that period.

    2.   No adverse change in business conditions. In the event of adverse business conditions the station will be relieved of the specific obligation of adding 9 women by 12/1/77. However, the station will continue to hire and terminate without regard to race, color, creed, age or sex.

    3.   Availability of applicants who, in the good faith opinion of KNBC, are qualified for the position KNBC is seeking to fill.

    (b) KNBC will continue to encourage women to enter all phases of the broadcasting industry . . . providing full opportunities for the hire, transfer, and promotion of women into positions of greater responsibility in this connection:

    1.   When recruitment takes place at universities or colleges, female students will be affirmatively encouraged to apply for all positions for which applicants are being sought. Further, if recruitment takes place at primarily male institutions, like recruitment efforts will take place at institutions where there is significant female enrollment and affirmative efforts will be made to secure female interviewers.

    2.   Where advertisements are utilized to solicit applicants for positions at KNBC, such employment advertisements will be placed in media which have significant circulation among women in the Los Angeles area. The Coalition will furnish KNBC with a list of such media.

    (c) In its application for employment KNBC will eliminate questions relating to marital status, number of children, height, weight, and number of persons dependent upon the applicant for support, nor will the above factors be considered as criteria for employment. . . .

    (d) KNBC does not and will not penalize female employees requiring maternity leave with respect to job status or seniority.

    (e) KNBC has urged and will continue to urge unions with which it has agreements to cooperate in the development of programs to assure qualified female persons equal opportunity in employment and such union contracts include a provision designed to eliminate discrimination based upon sex.

The Los Angeles Coalition for Better Broadcasting consisted of the following groups at the time of the KNBC-TV and KABC-TV negotiations: The Los Angeles Metro Caucus of the National Women's Political Caucus, the Media Group of the Los Angeles Women's Liberation Union, the California Public Interest Research Group, the Women's Equity Action League of Los Angeles, the National Organization for Women, the Comision Feminil de Los Angeles, the California Citizen Research Group, and the Career Planning Center.

CHAPTER 23

Monitoring Newspapers: *The Oregonian*

At many newspapers in this country a special section of the newsroom is set aside for production of the women's pages. Out of this corner comes the society news, the club notes, the advice and health columns, the recipes, and the horoscopes. More recently traditional women's pages have included consumer features and human interest stories. But many women journalists say the women's section isn't taken very seriously by hard news reporters; *Washington Post* Virginia editor Judy Nicol recalls that reporters at the Chicago paper for which she had worked previously called the women's department "Birdland."

Some women's sections have been revamped as "lifestyle" sections, focusing on men and women, entertainment, and leisure. But if readers and reporters thought this redesigning would free more of the newshole for profiles and investigative pieces about people in the community, women as well as men, they were disappointed. A study by Zena Beth McGlashan found that entertainment material had replaced traditional content in "lifestyle" sections; and Susan Miller, a reporter for the *Bremerton* (Washington) *Sun*, said that these sections still tend to look like women's pages because "they retain the traditional slick ornamentation of women's photos and fashion and cosmetic ads."

Writer Lindsy Van Gelder complained in the 1970's that this section "is still a dumping ground for anything the male editors consider a 'woman's story.' So we get all the serious news stories about ERA, rape-law changes, back-pay lawsuits, and so forth, back among the girdle ads instead of on page one or two or three where they belong."

At the same time, some women's page reporters said that in-depth features they've developed often are "stolen" for play in other sections of the paper, depriving the women's pages of an attention-getter.

Change in the format of the women's pages was introduced to attract more readers to the pages, to bring a more contemporary view to women's changing role and to explore lifestyles pursued by men as well as women. How many women readers have benefited by these changes is a tough question to answer. McGlashan suggested that women actually may have been disadvantaged by the change, since the trend among newspapers with "lifestyle" sections has been to replace traditional women's content with entertainment, rather than more imaginative coverage of women.

The experimentation with "lifestyle" sections attracted the interest of the Beaverton and Portland, Oregon, chapters of the American Association of University Women, which conducted a content analysis of the "Day" section of the Portland *Oregonian*. The members said they chose the *Oregonian* because it was their community's largest daily newspaper, it was the most easily accessible to them. They did not include Saturday and Sunday editions because they felt the "specialized nature" of those editions did not give a typical picture of the section. They studied women's pages produced during the early fall of 1974 — August, September and October — on the grounds that those months would best reflect the variety of activities or themes involved in seasonal changes.

Their interpretations of the categories they used to code the stories and each category's percentage of total space allotted to the women's pages each month are reprinted here.

"DAY" SECTION OF PORTLAND OREGONIAN

All interpretation items will commence with the August allocations of space but will include the other two months.

A. *Advertising* consumes 62, 62 and 62-plus percentage of total space of the "Day" section. This fact brings home in a startlingly visible way the fact that we are universal captives to the advertising industry with all its built-in deception techniques; newspaper policy can be assumed to be commonly made in the business offices, not the editorial or news ones, therefore.

The metropolitan paper, increasingly squeezed by suburban growth, with advertising competition from suburban papers, with ad handouts, and by the radio and visual media as well, must meet this competition to survive.

* * *

B. *General news*, unrelated to the activities of Oregon women, consumed second place in August and October (10%) and came in a close third (8%) in September. How much news of the productivity, contribution and real newsworthy activity of Oregon women had to be dumped to allow for these news items.

It's also instructive that many of the "hard" news items which wander into the "Day" section are of obviously lesser significance, a blatant announcement that "Day" section concerns are where the more trivial news — even hard news — appears.

C. In August and October *entertainment* (comics, puzzles, radio, tv and bridge) came in third (7 and 8%) and second in September (9%).

While entertainment is undoubtedly a sales feature of any newspaper, this committee protests the inclusion of *all* these entertainment features in the "Day" section, at obvious expense to women's hard news.

D. *Feature articles about local women and women's concerns,* or syndicated articles on those subjects, ranked 4th in August and September (5 and 6% of total space) and 5th in October (3% of total space). In each case local articles written by local reporters slightly outranked those purchased from wire services by syndicated writers. We have five observations to make in this area:

1. To the extent that women, or so-called women's issues, seem to receive maximized space, they are handled as features. There is an inescapable conclusion to be drawn: handled as the subject of straight news they would often not appear in print, a fact which seems to reflect either the true power-status of women in American society or the power-importance assigned to them.

2. Although a qualitative comment (and it's nearly impossible to untie the two), the tone of features about individual women often contains comments which would never appear in the hard news section. It is unlikely that President Ford's socks, shirts and width of lapels would routinely be commented on when he makes a major speech on inflation; women who are so-called newsmakers are often described, not only as to appearance but as to personality qualities. While this makes entertaining reading, it definitely sets women apart from the straight-forward reporting about men and male activities, and its subliminal effect is to reduce the seriousness with which the reader takes the news item he/she reads. (Example: a woman dentist is described as "pert, lively, blonde, trim..." A male dentist would likely call up the paper and complain if he were described in an article as "flip, nervous, fair and skinny...")

3. While syndicated articles about women or women's issues accurately reflect the intent of the *Oregonian* to be a metropolitan newspaper adequately covering national and international news, and while these features expand the knowledge of Portland readers, sometimes locality space seems crucially sacrificed.

4. Again qualitatively, feature headlines sometimes cutely reflect all these prejudices. An article about Anne Armstrong, assistant to President Ford for women's concerns, reads: "Anne Armstrong Exudes the Perfume of Power..." No one yet has referred in headlines, nor is likely to, to the smell of President Ford's aftershave lotion as related to his position.

5. Sometimes our analysts felt an unconscionable amount of space

given over to really trivial, if not outright bizarre, features such as the full-time front page of the "Day" section devoted to animals dressed in various types of coats and sweaters. (Apart from the obvious question of humaneness to animals, this sort of anthropomorphism is frowned on even in children's school books.)

Men reporters, seeing this use of hard-to-come-by space, can't be blamed for sometimes feeling sounder priorities ought to be set in the women's cubicles.

E.   *Food news* ranked fifth in use of total space in August and September and 4th in October. When prepared foods are a resource for millions of women who work, we are skeptical that recipes in that quantity or complexity have all that relevance in an increasingly technologized world. It might also be added that in days when serious food shortages threaten for all elements of the world population and when inflation is a disaster as a food factor, conventional emphases on food preparation ought — in the interests of reality — yield to more practical uses of food space. Our committee also noted how much of food space was purchased, again at the expense of the writing and newsgathering talents of local women reporters.

F.   In August and September *styles* took 6th place; in October 10th. As women become more determinedly individual in the way they dress, style news may perhaps diminish. . . . .

G.   In August *advice* (Jennifer, Abby) ranked 7th in use of space; in September it tied with community meetings and events; in October it was 8th. The stereotype of girls and women traditional to literature and law is one of dependence and inability to decide or choose to act with courage and resolution without males. (This influential image permeates primary text books, for instance.) It's perhaps not surprising, therefore, that Advice allocations are high. Though we realize the publishing of an American newspaper is first of all a commercial undertaking, and we know readership of these advice columns is extremely high, we respectfully suggest that once in a while *Dear Abby* — with its traditional and authoritarian approach — be absorbed into some other section.

H.   *Women's community events* in August ranked 8th, tied with Advice (7-8th) in September; in October it was 6th. In all months there was only a fractional difference between space given to reports of community meetings and events, non-female, and community meetings and events, female. While the prevailing trend is away from sexually segregated community organizations, a true picture *as of this moment* is obviously not achieved in reporting what is actually going on in the infrastructure and organizational life of Portland women.

*   *   *

I.   *Family news* ranked 10th in August, 11th in September and tied 11-12 in October. We applaud the *Oregonian* for its shrinkage in coverage of limited-appeal news: weddings, engagements and the like. Since the

Harris poll reports that wedding readership stands at 3% it seems justifiable for a newspaper to charge for this ego-massaging space. Wedding and engagement space in European papers is unheard of, according to Colleen Dishon, who suggests that, like the *Washington Post*, there be a guarantee of a 2" announcement, after which space must be paid for as in a classified ad.

J. Ranking 11th, 10th and 9th respectively were space allocations to *gossip* (local and syndicated!). Personal recitals of this kind are uniformly deplored in journalism schools and ubiquitously practiced by newspapers as necessary to sell them. But analysts question how *many* readers are really all that enthralled by the news that Mrs. Myhave I. Gotrocks wore a spangled tunic to a fundraiser to buy a hydraulic crane for lifting wheel chairs to sporting events. (We are sympathetic to the needs of the handicapped but whatever has happened to old-fashioned volunteer muscles?)

K. *Health* — ranking 12-13, 12-13 and 11-12-14 — was interesting in that even in this area general health took fractionally more space than women's health news. In light of the considerable agitation for better and more equitable health care by the medical establishment and more research attention to women's health needs, this fact is notable. (Example: in a recent national study it was shown that men and children are routinely treated before women in a large urban hospital emergency ward).

L. Perhaps one of the most noteworthy — and staggering — practices of the "Day" section was to give straight-forward, *hard news about women* exactly .27, .17 and .27% respectively of available space in the three months studied. This undoubtedly reflects the less powerful position of women in all aspects of metropolitan, national and international life, but it is difficult to believe, even with obvious inequities, how 51% of the population could be such pitiful failures as newsmakers.

Category	(August, 1973)	Percentage of Space
Advertising		62.6%
General news—non-female		10.1%
Entertainment		7.8%
Feature articles about women		5.1%
Food and household advice		5.0%
Styles		3.3%
Advice		2.2%
Community meetings and events (female)		1.7%
Community meetings and events (non-female)		1.4%
Family news		.7%
Gossip and society		.6%
General health		.6%
Female health		.3%
Straight news about women		.3%

Table from Media Report to Women, February 1, 1976, p. 5.

CHAPTER 24

Monitoring Prime Time: United Methodist Women

The most common way for TV viewers to track sex stereotyping in programming is to conduct a "monitoring study." Monitoring, when done systematically, can focus and substantiate viewer complaints and provide the information necessary for any action before the Federal Communications Commission with respect to a licensee's programming. For a citizen group to refute a licensee's claim that it has shown "overall balance in its programming," the group's monitoring study must be carefully and thoughtfully planned and carried out. The FCC does not readily question a licensee's "discretion" in choosing programming content.

The American Association of University Women issues to its chapters an "Implementation Guide for Media" which suggests ways to begin dialogues with radio and television station managers. It also contains brief summaries of communication issues, sourcebooks, article reprints and a bibliography of background information for members on freedom of the press. As a result, the AAUW has been very active in monitoring television programming. In 1974 the AAUW conducted a nationwide monitoring study for the Columbia University's Alfred I. Dupont Survey of Broadcast Journalism.

AAUW chapters also conduct monitoring to press for broadcasting changes in each chapter's area. The Erie, Pennsylvania chapter timed its 1974 monitoring study so that its report would be finished at about the time local radio and television stations would be applying for license renewals. The chapter set aside seven months for the project, beginning with an intensive recruiting and training session. Each month the monitors concentrated on a special aspect: commercials in October, soap operas in November, stereotyping in children's programs in December, employment discrimination in January, local news in February. The chapter's media committee participated in ascertainment hearings held by the three stations whose licenses were up for renewal. After a number of meetings and phone calls with station managers, and some helpful coverage of the AAUW's study in the local newspaper, all three station managers agreed to increase the amount of local news they devote to women, and to set up a Women's Advisory Council to recommend programming of interest to women.

The AAUW's Sacramento, California chapter conducted its monitoring study in 1974 to be able to show managers at the Sacramento stations precisely where the weaknesses were in their programming for and about women, and to publish a booklet about the methodology of the study which could serve as a guide for other women's groups throughout the country. Their study was more concentrated — focused on one month (April) of news programming and commercials. Entertainment programs were not included. The monitors studied content in 5,353 hard news stories and 1,668 news features.

One monitor commented, "After watching television news for a while, you get the feeling that women just don't exist."

The Sacramento chapter's media monitoring committee visited the managers of KCRA-TV, KXTV-TV, and KOVR-TV after the study was printed. All were cordial, the chairwoman reported, but not any of them wanted to commit themselves to programming adjustments.

The Sacramento Community Commission for Women, using the AAUW monitoring study as leverage, visited the stations and pushed for more programming featuring women as well as the hiring of more women professionals by the stations.

One station agreed to let the Commission for Women write and produce programs on women in art, sports and advertising. The station also aired a program on "International Women's Year."

The AAUW chairwoman said coverage of women in sports improved after the study was released. A coalition of women's groups in Sacramento also was formed to keep broadcasters aware of women's interest in their programming.

Many other groups have been active in monitoring television. The United Church of Christ's Office of Communication is well known for the studies of employment in broadcasting as well as for its surveys of programming content. NOW's Media Reform Task Force has established itself as an expert on women's programming and employment conditions in all areas of mass media.

The Women's Division of the Board of Global Ministries of the United Methodist Church in March 1976 published the results of its nationwide study, *Sex Role Stereotyping in Prime Time Television.* In this study, 187 monitors across the United States coded programs telecast on the three commercial networks for a 12-week period (November 1975 through February 1976). The study included programs shown during the family hour (8-9 p.m. in most states) and the adult viewing period (9-11 p.m.).

The United Methodist Women found that programming in 1976 continued the patterns of sex role stereotyping found in studies of previous years. The "Character Analysis Checklist" used by the UMW monitors to obtain profiles of female and male roles in prime time programs, and some of the charts comparing their findings, are reprinted here.

MAJOR FINDINGS

The 1975-76 television season continues the patterns of sex role stereotyping found in studies of prior years. Statistical comparison of variable 06, sex of character, with other variables, showed significant correlation in a number of important areas:

Women were under-represented in the world of television. A total of 1,095 characters appeared in the episodes coded; 345 or 32% were female. In the United States, 51% of the population is female.

The percentage of women portrayed in leading roles was even less than their distorted 32% representation on television.

A larger percentage of women were portrayed in the 20-39-year-old age group than were men. (While the project did not attempt to code physical appearance, a number of monitors wrote comments suggesting that younger women were also portrayed as "sexier.")

Women were more likely to be portrayed as inner directed, men as outer directed. Women's categories of problems and relationship roles clustered around family and romance. Those of men clustered around business and acquaintances.

Women were less frequently portrayed as being recipients of help from others in problem solving than were men. The episodes coded from *Maude, Mary Tyler Moore,* and *One Day at a Time* were exceptions to this pattern.

In problem solving, men were portrayed primarily as being resolvers of problems faced by others. They were also more likely to be of primary concern in the problems faced.

Women were most likely to be portrayed in traditional female occupations (secretary, nurse) having low occupational authority. Women were supervisees, men were more likely to be supervisors.

Women generally did not use aggressive or defensive force, but were victims of force; they rarely appeared in programs in which these variables occurred.

CHAPTER 25

Public Broadcasting:
2 Self-Examinations
U.S. and Canada

The impact of media monitoring was not lost on the trustees of the nation's noncommercial broadcasting unit. In May 1974 the Corporation for Public Broadcasting's Board of Directors received a position paper on women's programming from its Advisory Council of National Organizations. ACNO told the Corporation that a *definition* of women's programming was needed. Women were not being presented fairly in public broadcasting media. Rather than portraying a full range of women's roles in society, ACNO said, public broadcasting was showing a distorted image of women. In November of that year, CPB's Board of Directors endorsed the creation of a Task Force on Women in Public Broadcasting.

Interestingly, the Task Force found that women were not *stereotyped* on public television, they were *overlooked*.

At the time the Task Force conducted its study on women, 245 television stations and 159 radio stations comprised the structure of the Corporation, which was an entity created by the Public Broadcasting Act in 1967. Public television was estimated to attract viewers in about 20 million homes per week. Its mission was to provide "high quality, alternative programming" unavailable from commercially operated stations. The Corporation receives funds from the federal government and solicits grants from foundations and other philanthropic associations. Member stations also raise funds to underwrite their programming.

Deciding which programs will be funded is done through the "Station Program Cooperative," a catalog of about 200 proposed programs distributed to public broadcasting stations by the Public Broadcasting Service. The stations allocate portions of their budgets to fund the proposed programs they think will have appeal in their areas. Programming for women has not fared well in the SPC selection process. A number of radio and television stations produce their own programs for women, rather than opting to buy a national program through SPC.

Employment of women in professional and managerial positions in public broadcasting lags behind employment of men, as it does in commercial broadcasting. The Task Force on Women used CPB's own statistics and a mail survey of radio and TV employees in public broadcasting to develop recommendations about the employment of women. Interviews were conducted at selected radio and television facilities and at one production house to document attitudes about the employment and on-air performance of women.

To develop recommendations about the portrayal of women in programming, the Task Force staff monitored one week of television programming distributed through the Public Broadcasting interconnection service. They also monitored one week of National Public Radio programming distributed through its interconnection service and network tapes.

The sample week chosen for monitoring was January 19-25, 1975 All regularly scheduled programs (except *Soundstage*) of the 1974-1975 season were broadcast during the sample week. The profiles of women in public broadcasting developed by the Task Force's monitoring study and employment survey are described here.

PROGRAMMING

The Task Force, in an effort to find out what image is projected through public radio and televison, conducted a content analysis of programs broadcast over the Public Broadcasting Service (PBS) and National Public Radio (NPR). The rationale behind this analysis is that the portrayal of women and girls through the media is a dynamic force in determining attitudes about women and that television, in particular, is a major socializing agent of young children. Because this is the first systemized information concerning the content of public radio and television, the analysis provides information unavailable elsewhere.

*   *   *

In order to find out how females are portrayed as compared to males in public broadcasting, the Task Force staff monitored one week of television programming distributed through the PBS interconnection system (approximately 37½ hours) and one week of radio programming distributed by NPR (44 hours) through its interconnection service and network tapes. Because of the nature of public broadcasting, it is impossible to know if and when these programs were broadcast in each local market area. Program schedules vary in different localities because each public licensee retains control of its program scheduling. Public television stations do not show the same degree of homogeneity in programming as do commercial stations.

All radio in the United States is locally controlled and different kinds of stations have different program formats. Most, but not all, community television stations broadcast programs transmitted over the interconnection. There are localities in which the NPR programs and tapes are not heard. Also, locally originated programs shown on television and heard on radio may portray women differently from the way they are portrayed on national broadcasting. The practical limitations of this research (time and money) did not allow the staff to explore local programming. . . .

CATEGORY 1–GENERAL ADULT PROGRAMMING

In the adult television programs monitored, 200 men (85%) and only 36 women (15%) appeared. Of the 28 adult programs listed in this classification, 11 [representing a total of six hours, 17 minutes out of 18 hours (36%) of programming] had no women participants. . . .

There were only four black women out of the total 236 participants. Of 11 public affairs programs (see starred programs in "Programs Monitored") in which issues and events of topical importance were discussed and/or reported, seven excluded women completely. In the remaining public affairs programs there were 11 females, as compared to 90 males. Thus, programming directed to timely issues, dealing with events of major importance, such as the economy, government, and foreign policy issues, almost ignored women completely. Moreover, there was only one program which dealt with a woman's issue—*Woman*—a weekly series for and about women.

* * *

In adult radio programming, the results are similar, though females fare slightly better. There were 428 men (77%) and 127 women (23%). Ten radio programs (9½ hours) had no women participants. This is approximately 20% of the broadcast time. Because of the nature of radio, it is impossible to find out the race of the participants. Men participated on the air proportionately more of the time. For instance, 16% of the men, as compared to 9% of the women, were on the air over five minutes, and 47% of the men, compared to 36% of the women, were on the air between one and five minutes. Thus there are not only fewer women than men, but also those women who are on the air participate less. . . .

There were no radio programs at the national level which addressed women's issues specifically. During the week of broadcasting, only one female and no males discussed human rights—sexual. This, however, must be interpreted with care because, according to Katzman (1973), almost three-fourths of all air time during the sample week of public radio he studied originated with the local stations. At the national level, women's issues were ignored during the sample week.

* * *

CATEGORY III – DRAMA

Two television dramas were monitored during the sample week: *Theater in America* and *Upstairs, Downstairs.* In *Theater in America,* 80% of the characters analyzed were men and 20% women. In *Upstairs, Downstairs,* 45% of the characters were male and 55% female. The women were cast in female sex-typed occupations.

Two radio dramas were monitored during the sample week: *NPR Theatre* and *I'm Sorry, I'll Read That Again.* Six characters were monitored for *NPR Theatre;* two were women. In *I'm Sorry, I'll Read That Again,* 31 characters were noted, of whom six were women. Again, women were cast in sex-typed occupations.

CATEGORY IV – MUSIC

The musical programs were more difficult to analyze because performers in orchestras and choruses cannot be counted accurately. This is especially true for radio performers. From impressions of the monitors almost all orchestral musicians were men. Performers such as soloists, duos, and trios who appeared on television during the week monitored were almost evenly divided between the sexes. In radio, 75% of such performers were male.

CATEGORY V – CHILDREN'S PROGRAMMING

The programs directed to children on television represent a very important part of public broadcasting's offerings. Not only do the children's programs account for a large segment of the time (15½ hours of programming), but they attract the largest audience. Moreover, the audience for the children's shows is drawn from all socio-economic groups and from the various ethnic and racial minorities in the U. S. *Sesame Street* is shown in several foreign countries as well. Six series of children's programs were monitored for television. (There were no programs specifically directed to children on radio.) . . .

In all there were 793 male characters (69%) and 362 female characters (32%). The variations from program to program are large. *Sesame Street* had the smallest proportion of females, and *Carrascolendas*, the highest. It must be remembered that *Sesame Street* was also on the air more than any other program.

Twenty-six percent of the male characters were assigned occupational roles and 16% of the female characters. In all programs the proportion of males in occupations was greater than the proportion of females. Of those assigned occupations in *Sesame Street*, 88% were male, 12% female; in *Electric Company*, 70% male, 30% female; in *Villa Alegre*, 81% male, 19% female; in *Carrascolendas*, 69% male, 31% female, and in *Mister Rogers' Neighborhood,* 79% male, 21% female. . . .

Because the absolute number of role assignments for males is so much greater than for females, the range of occupations is also greater for the males. Females were shown in a few non-traditional occupations such as assistant boiler engineer, clown, theater and film director, and ice cream vendor, but the males were shown in a wider range of occupations such as doctor, librarian, actor, chef, newscaster, customs agent, and hockey player. Also 58% of the females with occupations were shown in female sex-typed occupations, and only 17% were in male sex-typed occupations which can be considered non-traditional roles for females.

* * *

EMPLOYMENT

According to fiscal year 1974 employment statistics reported by the licensees to CPB and supplied the Task Force, women held slightly fewer than 30% of all jobs in public broadcasting (2,357 full-time jobs and 1,095 part-time jobs, almost exactly 30% of all jobs in each category). Women held 30% of all jobs in television stations and 29% of full-time jobs. In radio stations, women were employed in only 26% of all jobs, both full- and part-time. . . . Among the types of public television licensees, community stations had the most female employees: 35% of all full-time positions and 38% of the part-time ones were held by women. Participation rates were similar for joint licensees of community stations. . . .

At the highest managerial level, men outnumber women by ten to one. This corroborates the data from the CPB station surveys. The Task Force mail survey revealed that the majority of women respondents (51%) at all types of facilities entered their present job at level three while the majority of the men respondents (54%) entered at level four. Thirty-seven percent of the females began their careers at the secretarial/clerical position (level three). Twenty-two percent of the men respondents entered as broadcast engineers (level five).

For men, educational attainment related positively to their entry level into public broadcasting. Twelve percent of those with a college degree plus a graduate education entered at levels six or seven, and seven percent of those with only college degrees entered at those levels. For women, only three percent of the women with college educations and two percent with graduate degrees entered at level six or seven. The remainder of those women with college degrees or above entered at lower levels.

The survey provides evidence concerning the salary differential between men and women. At all three types of stations examined, 65% of the women employees earned less than $9,000 a year compared with 25% of the men. Only two women were making between $21,000-22,999 annually, and only one was making more than $22,999. Twenty-three men were earning between $21,000-$22,999 and 43 were receiving salaries in excess of $23,000.

To determine the longevity of employment between men and women in the industry, employees were questioned on both the number of years they had worked in public broadcasting and the number of years worked at their present employment. A large percentage of the [women], 27%, reported they had been employed one year or less at their present stations, compared to only 10% of the men. As length of service progressed, this is reversed. For example, of those who had been employed for 10 years or longer in television, only 8% of the employees were women, compared to 30% of the men. This finding can be interpreted to mean that hiring practices are changing and women are more likely to be hired presently than in the past. However, it should be recalled that even though a higher proportion of women have been hired in the last few years, most of the women have entered their present jobs at level three while men entered at level four.

* * *

Also men were more likely to be promoted than women. In radio 51% of the men and 40% of the women had been promoted, whereas in television, 35% of the men had been, compared to 21% of the women, and at joint stations, 42% compared to 35%. Related to this, it was found that more women than men were working in jobs for which they were hired at their present stations. In television, 72% of the women and 51% of the men were still working at their first jobs at the station. In radio, 53% of the women had not advanced past their entry level, compared with 38% of the men. In joint facilities, 61% of the women had not, compared with 48% of the men.

TASK FORCE ON THE STATUS OF WOMEN IN THE CANADIAN BROADCASTING CORPORATION

Women employees of the Canadian Broadcasting Corporation, a corporation created by the Canadian Parliament, became increasingly dissatisfied in the late 1960's with their treatment by the CBC. In February 1971, CBC women in Montreal formed a group to do something about the situation. Two years later a similar group formed in Ottawa. CBC women in Toronto and other cities shortly thereafter also formed Women's Associations.

On May 23, 1974, the president of CBC, Laurent Picard, appointed a Task Force on the Status of Women at CBC to "compile information on the situation of women and identify the problems they face; establish priorities for solving the important problems that are identified; and develop specific action programs for each priority area and establish any organizational mechanisms required for implementation." The CBC Task Force was not directed to study the portrayal of women in CBC programming, although, in its final report, the Task Force recommended such a study be made.

The six-person Task Force (4 women, 2 men), headed by Catherine MacIver, Director of Radio, English Services, Montreal, included the Deputy Manager of Station Relations, French Services; a script assistant; a secretary; the Director of Personnel, Head Office; and a management consultant.

Chair of the Royal Commission on the Status of Women, Florence Bird, served as a consultant to the team. They were given complete independence. Several of the Task Force were members of the Women's Associations.

The Task Force studied the CBC staff of 10,445, interviewing 2,000, one-third of them women, and in addition invited private letters of comment from employees who were reluctant to speak out.

They found, on the one hand, that the most serious complaint of women was the "limited access to the majority of jobs" and, on the other hand, that many of the men responsible for hiring and promotion held stereotyped views of women, including four myths which the Task Force countered with specific evidence in its final report, as for example, that women are not career-oriented or are less suited for certain jobs than men.

The Task Force also found that three fourths of the employees were male and that 93% of the management-level jobs were held by men. Women were found to receive 30% of the advancements and promotions but that these were generally paths into sex-segregated jobs. Of the CBC's 1,425 job titles, 1,086 were occupied by men only.

The management of the Canadian Broadcasting Corporation accepted, in full, 43 of the Task Force's 56 recommendations, accepted 12 with reservations, and rejected only one (creation of an "ombudsman capability" for employees). A number of the recommendations are reprinted here.

TASK FORCE RECOMMENDATIONS TO THE CBC

Job Access

1. Develop and communicate throughout the Corporation an equal opportunity policy with detailed guidelines for its implementation.

2. Revise all recruitment materials to eliminate sex stereotyping.

3. Communicate new equal opportunity policy to all major sources of outside candidates for employment.

4. Ensure that all external employment advertising invites both men and women applicants.

5. Work with unions to remove — where practical — sex from position titles.

6. Revise application forms to remove questions on sex and marital status, and encourage use of initials rather than first names.

7. Redesign notice of vacancy form to include invitation to both men and women applicants.

8. Develop new interview guidelines and circulate to all employment personnel and supervisors.

9. Post all jobs up to and including MS V.*

---

*Fifth level of Management Scale positions.

10. Have manpower planning personnel, working with the Office of Equal Opportunity, develop an inventory of women, to be consulted by decision makers.

11. Establish selection boards for all vacancies from above lowest entry level up to and including MS V.

12. Ensure that awareness sessions are built into the supervisory training program that is being developed in 1975/76.

13. Conduct pilot awareness sessions outside supervisory training, using professional resources; extend these sessions across the CBC if they are successful.

14. Develop and implement affirmative action programs to increase the proportion of women in management and other key jobs, and to break down segregation by sex in positions at lower levels.

* * *

Compensation

25. Develop and distribute to all employees an overall equal pay policy and guidelines for its administration.

26. Request, following the issuance of that policy, that all supervisors review the salaries of men and women in identical position categories, to determine whether differences are justified.

27. Review annually all entry salaries and position-by-position comparisons, and follow up apparent anomalies with the supervisors concerned.

28. Incorporate materials on unconscious discrimination in salary administration into general supervisory training.

* * *

35. Change all references from "wife" to "spouse" in both policy and forms that describe Transfer and Removal Allowances.

Responsibilities of Parenthood

36. Establish, for employees with 1 year of service or more, a separate paid paternity leave, to be included in an overall birth policy.

37. Set the leave entitlement at 3 days.

38. Pay, for women with a minimum of 1 year's service, full salary and the Corporation's share of benefit costs during maternity leave for a period of up to 15 weeks, to be taken at her discretion, provided she signifies her intention to return.

39. Guarantee the new mother the identical position upon her return.

40. Undertake to provide assistance to employees in obtaining improved child care facilities.

* * *

Additional Issues

50. Determine the extent of sexism in CBC programs, and work with program personnel to develop a policy statement on program standards.

51. Establish more clear-cut commercial acceptance guidelines.

52. Alert outside sources of broadcast material to CBC policies with regard to the portrayal of women.

CHAPTER 26

Advertising Industry: A Checklist

Among the areas most criticized by feminists, none has received such stinging criticism as advertising. And no source of images of women has been harder to "liberate." The Federal Trade Commission can prohibit false claims by advertisers, and in some special cases, the Federal Communications Commission has upheld citizens' complaints about advertising under the fairness doctrine. But freedom of expression is a Constitutional right, so context and interpretation of advertising cannot be regulated.

Pressure has been applied on advertisers through demonstrations, mail and telephone complaints, and in some cases, boycotting of a product marketed via a sexist ad. Advertisers have yielded to the pressure, knowing that women spend more dollars in the American marketplace than men or teenagers. Although many ads have been modified or designed to appeal to a more shrewd, savvy female consumer, researchers say that a residue of sexism and paternalism can still be detected in many of the advertising spots sold on radio and television, and in the columns of newspapers and magazines.

In "Madison Avenue Brainwashing — the Facts," Alice Embree debunked what she called "a prevailing myth of the consumer economy that the new innovations create leisure time for the consumers." The many household products a woman is told she needs merely lock her into a more elaborate routine of home care, Embree said.

Embree identified "a theme of containment and control" which is threaded through many of the ads aimed at women — control of full figures, dirt, germs and odors. "But women are not only particularly exploited because of their special consumer role," she said. "They are doubly used as sexual objects to *sell* products."

Alice Courtney and Sarah Lockeretz found that women in magazine advertisements rarely were depicted in important activities outside their homes, and women in the ads were limited even in making decisions about their homes. They made independent decisions only for relatively inexpensive purchases — food, cosmetics, and cleaning products. Men were brought into the ads which sold more expensive household products. Banks, industrial manufacturers, mass media, and institutions featured men in advertisements.

In March 1975, the National Advertising Review Board released a study which examined industry practices and complaints about them. The NARB panel issued a list of recommendations about portrayal of women which, although not binding on member agencies, urged them to look at their advertising compaigns from an "If-the-shoe-were-on-the-other-foot" perspective. Following here are excerpts from its study, *Advertising and Women: A Report on Advertising Portraying or Directed to Women*.

NARB: ADVERTISING AND WOMEN

The Panel's assignment was to examine the basis for complaints about advertising that portrays women or is directed to them. In carrying out its work the Panel drew upon various resources, both inside and outside the industry. It analyzed a broad sampling of current advertising, as well as reviewing in depth the current literature on the subject, both supportive and critical of what is known as "Women's Liberation."

The Panel found that people differ widely in their reactions to woman-related advertising. Some find much of it offensive, demeaning, and contributory to the continued stereotyping of women's role in society. Others seem unaware of any social implication.

The Panel interviewed many in the concerned group. Some were outspoken feminists, some were at the other end of the spectrum. The Panel found that, while there was often considerable difference in their rhetoric, frequently there were only small differences in their attitudes toward advertising that involved women. Their concern is based upon a belief in the power of advertising.

The problem is real.

To deny that the problem exists, in fact, is to deny the effectiveness of advertising. For what the critics are saying is that advertising, in selling a product, often sells a supplementary image as well. Sometimes, in woman-related advertising, that image is negative and depreciatory. Unfortunately, such images may be accepted as true to life by many men, women, and children, especially when they reinforce stereotypes of time gone by.

Seen in this light, advertising must be regarded as one of the forces molding society. Those who protest that advertising merely reflects society must reckon with the criticism that much of the current reflection of women in advertising is out of date. To the extent that this is true, advertising is neglecting its responsibility to be fair, accurate, and truthful, not only in the presentation of products and services, but also in the presentation of men and women.

*   *   *

In this connection it might be noted that during the course of the investigation the members of the Panel experienced a distinct change in the levels of their individual awareness of the problem. They found themselves increasingly sensitive to the implications of advertising that portrays women or is directed to women and to the attitudes that many people hold toward this kind of advertising. It is the unanimous conclusion of the Panel that any attempt to improve the situation will accomplish two important goals. First, it will provide a greater measure of fair treatment for women. Second, it will be an intelligent marketing decision.

*   *   *

Scope of the Problem

Society is undergoing a period of rapid transition. Whether or not you call it a "revolution," the fact is that relationships between the sexes and patterns of social behavior are changing at a swift pace.

Among the pervasive ramifications of this trend, the Panel has noted the following random examples:

Educators are rewriting textbooks at every grade level to elimin-
  traditional sexual stereotypes.

*   *   *

The leaders of the United Church of Christ were charged by the
  delegates to the Church's Ninth General Synod "to take steps
  to translate the Bible in a manner sensitive to the experiences
  of both women and men" and to use "deliberately inclusive
  language" in hymnals and worship materials.
"Ms." as a new form of address for women is gaining acceptance
  at a steadily increasing pace.

*   *   *

These random statements could be multiplied many times over without including all the important indicators such as the number of women elected to political office, the amount of back pay awarded to women in cases of employment discrimination, admission of women to professional graduate schools, etc.

In the midst of such far-reaching social change, therefore, it would be surprising if as vital a part of our society as advertising were not affected. It has been. In many instances advertising has already reflected the changing status of women. But it has been attacked for not going far enough and in some cases for allegedly furthering traditional forms of discrimination against women.

*   *   *

WHAT THE PANEL RECOMMENDS

Recognizing that principles are more enduring than specific cases, the Panel has distilled its many months of study into a checklist of questions for advertisers and agency personnel to consider when creating or approving an advertisement.

*   *   *

Checklist: Constructive Portrayals

— Are the attitudes and behavior of the women in my ads suitable models for my own daughter to copy? Will I be happy if my own female children grow up to act and react the way the women in my ads act and react?

— Do my ads reflect the fact that girls may aspire to careers in business and the professions? Do they show, for example, female doctors and female executives? Some women with both male and female assistants?

— Do my ads portray women and men (and children) sharing in the chores of family living? For example, grocery shopping, doing laundry, cooking (not just outdoor barbecueing), washing dishes, cleaning house, taking care of children, mowing the lawn, and other house and yard work?

— Do the women in my ads make decisions (or help make them) about the purchase of high-priced items and major family investments? Do they take an informed interest, for example, in insurance and financial matters?

— Do my ads portray women actually driving cars and showing an intelligent interest in mechanical features, not just in the color and upholstery?

— Are two-income families portrayed in my ads? For example, husband and wife leaving home or returning from work together?

— Are the women in my ads doing creative or exciting things? Older women, too? In social and occupational environments? For example, making a speech, in a laboratory, or approving an ad?

Checklist: Positive Appeals

— Is the product presented as a means for a woman to enhance her own self-esteem, to be a beautiful human being, to realize her full potential?

— Does my advertisement promise women realistic rewards for using the product? Does it assume intelligence on the part of women?

CHAPTER 27

IWY Commission:
The Ten Guidelines

In 1975 the National Commission on the Observance of International Women's Year, appointed by President Gerald R. Ford, devoted part of its activities to evaluating the role of women in the media. In addition to compiling *Ten Guidelines for the Treatment of Women in the Media* (which are reprinted here), the Commission drew up a *Checklist for the Portrayal of Women in Entertainment Programming and Advertising*. It also recommended that the Department of Health, Education, and Welfare study the impact of television on sex discrimination and sex-role stereotyping, and schedule hearings, to be conducted by the U.S. Commission on Civil Rights, on the impact of mass media on women.

The IWY Commission's *Ten Guidelines* is a roundup of ideas that, by 1975, were showing the first signs of having an impact on the treatment of women in the news and the newsroom. Newspapers, magazines, and the wire services have begun to adjust their stylebooks to eliminate differences in writing about men and women newsmakers. Many newspapers are dropping "Mr.," "Miss," and "Mrs." before surnames, and if they retain such titles, often they will follow the woman's preferred usage — including "Ms." Nonessential references to the appearance of a woman are being discouraged.

The Stanford University Women's News Service has recommended an "appropriateness" test to reporters: "When you have completed a story about a woman, go through it and ask yourself whether you would have written about a man in the same style. If not, something may be wrong with the tone or even the conception of your article. Think it through again."

The members of the Media Committee that designed the IWY guidelines were: Chair, Patricia T. Carbine, *Ms.* publisher and editor; actor

167

Alan Alda; Margaret Long Arnold, past president of the General Federation of Women's Clubs and radio commentator; Richard Cornuelle, writer; Helen K. Copley, Copley Newspapers; Winfield Dunn, former governor of Tennessee; Casey Eike, assistant dean, University of Kansas; *Ladies Home Journal* editor Lenore Hershey; Dr. Donna Allen, editor, *Media Report to Women*; Midge Kovacs, National Organization for Women and president, Midge Kovacs Ads Unlimited; Kathryn C. Pelgrift, Vice President of Planning, Columbia Broadcasting System. Kathy Bonk, chair of NOW's Task Force on Media, and Pamela Curtis served as staff members to the committee.

The *Ten Guidelines* follow here.

THE TEN GUIDELINES

1. The media should establish as an ultimate goal the employment of women in policymaking positions in proportion to their participation in the labor force. The media should make special efforts to employ women who are knowledgeable about and sensitive to women's changing roles.

2. Women in media should be employed at all job levels — and, in accordance with the law, should be paid equally for work of equal value and be given equal opportunity for training and promotion.

3. The present definition of news should be expanded to include more coverage of women's activities locally, nationally, and internationally. In addition, general news stories should be reported to show their effect on women. For example, the impact of foreign aid of women in recipient countries is often overlooked, as is the effect of public transportation on women's mobility, safety, and ability to take jobs.

4. The media should make special, sustained efforts to seek out news of women. Women now figure in less than 10 percent of the stories currently defined as news.

5. Placement of news should be decided by subject matter, not by sex. The practice of segregating material thought to be of interest to women only into certain sections of a newspaper or broadcast implies that news, when no longer segregated, is not covered at all. Wherever news of women is placed, it should be treated with the same dignity, scope, and accuracy as is news of men. Women's activities should not be located in the last 30-60 seconds of a broadcast or used as fillers in certain sections or back pages of a newspaper or magazine.

6. Women's bodies should not be used in an exploitative way to add irrelevant sexual interest in any medium. This includes news and feature coverage by both the press and television, movie and movie promotion,

"skin" magazines and advertising messages of all sorts. The public violation of women's physical privacy tends to vioate the individual integrity of all women.

7. The presentation of personal details when irrelevant to a story — sex, sexual preference, religious or political orientation — should be eliminated for both women and men.

8. It is to be hoped that one day all titles will be unnecessary. But in the meantime, a person's right to determine her (or his) own title should be respected without slurs or innuendoes. If men are called Doctor or Reverend, the same titles should be used for women. And a woman should be able to choose Ms., Miss, or Mrs.

9. Gender designations are a rapidly changing area of the language, and a decision to use or not to use a specific word should be subject to periodic review. Terms incorporating gender reference should be avoided. Use firefighter instead of fireman, business executive instead of businessman, letter carrier instead of mailman. In addition, women, at least from age 16, should be called women, not girls. And at no time should a female be referred to as "broad," "chick," or the like.

10. Women's activities and organizations should be treated with the same respect accorded men's activities and organizations. The women's movement should be reported as seriously as any other civil rights movement; it should not be made fun of, ridiculed, or belittled. Just as the terms "black libbers" or "Palestine libbers" are not used, the terms "women's libbers" should not be used. Just as jokes at the expense of blacks are no longer made, jokes should not be made at women's expense. The news of women should not be sensationalized. Too often news media have reported conflict among women and ignored unity. Coverage of women's conferences is often limited solely to so-called "splits" or fights. These same disputes at conferences attended by men would be considered serious policy debates.

CHAPTER 28

Publishers' Guidelines

For the most part, children's comsumption of media is guided by their parents. Mothers and fathers decide when the television will be on, if it must be forsaken for homework or chores, or which of its programs are appropriate for young eyes and ears. Some parents use the television as a babysitter, a habit that gives youngsters carte blanche to view whatever they want when their parents are occupied with something else.

Since parents control the purse strings, they also decide which books their child will own and which movies he or she will see. Children also are affected by their parents' own taste in magazines, newspapers, radio, television, film, theater, and art.

But there is another authority which exposes children to media that lies outside the control of parents: the schools. The socialization of children is deeply influenced by the role models they find in their schoolbooks, the audio-visual resources of their school, and the learning situations their teachers create for them.

Parents, particularly mothers, who have grown concerned about stereotyping in textbooks and teacher's manuals, have banded together in many cities to evaluate the content and language of books being used in their schools. This scrutiny has also been extended to films, filmstrips, and programs on educational television used by the schools as part of their curriculum.

One of the first intensive studies, which evaluated 134 elementary school readers from 14 different publishers, was *Dick and Jane as Victims: Sex Stereotyping in Children's Readers*, compiled by Women on Words and Images, Princeton, N.J., in 1972. Their content analysis exposed a pattern of omission of women in American and world history, and compartmentalization of lifestyles and roles assigned to women. The Women on Words and

Images could find almost no mention of single parents or working mothers.

The little girls in the readers studied had low expectations of their ability to achieve. They joined little boys in putting themselves down. Neither girls nor boys expressed a realistic range of emotions, and little boys were further stifled in their need to express sorrow, joy, or compassion. The researchers noted a lack of closeness between husbands and wives. Most interaction, they said, was between parent and child.

Complaints about the sex role assignments in children's textbooks soon reached the school boards in many cities and counties. Parents and teachers in many locales have organized committees against sex stereotyping, which monitor acquisitions of teaching materials in their school districts and file complaints if the books, filmstrips, or TV programs are found to be sexist. These groups find support in Title IX of the Civil Rights Act, which prohibits discrimination on the basis of sex in any education program or activity receiving federal financial assistance.

The publishing companies began to feel the pressure mounted by coalitions of parents, school board members, and women's groups. They also began to hear from their own employees, both women and men. Several textbook companies, working through committees formed internally, drew up and issued guidelines to prevent sex stereotyping in the educational materials they published. Excerpts from three of these manuals appear here.

GUIDELINES FOR EQUAL TREATMENT OF THE SEXES IN MCGRAW-HILL BOOK COMPANY PUBLICATIONS
McGraw-Hill Book Company

The word *sexism* was coined, by analogy to *racism*, to denote discrimination based on gender. In its original sense, *sexism* referred to prejudice against the female sex. In a broader sense, the term now indicates any arbitrary stereotyping of males and females on the basis of their gender.

We are endeavoring through these guidelines to eliminate sexist assumptions from McGraw-Hill Book Company publications and to encourage a greater freedom for all individuals to pursue their interests and realize their potentials. Specifically, these guidelines are designed to make McGraw-Hill staff members and McGraw-Hill authors aware of the ways in which males and females have been stereotyped in publications; to show the role language has played in reinforcing inequality; and to indicate positive approaches toward providing fair, accurate, and balanced treatment of both sexes in our publications.

One approach is to recruit more women as authors and contributors in all fields. The writings and viewpoints of women should be represented in quotations and references whenever possible. Anthologies should include a larger proportion of selections by and about women in fields where suitable materials are available but women are currently underrepresented.

Women as well as men have been leaders and heroes, explorers and pioneers, and have made notable contributions to science, medicine, law, business, politics, civics, economics, literature, the arts, sports, and other areas of endeavor. Books dealing with subjects like these, as well as general histories, should acknowledge the achievements of women. The fact that women's rights, opportunities, and accomplishments have been limited by the social customs and conditions of their time should be openly discussed whenever relevant to the topic at hand.

We realize that the language of literature cannot be prescribed. The recommendations in these guidelines, thus, are intended primarily for use in teaching materials, reference works, and nonfiction works in general.

*   *   *

PORTRAYALS: HUMAN TERMS

Members of both sexes should be represented as whole human beings with *human* strengths and weaknesses, not masculine or feminine ones. Women and girls should be shown as having the same abilities, interests, and ambitions as men and boys. Characteristics that have been praised in females — such as gentleness, compassion, and sensitivity — should also be praised in males.

Like men and boys, women and girls should be portrayed as independent, active, strong, courageous, competent, decisive, persistent, serious-minded, and successful. They should appear as logical thinkers, problem solvers, and decision makers. They should be shown as interested in their work, pursuing a variety of career goals, and both deserving of and receiving public recognition for their accomplishments.

Sometimes men should be shown as quiet and passive, or fearful and indecisive, or illogical and immature. Similarly, women should sometimes be shown as tough, aggressive, and insensitive. Stereotypes of the logical male and the emotional, subjective female are to be avoided. In descriptions, the smarter, braver, or more successful person should be a woman or girl as often as a man or boy. In illustrations, the taller, heavier, stronger, or more active person should not always be male, especially when children are portrayed.

*   *   *

DESCRIPTIONS OF MEN AND WOMEN

Women and men should be treated with the same respect, dignity, and seriousness. Neither should be trivialized or stereotyped, either in text or in illustrations. Women should not be described by physical attributes when men are being described by mental attributes or professional position. Instead, both sexes should be dealt with in the same terms. References to a man's or a woman's appearance, charm, or intuition should be avoided when irrelevant.

* * *

In descriptions of men, especially men in the home, references to general ineptness should be avoided. Men should not be characterized as dependent on women for meals, or clumsy in household maintenance, or as foolish in self-care.

To be avoided: characterizations that stress men's dependence on women for advice on what to wear and what to eat, inability of men to care for themselves in times of illness, and men as objects of fun (the henpecked husband).

Women should be treated as part of the rule, not as the exception. Generic terms, such as doctor and nurse, should be assumed to include both men and women, and modified titles such as "woman doctor" or "male nurse," should be avoided. Work should never be stereotyped as "woman's work" or as "a man-sized job." Writers should avoid showing a "gee-whiz" attitude toward women who perform competently. ("Though a woman, she ran the business as well as any man" or "Though a woman, she ran the business efficiently.")

GUIDELINES FOR CREATING POSITIVE SEXUAL AND RACIAL IMAGES IN EDUCATIONAL MATERIALS

Macmillan Publishing Company

THE 51% MINORITY

More than one-half of the population is female; yet a visitor from another planet, after examining most texts and readers, might assume that males outnumber females by at least ten to one.

GUIDEPOST:

In selecting authors, illustrators, and content of artwork, stories, poetry, non-fiction accounts, and examples, remember that half of the human population is female and should be represented appropriately in our textbooks.

* * *

THE "CHEERLEADER" SYNDROME

Girls watch boys build a treehouse, reward their big brothers with smiles when they solve a mystery; a mother stands at the kitchen door wiping her hands on an apron while father rescues a treed cat; women urge their husbands on to greater achievements and allow males to take credit for their ideas.

These prevalent images reinforce the notion of woman as passive onlooker, giver-of-support, and non-achiever. Such images act as a straitjacket to

females and a painful hairshirt to males who suffer from constant pressure
to prove themselves.

GUIDEPOST:

Emphasis should be placed frequently on portrayals of girls and women
participating actively and positively in exciting, worthwhile pursuits, while
males should be permitted often to observe and lend support.

* * *

"THE EMOTIONAL SEX"

*"I'm scared," said Susan, clutching her brother's hand. She began to
sob uncontrollably.*

*"That love stuff is for girls," said Jerry to his friend as they left the
movie theater.*

Once in a great while, traditional textbooks show little boys on the verge of
tears, but they nearly always manage to choke them back bravely. Girls in
such books, on the other hand, usually surrender to their fears and dislikes,
to the point where they seldom take positive action. In this way, girls are
used as a kind of foil to highlight male achievements. Thus girls are programmed to feel that "feminine" emotional weakness is desirable because it
helps males build their self-esteem and, in turn, will spur males to solve all
of life's problems. This attitude cripples males, too: they are learning contempt for females and an exaggerated image of masculine strength impossible to fulfill. They are being taught to be dishonest about their own feelings and to deny their expression. Boys and girls are further learning to be
less than whole human beings when we reinforce the notion that tender
emotions, such as love, sympathy, and caring, are acceptable only for one
sex.

GUIDEPOST:

Boys as well as girls, women as well as men, should cry or otherwise
respond emotionally when appropriate. They may also exhibit self-control
and emotional courage in trying circumstances, especially when such restraint enables them to act positively.

* * *

WOMEN'S INFERIOR STATUS – CULTURAL PERSPECTIVES

*"The wives were not permitted to vote because the chairman felt they
would, in effect, give their husbands a double vote for the same candidate."*

"Colonial women were not allowed to own property."

"Cortez received an Indian girl as a present."

Statements such as the above that describe past sexism should be amplified
by an explanation of the customs, discriminations, and economics involved.
This should include the historical forces that created the inequality, the
changes occurring today to ameliorate the situation, and the need for con-

tinued efforts to make equal opportunity a reality for women. When discussing male-dominated cultures, try to include specific statements about the suppression of women, and describe the contribution — however submerged — of women within the culture. Sexist statements and events might be included in stories and quotations, but should be cited as examples of attitudes no longer acceptable in our culture.

GUIDEPOST:

Sexist behavior and customs must not be accepted as "givens" but must be explained in the context of the culture and point in history. These explanations should appear in the student's materials, although they might be further amplified in the teacher's editions.

GUIDELINES FOR IMPROVING THE IMAGE
OF WOMEN IN TEXTBOOKS
Scott, Foresman and Company

SEX-ROLE STEREOTYPING

Editors and authors should be cautious when they assign certain activities or roles to people purely on the basis of sex. Many such assumptions misrepresent reality and ignore the actual contributions of both sexes to the activity or role.

EXAMPLES OF SEXIST LANGUAGE:

In New England, the typical farm was so small that the owner and his sons could take care of it by themselves.

Children had once learned about life by listening to aunts, uncles, grandparents, and the wise men of their town or neighborhood.

POSSIBLE ALTERNATIVES:

In New England, the typical farm was so small that the family members could take care of it by themselves.

Children had once learned about life by listening to aunts, uncles, grandparents, and the wise people of their town or neighborhood.

* * *

Care must be taken to avoid sexist assumptions and stereotypes in teachers' manuals and other teacher aids.

EXAMPLES OF SEXIST LANGUAGE:

Hammers and scissors are good eye-hand coordinators. Hitting the nail instead of the thumb is a triumph for the boys. Cutting out paper dolls and their garments is good for the girls.

POSSIBLE ALTERNATIVES:

Hammers and scissors are good eye-hand coordinators. For a child, hitting the nail instead of the thumb or cutting out a recognizable shape is a triumph.

CHAPTER 29

Three Principles of Feminist Journalism

Still another type of guidelines has been proposed by the feminist press both in practice and in theory. In 1973 *her-self* said editorials were unnecessary. "Who can speak for the women of Ann Arbor? Why not let them speak for themselves?" The *Marin Women's News Journal* asked whether it should decide what information the reader should have or whether the reader should give her own information. *WOMEN* let women supervise the editing of their articles. In France, Francoise Benedicte said, "Women must set up their own film crews, structure of film production, the language of the film, to fit what we have to say." Women need a new language for new ways of thinking, said the *Women's Free Express*, not just the addition of *she* and *her* to masculine pronouns. *the second wave* said the feminist media must be a means of discovering "our own language." Sandia in *Big Mama Rag* wrote that women must stop copying the male model and establish media as a new means of communication for self-definition with "a person-to-person perspective." Several women's conferences insisted that women cover their own events.

Media Report to Women, which has been chronicling women's progress in obtaining a means of communication, wrote its only editorial in five years on the subject, on January 1, 1976. It is reprinted here.

FEMALE JOURNALISM IS SOMETHING DIFFERENT

As *Media Report to Women* begins its fifth year of publishing, and its fourth volume (Volume 1, published by the Women's Institute for Freedom of the Press which founded *Media Report to Women*, encompassed both 1972 and 1973), it seems a good time to state the journalistic principles which have guided our news information decisions.

Media Report to Women has three criteria for the selection and presentation of its news information. (We have also found the three criteria useful as a standard for examining the performance of other media as well as our own.)

We believe that journalism based on these three principles is more respectful of people.

Recognizing that people are capable of interpreting news information for themselves, we see our function as supplying factual information that is not easily available elsewhere, and we leave the formation of opinions about it to each individual. (We do *not* consider that our judgment can be better for another person than her own.)

The public has more to tell newspeople than vice versa, we have observed, because news information resides in people. Therefore we believe that people should convey their information to the public as directly as possible.

Our criteria would redefine "news" and redefine the role of the newsperson.

We propose a new and feminist, here meaning female, set of standards to improve or replace the existing male journalism. The following are our *Three Principles of Feminist Journalism:*

1. NO ATTACKS ON PEOPLE

In *Media Report to Women* we do not attack anyone, call names, use opinion nouns or adjectives that characterize, label or pass judgment on the opinions, actions, ideas, or attitudes of other women — or men. We know that they are just as entitled to their views as we are to ours. We also know that media characterizations of people can be inhibiting and restrictive — both to the person characterized and to those among the public who may wish to pick up on an idea or take an action — be they children or adults. To the contrary, public news media, we believe, should work to *widen* the social, political, or economic options for people, not inhibit them. In *Media Report to Women*, we do not say, for example, that a book or speech is good or bad, or fair or biased; rather we report what is in it and let each woman judge for herself.

2. MORE FACTUAL INFORMATION

Priority is given to facts over opinion in *Media Report to Women*. We include full texts wherever possible. Although entitled to express our opinions, even without giving the facts on which we based them, we believe that all people must find, as we do, that others' conclusions are nearly useless without their facts to enable us to judge the opinion's merit for ourselves, or to form our own. Conclusions without facts keep us apathetic, powerless to act, and dependent upon the decision-making of others.

We emphasize fact over opinion in *Media Report to Women*'s limited space also because the existing media carry so little information from women, for or about women (as well as other parts of the public) — especially compared to the abundance of information available to be known. Therefore, as long as there is information people do not yet know about, we cannot justify using our limited space for our opinions of the information they already do know about. We thus avoid the *repetition* which is customary in the "issue-making" of conventional journalism, as well as its emphasis on opinion.

3. PEOPLE SHOULD SPEAK FOR THEMSELVES

We believe that the surest way to dispel stereotypes, to achieve accuracy, and to add more, new factual information, is for people to make their own case directly to the public and thus to define themselves. Therefore, to the greatest extent possible, in *Media Report to Women* we do not tell *about* what women do and think, as we would in conventional journalism, but we let them tell it themselves. People know their own information best, and we believe that neither the person with the information nor the public needs an intermediary reporter to be an interpreter — but only to help the person get her own account down on paper, on the air, or into some other medium.

People speaking for themselves provide not only more accurate information but information that is more diverse, complex, direct, honest and reliable, imaginative and lively than anyone else can make it in reporting it second hand. Even the simplest statements of information are better direct from the source. For example, " 'I think we ought to have more women represented,' " is far preferable, we believe, to the conventional journalism's "She said she thought that there ought to be more women represented."

These three basic criteria also address the three most common complaints women have about the communications media, as we at *Media Report to Women* hear them, and we believe that the application of the Three Principles could constructively improve the conditions that give rise to each type of criticism: 1) that the *image* of women in media too often is derogatory, restrictive, and inaccurate; 2) that the media do not carry enough *news coverage of women's activities and issues*, especially in light of the proportion of the public that are women; and 3) that insufficient *employment* of women in the media, particularly in policy-making positions, results in men speaking for the female 53% of the population.

Although the *Three Principles of Feminist Journalism* may help in these respects to improve the mass media as a means of communication with others both at home and abroad, their first purpose is to serve women as guidelines for our own media.

Dr. Donna Allen, Editor
Martha Leslie Allen, Associate Editor

CHAPTER 30

Satellite Communication: Women in Media of the Future

A document as up-to-date as tomorrow is the letter proposing satellite communication for women, which begins on the next page. It was written by Madeline Lee, director of the National Women's Agenda Project to the Project's 106 participating national women's organizations, representing over 33 million members. The National Women's Agenda is in the process of forming a national coalition of women's organizations.

The importance of having a means of communication with each other registered forcefully with women during International Women's Year 1975, when as never before women began to find each other, across national, international, state and local borders. They discovered that their interests were more common than different. The vast new network that began to arise from these contacts convinced many that if they could continue to communicate, they could work together and indeed achieve goals of equality never before approached.

This belief gave rise to the National Women's Agenda, which began as a project of the Women's Action Alliance, under the direction of Ruth J. Abram. By the end of 1975, more than 90 national women's organizations were cooperating in the formulation of an eleven-point Agenda which was presented to Congress and the governments of more than 40 states and localities on "Agenda Day," December 2. The National Women's Agenda called for progress in these respects: 1) fair representation and participation in the political process, 2) equal education and training, 3) meaningful work and adequate compensation, 4) equal access to economic power, 5) quality child care for all children, 6) quality health care and services, 7) adequate housing, 8) just and humane treatment in the criminal justice system, 9) fair treatment by and equal access to media and the arts, 10) physical safety, and 11) respect for the individual.

Task Forces were formed for each of these goals to recommend Plans of Action that would accomplish the goals during the next decade, designated by the United Nations as International Decade for Women and Development.

But clearly, for 100 national women's organizations with many millions of members to accomplish these goals in a coordinated way, a new and vastly greater communication system would be needed.

It was at this critical point that the possibility of satellite communication was suggested.

The document below, which describes its own sense of historical significance, was mailed to the participating organizations on June 17, 1977.

NATIONAL WOMEN'S AGENDA SATELLITE PROPOSAL

I am writing all members of the large informal network that has grown up around the National Women's Agenda to share a remarkable piece of news. Within the next year, women's organizations may well have access to time on a communications satellite, making possible such vital resources as a feminist news service, teleconferencing by phone, and a Washington "hot line" on national legislative activity affecting women. Organizations could experiment with satellite link-ups to their regional chapters, with instantaneous long-distance document transmission, with their own teleconferences.

Our first problem will be to overcome reactions of disbelief or incomprehension. Women have traditionally been the last to benefit from technological change. The typewriter was thought too complicated for women to use; women driving automobiles was shocking; we have yet to have much direct access to jets or spacecraft. This need *not* be true of satellites. If we can use phones, we can have those phones hooked up to satellites instead of long-distance phone cables.

Some history. In the fall of 1975, a New York based organization called Public Interest Satellite Association was formed. PISA's purpose is to see that the *public* benefits from advances in communications technology. Their excellent booklet, *Toward the Public Dividend*, offers a complete introduction to the history, the politics, and the critical next years of the use of satellites for long-distance communication. I urge you to request a copy from them.

In brief, the National Aeronautics and Space Administration, in addition to its space exploration program, has been a major developer of satellites for long-distance television, telephone, and information transmission.

The communications satellites designed, built and launched by NASA were financed by your tax dollars. What NASA learned, private industry gained. The communications industry (Western Union, AT&T, and so on) proceeded to build communications satellites of their own, as part of the service they charge for. This led to a sort of crisis as they sought guidelines for launching their satellites. There is a limit to how many satellites can circle the earth for communications purposes. Who was to regulate them? The FCC was the logical answer, but in 1973, the Nixon Administration announced an "open skies" policy. Seductively named, it meant the government would *not* regulate space. Anyone can design and launch a satellite. And NASA's experimentation with more advanced forms of satellite communication would end. Private industry would continue the research and development.

The public will *not* benefit from their arrangement. Few public service groups and even fewer ordinary citizens have the capacity to build or buy a satellite. Almost none of us even knows what we would do with one.

The Technology

A communication satellite circles the earth at a distance above the earth which means its position remains relatively constant. A signal sent to it from, say, Boston, is bounced down to, say, Los Angeles. Because the satellite is so far up, the distance the signal travels is the same up and down — and the distance between Boston and Los Angeles is virtually irrelevant.

The signals a satellite can handle include signals from telephones, television transmitters, computers, and copying machines. All that is required is the *ground station* which talks to the satellite, and some connection to our more familiar office machines (copiers, phones, wire services, computers). This is called a *micro-wave link.*

Understanding more than this is not necessary, any more than a degree degree in electronics is required to operate a telephone. Political sense and ability to organize are far more important to us at this stage.

The Agenda

PISA learned of the National Women's Agenda through Jan Zimmerman of the Media Task Force. Without this contact, women and women's organizations might never appear in the story of the "public" and the development of communications systems using satellites. Just as television followed a course away from direct public access, leaving women especially far from contact, so may this new potential for human communication.

NASA, for its own complex reasons, would like to re-enter the field of satellite communication. To do so, it needs evidence of public interest in satellites for communication. It currently allows "experiments on its existing equipment." Experimenters include medical groups educating rural health services, library associations using satellites for information retrieval, state governments and police systems, and education departments reaching isolated areas with television programming.

The National Women's Agenda Project submitted a proposal to NASA to become experimenters on current equipment linking women's organizations with one another, and with their chapters, and creating an information network for women. It can include a legislative hot-line from Washington, giving us information on emerging issues for women; a women's news service; and even data banks on women's issues. We have just received word that our request has an excellent chance of being granted. Funding is being sought for the necessary research, coordination, and staffing of the experiment's early stages.

This alternative communication system can greatly increase the efficiency of communications in the Coalition. Organizations joining the National Women's Agenda Coalition are expected to keep their membership informed of Coalition activities. Members must also coordinate their activities within the Coalition. The Plans of Action written by the Task Forces stress again and again the need for wide dissemination of information on the Agenda's issues.

As you consider whether your organization will join the Coalition, try to assess the potential of this extraordinary possibility. Read the enclosed questionnaire and see how much your organization spends (and depends) on communication.

In addition, please complete the enclosed questionnaire on your organization's communication needs. Responses of Agenda groups will be used to design the use of the satellite when the experiment begins, possibly as early as December, 1977. Since the establishment of such a network is enormously complex, the first stages will be planned to link as many Coalition members as possible. Our current plan starts in San Francisco and Washington, where ground terminals are already available to us at no charge.

Please complete the questionnaire as soon as humanly possible, so we can best use this amazing opportunity.

The title of an article on the satellite in May's *Women's Agenda* magazine is "Women Hold Up Half the Sky But Men Are Using All of It." We can work together to change that. The idea of a coalition of women's organizations stunned NASA officials at an experimenters' conference in March. The idea of 33 million women learning about satellite technology through their groups had a decided impact. I hope you will call me – via conventional telephone for the moment – with any questions you may have on the satellite.

Sincerely yours,
Madeline Lee, Director
National Women's
Agenda Project

BIBLIOGRAPHICAL NOTES

GENERAL

The story of women journalists is told in *Up From the Footnote: A History of Women Journalists* by Marion Marzolf (New York: Hastings House, 1977). Material from the book ran in two parts in *Journalism History*, Vol. 1, Winter 1974-75 and Vol. 2, Spring 1975, titled "The Woman Journalist: Colonial Printer to City Desk." The winter issues of *Journalism History* for 1974-75 and 1976-77 each were devoted to the literature of women journalists. The Winter 1974-75 issue contained a comprehensive bibliography by Marzolf, Ramona R. Rush and Darlene Stern titled, "The Literature of Women in Journalism History." A bibliographic supplement compiled by Marzolf appeared in the Winter 1976-77 issue.

Other general source material may be found in *Notable American Women: 1607-1950* (Cambridge, MA: Belknap Press, 1971), an excellent three volume biographical dictionary which contains short biographies of individual outstanding women. Edith May Marken, "Women in American Journalism Before 1900" (unpublished master's thesis, University of Missouri, 1932) has useful lists of journalists.

MARY KATHERINE GODDARD AND EARLY WOMEN PRINTERS

No biographies exist of colonial women printers and publishers, although some material on Mary Katherine Goddard and her mother, Sarah Updike Goddard, is included in Ward L. Miner, *William Goddard, Newspaperman* (Durham, NC: Duke University Press, 1962). The best sources of information are their publications, many of which are preserved in state archives. Files of Mary Katherine Goddard's *Maryland Journal* are in the Maryland Historical Society at Baltimore, which also has photostats of her account book and petitions to retain the post of postmistress. A copy of the Declaration of Independence printed by her is at the National Archives in Washington, D.C. Lists of the imprints from her print shop appear in Lawrence C. Wroth, *History of Printing in Colonial Maryland* (Baltimore: Typolhetae, 1922) and Joseph T. Wheeler, *The Maryland Press, 1770-1790* (Baltimore: Maryland Historical Society, 1938).

Secondary sources on colonial women printers include Isaiah Thomas, *The History of Printing in America* (2 vols., Worcester, MA: Isaiah Thomas, Jr., 1810); Elisabeth A. Dexter, *Colonial Women of Affairs* (Boston: Houghton Mifflin, 1931) and *Career Women of America: 1776-1840* (Francestown, NH: Jones, 1950); Eugenia A. Leonard, *The Dear-Bought Heritage* (Philadelphia: University of Pennsylvania, 1965); Alice M. Earle, *Colonial Dames and Good Wives* (New York: Ungar, 1962); Julia C. Spruill, *Women's Life and Work in the Southern Colonies* (Chapel Hill, NC: University of North Carolina, 1938); and Barbara Mayer Wertheimer, *We Were There: The Story of Working Women in America* (New York: Pantheon Books, 1977).

Sources on Sarah Updike Goddard include Nancy Fisher Chudacoff, "Women in the News 1762-1770 — Sarah Updike Goddard" (*Rhode Island History*, Vol. 32, November 1973, pp. 98-105) and "Sarah Updike Goddard, Gentlewoman Printer," a paper presented at the 1976 Association for Education in Journalism convention by Susan Henry, a doctoral candidate in communications at Syracuse University.

ANNE ROYALL

Source material on Anne Royall is scattered among various libraries. The Library of Congress holds a complete file of *Paul Pry* from 1831 to 1836. Fortunately,

The Huntress, which appeared from 1836 until 1854, has been microfilmed and is available in many libraries. Anne Royall's letters, are preserved in the University of Virginia Library, the New York Public Library, the Yale University Library, the Duke University Library and the Library of Congress, but they pertain more to her career as a bookseller than to her career as a Washington editor.

Copies of her books are in the Library of Congress including *Sketches of History, Life and Manners in the United States* (1826); a novel, *The Tennessean* (1827); the three-volume *Black Book* (1828-29); the ' two-volume *Pennsylvania* (1829); and the three-volume *Southern Tour* (1830-31). All were published by her. With the exception of the first two, which were printed in New Haven, all were printed in Washington. *Letters from Alabama*, first published in 1830, was reprinted in 1969 by the University of Alabama Press with a helpful biographical introduction and notes by Lucille Griffith. Information on Anne Royall's pension claim may be found in Claim No. W-8566 in the Veteran's Administration in Washington. The Columbia Historical Society Library in Washington holds miscellaneous scrapbooks and clipping files on her.

Other biographical data may be gathered from her obituary in the *Washington Evening Star* (October 2, 1854) and in newspaper feature stories (*Washington Post*, February 22, 1891 and October 6, 1901 and *Baltimore Sun*, October 18, 1931). Descriptions of Anne Royall at the end of her life are contained in Allen C. Clark, "Joseph Gales, Junior Editor and Mayor" (*Columbia Historical Society Records*, Vol. 23, October 1919, pp. 86-146) and in the autobiography, *Life of P.T. Barnum Written by Himself* (New York: Redfield, 1855).

There are three full-length biographies of Anne Royall. Sarah H. Porter, *The Life and Times of Anne Royall* (Cedar Rapids, IA: Torch Press, 1909) argued that she had been unjustly treated by history and included original source material that was not footnoted. George S. Jackson, *Uncommon Scold* (Boston: Bruce Humphries, 1937) presented a psychological analysis of her activities. The most definitive, Bessie Rowland James, *Anne Royall's U.S.A.* (New Brunswick, NJ: Rutgers University Press, 1972), was amply footnoted but lacked a bibliography.

JANE GREY SWISSHELM

Jane G. Swisshelm said she burned all her papers and wrote her autobiography, *Half a Century* (Chicago: Jansen, McClurg, 1880) strictly from memory. Considerable manuscript material, however, is located at the Minnesota Historical Society in St. Paul. The Swisshelm papers are included in collections of the letters of Henry Z. Mitchell, her brother-in-law and a pioneer settler of St. Cloud. Other items are included in material on early life in Minnesota taken from the *Boston Daily Journal* and the *New York Tribune* and in the family papers of Alexander Ramsey and Sylvanus B. Lowry. The society also has complete files of her St. Cloud newspaper.

The Carnegie Library of Pittsburgh holds a file of the *Saturday Visiter* available only on microfilm. Copies of the *New York Tribune* containing her Washington correspondence are available in the Library of Congress. It also has copies of two rare books by her, *Letters to Country Girls* (New York: J.C. Ricker, 1853) and (written with others) *True Stories About Pets* (Boston: D. Lothrop & Co., 1879).

The best source on her life in Washington is *Crusader and Feminist* (St. Paul: Minnesota Historical Society,1934), a collection of her correspondence from the capital edited by Arthur J. Larsen. Some material appears in James Black, *A Brief History of Prohibition* (New York: National Committee of the Prohibition Reform Party,1880).

Two valuable articles are Lester B. Shippee, "Jane Grey Swisshelm, Agitator" (*Mississippi Valley Historical Review*, Vol. 7, December 1920, pp. 206-227) and Bertha Monica Sterns, "Reform Periodicals and Female Reformers: 1830-1860," (*American Historical Review*, Vol. 37, July 1932, pp. 689-693). Chapter three in Margaret Farrand Thorp, *Female Persuasion: Six Strong-Minded Women* (New Haven: Yale University Press, 1949) is devoted to Swisshelm.

Other material: Kathleen Endres, "Jane Grey Swisshelm: 19th Century Journalist and Feminist" (*Journalism History,* Vol. 2, Winter 1975-76, pp. 128-32) and Maurine Beasley, "Washington Correspondent: A Pioneer" (*Matrix*, Spring 1975).

MARGARET FULLER

Margaret Fuller has been the subject of numerous biographies, but they tend to treat her as a literary figure and philosopher, not as a journalist. Much of her correspondence for the *Tribune* appears in *At Home and Abroad* (1856), and *Life Without and Life Within* (1859), both edited by her brother, Arthur B. Fuller, and published in Boston, the first by Crosby, Nichols and the second by Brown, Taggert and Chase. Joseph Jay Deiss's *The Roman Years of Margaret Fuller* (New York: Thomas Y. Crowell, 1969) gives much detail about her role in the revolution and her marriage.

Standard biographies include Mason Wade, *Margaret Fuller: Whetstone of Genius* (New York: Viking, 1940), Katharine Anthony, *Margaret Fuller: A Psychological Biography* (New York: Harcourt, Brace, 1920), and Madeline B. Stern, *The Life of Margaret Fuller* (New York: Dutton, 1942). Yet, as Arthur W. Brown pointed out in *Margaret Fuller* (New York: Twayne, 1964), some of her biographers take a "Gee whiz!" approach toward her achievements, apparently due to their anti-feminist bias.

As noted by Deiss, modern scholarship has established that friends dealt somewhat unfairly with Fuller in *Memoirs of Margaret Fuller Ossoli* (2 vols., Boston: Phillips, Samson, 1852), edited by Emerson, William H. Channing, and James Freeman Clarke. Other early works on Fuller are biographies by Julia Ward Howe (Boston: Roberts, 1883) and Thomas Wentworth Higginson (Boston: Houghton Mifflin, 1884).

A listing of her contributions to periodicals appears in *The Writings of Margaret Fuller*, edited by Mason Wade (New York: Viking, 1941). Another source is *Margaret Fuller: American Romantic* (New York: Doubleday, 1963), edited by Perry Miller.

Her struggle to become a free individual is depicted in *The Woman and the Myth: Margaret Fuller's Life and Writings* edited by Bell Gale Chevigny (Old Westbury, NY: Feminist Press, 1977), which aims to correct some of the misconceptions of previous works.

SARAH J. HALE AND *GODEY'S LADY'S BOOK*

The primary source is *Godey's Lady's Book* available in the Library of Congress. It also has copies of the other books written or edited by Sarah J. Hale — some 50 in all — many of which were compendia of household advice. One of the most ambitious was *Woman's Record or Sketches of All Distinguished Women From the Beginning to A.D. 1868* (New York: Harper, 1870), an early biographical encyclopedia of notable women.

There are two biographies of Hale: Isabelle W. Entrikin, *Sarah Josepha Hale and 'Godey's Lady's Book'* (Philadelphia: Lancaster, 1946) and Ruth E. Finley, *The Lady of Godey's: Sarah Josepha Hale* (Philadelphia: Lippincott, 1931). William R. Taylor, *Cavalier and Yankee* (New York: Braziller, 1961) contains an evaluation of her writings. Information on *Godey's* appeared in Frank Luther Mott, *A History of American Magazines*, Vol. 1 (Cambridge: Harvard University Press, 1938-57, pp. 580-94). See also "The Genesis of Godey's Lady's Book" (*New England Quarterly*, Vol. 1, January 1928, pp. 41-70).

For valuable background on the period, see Barbara Welter, "The Cult of True Womanhood: 1820-1860" (*American Quarterly*, Vol. 18, Summer 1966, pp. 151-174). Also helpful: Fred Lewis Pattee, *The Feminine Fifties* (New York: D. Appleton-Century Co., 1940); Helen W. Papashvily, *All the Happy Endings* (New York: Harper, 1956); Frank Luther Mott, *Golden Multitudes: The Story of Best Sellers in the United*

States (New York: Macmillan, 1947); and James D. Hart, *The Popular Book: A History of America's Literary Taste* (New York: Oxford University Press, 1950).

THE REVOLUTION AND WOMAN'S JOURNAL

Files of both *The Revolution* and the *Woman's Journal* are available at the Library of Congress. Brief excerpts from *The Revolution* are contained in *Women Together: A History in Documents of the Women's Movement in the United States* by Judith Papachristou (New York: Alfred A. Knopf, 1976, p. 57).

The importance of *The Revolution* to the suffrage movement is stressed in Eleanor Flexner, *Century of Struggle* (Cambridge: Harvard University Press, 1959). The *Woman's Journal* is described in detail in Lynne Masel-Walters, "A Burning Cloud by Day: The History and Content of the 'Woman's Journal'" (*Journalism History*, Vol. 3, Winter 1976-77, pp. 103-110). Masel-Walters also wrote "Their Rights and Nothing More: A History of *The Revolution*, 1868-70" (*Journalism Quarterly*, Vol. 53, Summer 1976, pp. 242-251).

The Susan B. Anthony scrapbooks of press comments relating to Elizabeth Cady Stanton are in the Library of Congress. For other material on Stanton, see: Elizabeth Cady Stanton, Susan B. Anthony and Matilda J. Gage, eds., *History of Woman Suffrage* (3 vols., Rochester, NY: Susan B. Anthony, 1886); Theodore Stanton and Harriot Stanton Blatch, eds., *Elizabeth Cady Stanton as Revealed in Her Letters, Diary and Reminiscences* (2 vols., New York: Harper, 1922).

Alma Lutz has written biographies of both Elizabeth Cady Stanton and Susan B. Anthony: *Created Equal: A Biography of Elizabeth Cady Stanton, 1815-1902* (New York: John Day, 1940) and *Susan B. Anthony: Rebel, Crusader, Humanitarian* (Boston: Beacon, 1959). Other biographies of Anthony: Ida Husted Harper, *Life and Work of Susan B. Anthony* (3 vols., New York: Arno, 1969), a reprint of the 1898-08 edition; and Katharine Anthony, *Susan B. Anthony: Her Personal History and Her Era* (Garden City, NY; Doubleday, 1954).

Sources on the Blackwells: Elinor Rice Hays, *Morning Star: A Biography of Lucy Stone, 1818-1893* (New York: Harcourt, Brace and World, 1961) and Hays, *Those Extraordinary Blackwells: The Story of a Journey to a Better World* (New York: Harcourt, Brace and World, 1967); Alice Stone Blackwell, *Lucy Stone: Pioneer of Woman's Rights* (Boston: Little, Brown, 1930). See also Laura E. Richards and Maud Howe Elliott, *Julia Ward Howe, 1819-1910* (Boston: Houghton Mifflin, 1916).

For general background, see Robert E. Riegel, *American Feminists* (Lawrence, KS: University of Kansas Press, 1963); Aileen S. Kraditor, *The Ideas of the Woman Suffrage Movement: 1890-1920* (New York: Columbia University Press, 1965); and William L. O'Neill, *Everyone Was Brave: A History of Feminism in America* (Chicago: Quadrangle, 1969).

WASHINGTON CORRESPONDENTS LIPPINCOTT AND AMES

The careers of 19th century Washington women journalists are described in a monograph by Maurine Beasley, "The First Women Washington Correspondents," No. 4, George Washington Studies (Washington, D.C.: George Washington University, 1976). See also, Beasley, "Pens and Petticoats: Early Women Washington Correspondents (*Journalism History*, Vol. 1, Winter 1974-75, pp. 112-115, 136).

An interesting manuscript collection in the Rutherford B. Hayes Memorial Library, Fremont, Ohio, includes numerous letters sent to Hayes both during and after his Presidential term by several Washington women correspondents, chiefly social writers for Cincinnati newspapers. At least one, Austine Snead, complained of sex prejudice. The collection contains a few written by Mary Clemmer Ames plus some 50 letters sent to her during the late 1860's and 1870's by readers of the *New York Independent* and personal friends. The library holds a clipping file of Ames' columns in the

New York Independent from 1876 to 1881 and in the *Cincinnati Commercial* from 1876 to 1879. It also has a file of her obituaries.

For biographical material on Ames, see her novel, *Eirene or A Woman's Right* (New York: Putnam, 1871), which contains a realistic account of her Civil War experiences; two nonfiction works, *Ten Years in Washington: Life and Scenes in the National Capital as a Woman Sees Them* (Hartford, CT: Worthington, 1875) and *Outlines of Man, Women, and Things* (New York: Hurd and Houghton, 1873); the sentimental tribute by her husband, Edmund Hudson, *An American Woman's Life and Work: A Memorial of Mary Clemmer* (Boston: Ticknor, 1886); and a sympathetic sketch by Lilian Whiting in *Our Famous Women* (Hartford, CT: Worthington, 1884, pp. 250-75).

Primary sources on Sara J. Lippincott include her columns for the *New York Times* and her Washington correspondence for the *Saturday Evening Post* of Philadelphia from 1850 to 1852, much of which was reprinted in the *National Era*. A complete file of the *National Era* is available at the Library of Congress. Much of the *Post* correspondence also was published in the second volume of *Greenwood Leaves: A Collection of Sketches and Letters* (Boston: Ticknor, Reed and Fields, 1852) available at the Library of Congress. It also has *New Life in New Lands* (New York: Ford, 1873), a collection of Western correspondence, chiefly from Colorado, for the *New York Times*.

Some autobiographical material was included in *Recollections of My Childhood and Other Stories* (1852); *Records of Five Years* (1851); the first volume of *Greenwood Leaves* (1850); *History of My Pets* (1851); *Haps and Mishaps of a Tour in Europe* (1854); and a shelf of children's books, all published in Boston by Ticknor and Fields. Contemporary biographical data appeared in Sarah J. Hale, *Woman's Record* (New York: Harper, 1853, pp. 624-28) and James Parton (and others), *Eminent Women of the Age* (Hartford, CT: Betts, 1869, pp. 147-63). Lippincott is the subject of chapter five in Margaret Farrand Thorp, *Female Persuasion: Six Strong-Minded Women* (New Haven: Yale University Press, 1949).

Other material includes an article by Lippincott, "American Salon in Washington 1850-60" (*Cosmopolitan*, February 1890, pp. 437-477), and an unfavorable review of *Haps and Mishaps of a Tour in Europe* (London *Athenaeum*, November 18, 1854), available at the Library of Congress.

For other background, see lists of correspondents in the annual *U.S. Congressional Directory* from 1870 to 1879 and consult F.B. Marbut, *News from the Capital: The Story of Washington Reporting* (Carbondale, IL: Southern Illinois University Press, 1971).

BLACK WOMEN JOURNALISTS

Sources on Black women journalists are Alice E. Dunnigan, "Early History of Negro Women in Journalism" (*Negro History Bulletin*, Vol. 28, Summer 1965, pp. 178-79, 193-97). Frederick G. Detweiler, *The Negro Press in the United States* (Chicago: University of Chicago Press, 1922); and Garland I. Penn, *The Afro-American Press and Its Editors* (New York: Arno Press, 1969), a reprint of an 1891 edition.

For information on Ida Wells-Barnett, see her autobiography, *Crusade for Justice* (Chicago: University of Chicago Press, 1970), edited by her daughter, Alfreda M. Duster. Other sources: Mrs. N. F. Mossell, *The Work of the Afro-American Woman* (Freeport, NY: Books for Libraries Press, 1971, pp. 32-46), a reprint of an 1894 edition; August Meier, *Negro Thought in America: 1880-1915* (Ann Arbor: University of Michigan Press, 1968); and Herbert Aptheker, ed., *A Documentary History of the Negro People in the United States* (2 vols., New York: Citadel, 1966).

Some 19th century religious publications for which Black women journalists wrote are preserved in a collection at Drew University, Madison, NJ. Nineteenth-century Black newspapers, including the *New York Age,* are available on microfilm in many libraries through a project of the American Council of Learned Societies. Nineteenth-century Black magazines and pamphlets may be found in the Schomburg Collection of the New York Public Library and the Moorland-Spingarn Collection at Howard University.

"NELLIE BLY"

Primary sources on Elizabeth Cochrane are her "Nellie Bly" articles in the *New York World* from 1887 to 1895, available on microfilm in many libraries. Elizabeth Cochrane wrote three books: *Nellie Bly's Book: Around the World in 72 Days* (New York: Pictorial Weeklies, 1890); *Six Months in Mexico* (New York: American, 1888); and *Ten Days in a Mad-House* (New York: Munro, 1887). Her biography, *The Amazing Nellie Bly* by Mignon Rittenhouse (New York: Dutton, 1956), is undocumented. Her obituaries appeared in the *New York Times* and the *New York World,* January 28, 1922.

Other biographical sources are Frances E. Willard and Mary A. Livermore, eds., *A Woman of the Century* (Buffalo: Moulton, 1893) and Ishbel Ross, *Ladies of the Press* (New York: Harper, 1936). Some material on women stunt reporters appeared in Rheta Childe Dorr, *A Woman of Fifty* (New York: Funk and Wagnalls, 1924). "Sob sisters" are described in John K. Winkler, *W.R. Hearst — An American Phenomenon* (New York: Simon and Schuster, 1928). See also John W. Perry, "Women Leaders of the American Press" (*Editor & Publisher,* April 23, 1932, pp. 18-19) and Elizabeth Banks, *Autobiography of a Newspaper Girl* (London: Menthuen, 1902).

For general background, see Frank Luther Mott, *American Journalism: A History 1690-1960* (New York: Macmillan, 1962) and Edwin Emery, *The Press and America* (Englewood Cliffs, NJ: Prentice-Hall, 1962).

IDA TARBELL

In addition to her autobiography, primary sources include these other works, many of which contain articles originally published in *McClure's Magazine* or the *American Magazine*: *History of the Standard Oil Company* (New York: McClure, Phillips, 1904) and briefer edition edited by David M. Chalmers (New York: Harper & Row, 1966); *The Business of Being a Woman* (New York: Macmillan, 1912); and *The Ways of Woman* (New York: Macmillan, 1915).

For information on her muckraking period, see Louis Filler, *Crusaders for American Liberalism* (New York: Harcourt, Brace, 1939); Frank Luther Mott, *A History of American Magazines* Vols. 3 and 4 (Cambridge: Harvard University Press, 1938-57); Harold S. Wilson, *McClure's Magazine and the Muckrakers* (Princeton, NJ: Princeton University Press, 1970); David Mark Chalmers, *The Social and Political Ideas of the Muckrakers* (New York: Citadel Press, 1964); and Theodore Peterson, *Magazines in the Twentieth Century* (Urbana: University of Illinois Press, 1956).

Most of Tarbell's papers are at Allegheny College, Meadville, PA. Her career is discussed in Margaret Inman Meaders, "Ida Minerva Tarbell, Journalist and Historian, 1857-1944" (unpublished master's thesis, University of Wisconsin, 1947).

For general background on the muckraking period, see G. E. Mowry, *The Era of Theodore Roosevelt, 1900-1912* (New York: Harper, 1958). For a concise sketch, see Nelson M. Blake, *A History of American Life and Thought* (New York: McGraw-Hill, 1963, pp. 409-413).

RHETA CHILDE DORR

Primary sources on Rheta C. Dorr are two of her books: *Inside the Russian Revolution* (New York: Macmillan, 1917) and her autobiography, *A Woman of Fifty* (New York: Funk and Wagnalls, 1924). Other biographical information is contained in Ishbel Ross, *Ladies of the Press* (New York: Harper, 1936) and June Sochen, *Movers and Shakers* (New York: Quadrangle, 1973). See also Louis Filler, *Crusaders for American Liberalism* (New York: Harcourt, Brace, 1939) and her obituary in the *New York Times* (August 9, 1948).

For information on the first woman war correspondent, see Charles B. Brown, "A Woman's Odyssey: The War Correspondence of Anna Benjamin" (*Journalism Quarterly*, Vol. 46, Autumn 1969, pp. 523-30). Peggy Hull's career as a World War I correspondent is described in "Peggy Hull," *Ladies Home Journal* (April 1920, p. 83). Another source is a chapter, "Ladies on the Front Line," in M.L. Stein, *Under Fire: The Story of American War Correspondents* (New York: Messner, 1968).

For general background, see John Hohenberg, *Foreign Correspondence: The Great Reporters and Their Times* (New York: Columbia University Press, 1964); Eugene Lyons, ed., *We Cover the World* (New York: Harcourt, Brace, 1937); and Marguerite E. Harrison, *Marooned in Moscow* (New York: Doran, 1921).

FRONT-PAGE REPORTERS

For information on Ishbel Ross, see her obituary in the *New York Times* (September 23, 1975) and *AB Bookman's Weekly* (December 1, 1975). See also Ishbel Ross, "Shall Women Inherit the Fourth Estate?" (*Independent Woman*, April 1937, pp. 106-107, 119-120).

Other sources on early 20th-century women journalists: Florence Finch Kelly, *Flowing Stream* (New York: Dutton, 1939); Catherine Filene, ed., *Careers for Women: New Ideas, New Methods, New Opportunities — To Fit a New World* (Boston: Houghton Mifflin, 1934); Agness Underwood, *Newspaperwoman* (New York: Harper, 1949); Marion K. Sanders, *Dorothy Thompson: A Legend in Her Time* (Boston: Houghton Mifflin, 1973); Genevieve Boughner, *Women in Journalism* (New York: Appleton, 1926); Edna Ferber, *A Peculiar Treasure* (New York: Doubleday, 1939); and Elizabeth Jordan, *Three Rousing Cheers* (New York: Appleton-Century, 1938).

Stanley Walker's views on women reporters also appeared in a chapter titled "A Gallery of Angels" in *City Editor* (New York: Stokes, 1934).

Articles include Catharine Brody, "Newspaper Girls" (*American Mercury*, March 1926, pp. 273-277) and Catharine Oglesby, "Women in Journalism" (*Ladies Home Journal*, May 1930, pp. 29, 229).

MARGUERITE BOURKE-WHITE

Primary source material on Margaret Bourke-White includes her books, especially *Eyes on Russia* (1931); *Shooting the Russian War* (1942); *Purple Heart Valley* (1944); *Dear Fatherland, Rest Quietly* (1946); *Halfway to Freedom* (1949) and *Portrait of Myself* (1963), all published in New York by Simon and Schuster. See also Margaret Bourke-White with Erskine Caldwell, *You Have Seen Their Faces* (New York: Modern Age, 1937). Her obituary appeared in the *New York Times* (August 28, 1971) and in *Time* (September 6, 1971).

Other sources: Overseas Press Club of America, *I Can Tell It Now* (New York: Dutton, 1964), containing material on Bourke-White and Dickey Chapelle.

Background on World War II women correspondents may be found in Frank Luther Mott, ed., "The Newspaper Woman Joins Up" in *Journalism in Wartime* (Columbia, MO: University of Missouri, 1943). See also Ann O'Hare McCormick, *The World at Home* (New York: Alfred A. Knopf, 1956).

For material on women correspondents in Korea, see Marguerite Higgins, *News is a Singular Thing* (1955) and *War in Korea* (1961), both published in Garden City, NY, by Doubleday. See also her obituaries in the *New York Times* (January 4, 1966); the *New York Herald Tribune* (January 3, 1966); and *Newsweek* (January 17, 1966).

Dickey Chapelle, *What's A Woman Doing Here?* (New York: Morrow, 1962) describes the author's experiences as a correspondent in several wars. Her career is analyzed in Frederick R. Ellis, "Dickey Chapelle: A Reporter and Her Work" (unpublished master's thesis, University of Wisconsin, Madison, 1968).

Sources on Vietnam women correspondents include Gloria Emerson, "Hey Lady, What Are You Doing Here?" (*McCall's*, August 1971, pp. 61, 108) and "Arms and the Woman" (*Harper's*, April 1973, pp. 35-45 and June 1973, pp. 99-100); Margaret Kilgore, "The Female War Correspondent in Vietnam" (*The Quill*, May 1972, pp. 9-12); and "The Femininity at the Front" (*Time,* October 28, 1966, pp. 73-74).

EARLY DAYS IN BROADCASTING — RUTH CRANE

Source material on early women in radio and television may be obtained from the Broadcast Pioneers Library, Washington, DC. Helpful material titled "Our Radio and TV members," compiled by Ruth Crane Schaefer in 1969 is in the Women's National Press Club archives of the Washington Press Club. Gioia E. Diliberto, "Profiles of Three Newswomen" (unpublished master's thesis, University of Maryland, College Park, 1975) contains extensive material on Pauline Frederick based on personal interviews with her and others knowledgeable about her career.

For information on Mary Margaret McBride, see her books, *A Long Way From* day, 1960) and her obituary in the *New York Times* (April 8, 1975). Another early broadcaster was described in Mary E. Williamson, "Judith Cary Waller: Chicago Broadcasting Pioneer" (*Journalism History*, Vol. 3, Winter 1976-77, pp. 111-115).

Nancy Dickerson, the first female national network news correspondent, describes the period of the 1950's and 1960's in *Among Those Present: A Reporter's View of Twenty-five Years in Washington* (New York: Random House, 1976).

Other sources: Obituary of Margaret Cuthbert, *New York Times* (July 26, 1968); obituary of Martha Deane, *New York Times* (December 10, 1973); Beatrice Oppenheim, "Tune in on Radio Jobs" (*Independent Woman*, April 1943, pp. 104-106, 125); Paul W. White, "Women and Radio" in *News on the Air* (New York: Harcourt Brace, 1947); and Rebecca D. Scott, "Women 'On the Air' " (*Independent Woman*, November 1926, pp. 9-11).

Helen Hinchliff-Franzwa has prepared "The Image of Women in Television: An Annotated Bibliography," which is scheduled to appear in *Hearth and Home: Images of Women in the Mass Media*, edited by Gaye Tuchman, Arlene Kaplan Daniels, and James Benet and set for 1978 publication by the Oxford University Press, New York.

WOMEN'S MAGAZINES

An important source on this topic, as well as on many others, is Betty Friedan's *The Feminist Mystique* (New York: W. W. Norton & Co., 1963). A magazine writer, columnist and author, Friedan was among the first women to place women's magazines in the category of mythology.

For readers who want to explore the birth and development of women's magazines, *The Lady Persuaders* (New York: Ivan Obolensky, Inc., 1960) is a helpful source. Its author, Helen Woodward, established circulation departments at the *Woman's Home Companion, Pictorial Review* and *McCall's*, and had a 20-year career in advertising, during which she specialized in women's magazines.

Two other helpful histories are Theodore Peterson's *Magazines in the 20th Century* (Urbana: University of Illinois Press, 1958) and *Understanding Magazines*, 2nd edition, by Roland E. Wolseley (Ames: Iowa State University Press, 1969). Both books trace how magazines were born, bought, sold, revamped, merged, or dropped altogether.

Less involved with corporate wheeling-and-dealing, but specific and thorough in its analysis of the content of women's magazines, is "Women in the Popular Magazines for Women in America: 1830-1956" by Sarah Elizabeth McBride (unpublished dissertation, University of Minnesota, 1966).

Other pertinent studies are "Surviving the *Saturday Evening Post*" by Virginia Sammon (*The Antioch Review*, Vol. 29, Spring 1969, pp. 103-109); "Changing Concepts of Morality: 1948-1969" (a study of the *Ladies Home Journal*) by Margaret J. Zube (*Social Forces*, Vol. 50, March 1972, pp. 385-392); *Magazine Profiles: Studies of Magazines Today* (Medill School of Journalism, Northwestern University, December 1974); and "The Suburban Woman: Women's Roles in *McCall's* in 1964 and 1974" by Sheila Silver (*Magazine Studies Quarterly*, Vol. 1, Summer 1977).

Also of interest are Peter Clarke's and Virginia Esposito's "A Study of Occupational Advice for Women in Magazines" (*Journalism Quarterly*, Vol. 43, Fall 1966, pp. 477-485; "The Portrayal of Women in Selected Magazines from 1911-1930" (unpublished dissertation by Teresa M. Hynes, University of Wisconsin—Madison, 1975); and *Woman's Changing Place: A Look at Sexism* by Nancy Doyle (Pamphlet No. 509, 1972, Public Affairs Committee, 381 Park Avenue South, New York, NY 10016).

THE JOURNALISM OF WOMEN'S LIBERATION

The most comprehensive study of feminist periodicals to date is Anne Mather's "A History of Feminist Periodicals" (unpublished master's thesis, University of Georgia, 1974). Mather has adapted her thesis into a three-part series which appeared in *Journalism History*, Vol. 1, Autumn 1974 and Winter 1974-75 and Vol. 2, Spring 1975. Mather's thesis also includes a survey of editors of feminist periodicals.

Also helpful is Nancy Cooper's "Feminist Periodicals" (*Mass Communications Review*, Vol. 3, Summer 1976, pp. 15-23).

A continuing report on feminist periodicals is to be found in the monthly *Media Report to Women*, which covers both the feminist media and women in the established media, available by subscription from 3306 Ross Place, N.W., Washington, DC 20008.

An up-to-date list of feminist periodicals and other media can be found in the annual *Media Report to Women Index/Directory*, edited by Martha Leslie Allen (Washington, DC: Women's Institute for Freedom of the Press, 1975—). See also the *New Women's Survival Sourcebook* (New York: Alfred A. Knopf, Inc., 1975) edited by Kirsten Grimstad and Susan Rennie; and *Womanhood Media: Current Resources About Women* by Helen R. Wheeler (Metuchen, NJ: Scarecrow Press, 1972). See also the *Womanhood Media Supplement*, published in 1975.

The creation and growth of *Ms.* Magazine is analyzed in "Two Faces of the Same Eve: *Ms.* vs. *Cosmo*" by Stephanie Harrington (*New York Times Magazine*, August 11, 1974).

See also *Quest: a feminist quarterly* for a special issue, "Communications and Control" (Vol. 3, Fall 1976, pp. 3-10, 31-40).

Especially helpful for their overview of the women's liberation movement and journalism's role with and within the movement are *Rebirth of Feminism* by Judith Hole and Ellen Levine (New York: Quadrangle Books, Inc., 1971); and Maren Lockwood Carden's *The New Feminist Movement* (New York: Russell Sage Foundation, 1974). An update of Carden's research, *Feminism in the Mid-1970s: The Non-Estab-*

lishment, the Establishment, and the Future, was published in June 1977 (New York: The Ford Foundation Office of Reports).

LICENSE CHALLENGES, FEDERAL COMPLAINTS, AGREEMENTS, PRIME TIME/DAYTIME PORTRAYAL

Additional excerpts of NOW's challenge of WABC's license can be found in *Media Report to Women*, June 15, 1972.

The license challenge against WRC-TV, Washington, DC, filed by women's groups in the metropolitan Washington area, is chronicled in *Women in the Wasteland Fight Back: A Report on the Image of Women Portrayed in TV Programming*. It is available from Kathy Bonk, Media Task Force Coordinator for the National Organization for Women, 1424 16th Street, N.W., Washington, DC.

Agreements between women's groups and broadcast licensees have been excerpted in *Media Report to Women*. Excerpts of the following agreements can be located in these issues: KCST-TV, San Diego, CA and KWGN-TV, Denver, CO — July 1, 1974; KPRC-TV, Houston, TX — August 1, 1974; KABC-TV and KNBC-TV, Los Angeles, CA — February 1, 1975; and WGAL-TV, Lancaster, PA — June 1, 1977. *Media Report to Women* may be obtained by subscription or single issues from 3306 Ross Place, N.W., Washington, DC 20008.

The Los Angeles Women's Coalition for Better Broadcasting has worked to obtain agreements with every licensee in its area. It has filed license challenges against those stations which refused to negotiate agreements with the Coalition. The Coalition's office is located at 3514 Cody Road, Sherman Oaks, CA 91403.

Consulted by many citizen's groups for its explanation of procedures and strategies is the *Guide to Citizen Action in Radio and Television*, published by the Office of Communication of the United Church of Christ in 1971. Also of interest is *Television Station Employment Practices: The Status of Minorities and Women* by Ralph M. Jennings and Allan T. Walters, released in January 1977 by the United Church of Christ, Office of Communication, 289 Park Avenue South, New York, NY 10010, at a cost of $7.50. The Office of Communication prepares such reports annually, based on employment data submitted to the FCC by broadcasters.

NOW also has compiled a "FCC Action Kit," available from NOW's national office, 5 South Wabash, Suite 1615, Chicago, IL 60603.

More information on discrimination in broadcasting is contained in *The Rights of Women* by Susan Deller Ross (New York: Avon Books, 1974).

The complete report of the United Methodist Women's study of sex stereotyping in prime time programming may be obtained from Ellen Kirby, Room 1514, 475 Riverside Drive, New York, NY 10027.

A comprehensive reference on portrayal of females and males is *Sex Role Stereotyping in the Mass Media: An Annotated Bibliography* by Leslie Friedman (New York: Garland Publishing Co. Inc., 1977).

Content analyses of programming and commercials are not limited to those done by citizen groups. Michele L. Long and Rita J. Simon authored "The Roles and Statuses of Women on Children's and Family TV Programs" (*Journalism Quarterly*, Vol. 51, Spring 1974, pp. 107-110. *Washington Star* reporter Judy Flander described Action for Children's Television activities in "Some Parents Have Their ACT Together" (*Washington Star*, Section D, May 31, 1977). And a cluster of articles in the *Journal of Communication* (Vol. 24, Spring 1974) focused on women in the media: "Advising and Ordering," by Joseph Turow, a discussion of women and men's roles in prime time shows; "Women in Television Commercials" by Alice Courtney and Thomas Whipple; and "Heroine of the Daytime Serial" by Mildred Downing; "Fighting Sexism on the Airwaves" by Kay Mills.

A former FCC Commissioner's observations about the Commission, broadcasters, and the American public they serve are contained in *How to Talk Back to Your Television Set* by Nicholas Johnson (New York: Bantam Books, Inc., 1970). Johnson is head of the National Citizens Committee for Broadcasting, publishers of *Access* magazine, a digest of current activities in broadcasting. The Committee can be contacted at 1028 Connecticut Avenue, N.W., Room 402, Washington, DC 20036.

An analysis of contemporary broadcast coverage can be found in *Moments of Truth*, the fifth Alfred I. duPont-Columbia University Survey of Broadcast Journalism, edited by Marvin Barrett (New York: Thomas Y. Crowell, 1975). The volume illustrates "where the action was and wasn't" in 1974 and 1975, and analyzes the results of the AAUW's nationwide monitoring study of television.

Books on women in broadcasting seem to be written on a "case study" basis. Interviews with well-known women broadcasters are contained in *Women in Television News* by Judith S. Gelfman (New York: Columbia University Press, 1976). A book exploring the experiences of women who work off-camera is *Women in Television* by Anita Klever (Philadelphia: The Westminster Press, 1975).

An important volume is *Rooms With No View: A Woman's Guide to the Man's World of the Media*, edited by Ethel Strainchamps (New York: Harper and Row, Inc., 1974).

Other books are *Don't Quote Me* by Marie Torre (Garden City, NY: Doubleday, 1965) and *Don't Quote Me* by Winzola McLendon and Scottie Smith (New York: Dutton, 1970).

Studies of women who work in broadcasting also are helpful in pinpointing demographics and trends: "Women in Broadcasting," by Don C. Smith and Kenneth Harwood (*Journal of Broadcasting*, Vol. 15, Fall 1966); "Attitudes Toward Television Newswomen," by Vernon Stone (*Journal of Broadcasting*, Vol. 50, Winter 1973-74); and "Surveys Show Younger Women Becoming News Directors," also by Stone (Radio Television News Directors Association *Communicator*, Vol. 30, October 1976, pp. 10-12).

An interesting newspaper account of network hiring of women reporters is "CBS Network and WNBC-TV Get Their First Girl Reporters" by Val Adams (*New York Times*, May 7, 1965). A more contemporary view is contained in "Women in TV News," by Adam Shaw (*Cosmopolitan*, July 1977).

Press Woman, the monthly magazine of the National Federation of Press Women, Inc., can be ordered from 1105 Main St., Box 99, Blue Springs, MO 64015.

News and Views is a newsletter published 10 times per year by the American Women in Radio and Television, 1321 Connecticut Avenue, N.W., Washington, DC 20036.

Matrix is the quarterly magazine of Women in Communications, Inc. It runs commentary, history, information, and how-to articles on the communications industry. *Matrix* is available from WICI, P.O. Box 9561, Austin, TX 78766.

AFTRA's National Women's Committee publishes *WomeNews*. It is available through the Committee, American Federation of Television and Radio Artists, 1717 North Highland Avenue, Hollywood, CA 90028.

Two public interest law firms which specialize in citizens' access to broadcasting are the Citizens Communication Center, 1914 Sunderland Place, N.W., Washington, DC 20036; and the Media Access Project, 1609 Connecticut Ave., N.W., Washington, DC 20036.

MONITORING NEWSPAPERS

A roundup of problems in newspaper coverage of women is contained in a two-part series written by Gena Corea, a former women's page editor and author of a column, "Frankly Feminist." Her articles, "Writer says papers biased in covering news of women" and "How newspapers can conduct serious coverage of women," appeared in *Editor & Publisher*, April 21 and April 28, 1973.

Zena Beth McGlashan's "Women's Pages in American Newspapers: Missing Out on Contemporary Content" (*Journalism Quarterly*, Vol. 52, Spring 1975, pp. 66-69), and Susan Miller's "Changes in Women's Lifestyle Sections" (*Journalism Quarterly*, Vol. 53, Winter 1976, pp. 641-647) study news content in women's pages and "lifestyle" sections.

Recommendations for balancing content in the women's pages are suggested in Lenora Williamson's article, "Women's page 'relevancy' stories should go to 'subject' page, says Charlotte Curtis" (*Editor & Publisher*, April 6, 1974).

The influence of sex stereotyping on news judgment is explored by Jack E. Orwant and Muriel G. Cantor in "How Sex Stereotyping Affects Perceptions of News Preferences," and by Dan G. Drew and Susan H. Miller in "Sex Stereotyping and Reporting" (both in *Journalism Quarterly*, Vol. 54, Spring 1977, pp. 99-108 and pp. 142-146).

The manner in which sex stereotyping affects the shooting and cropping of news photos is discussed by Miller in "The Content of News Photos: Women's and Men's Roles" (*Journalism Quarterly*, Vol. 52, Spring 1975, pp. 70-75).

PUBLIC BROADCASTING

A copy of the *Report of the Task Force on Women in Public Broadcasting* is available free from the Corporation for Public Broadcasting, 1111 16th Street, N.W., Washington, D.C. 20036. A bi-monthly newsletter for women in public broadcasting may be obtained from the Corporation's Office of Women's Activities at the address above. Also available is *CPB Reports* from its Office of Public Affairs.

A copy of the *Report on the Status of Women in the CBC* is available for $3 from CBC Learning Systems and Publications, P.O. Box 500, Terminal A, Toronto, Ontario, Canada.

THE ADVERTISING INDUSTRY AND WOMEN

The full report of the National Advertising Review Board may be obtained by writing to NARB at 850 Third Avenue, New York, NY 10022. The report, "Advertising Portraying or Directed to Women," costs $1.

The principal feminist complaints about advertising are discussed in Lucy Komisar's "The Image of Women in Advertising," in *Women in Sexist Society*, edited by Vivian Gornick and Barbara Moran (New York: New American Library, 1972); and "Media Images I: Madison Avenue Brainwashing — The Facts" by Alice Embree. Embree's article appears in *Sisterhood is Powerful*, edited by Robin Morgan (New York: Random House, Inc., 1970).

"A Woman's Place: An Analysis of the Roles Portrayed by Women in Magazine Advertisements" by Alice E. Courtney and Sarah Wernick Lockeretz identified stereotypes in magazines which appeal to general audiences (*Journal of Marketing Research*, Vol. 8, February 1971, pp. 92-95).

A roundup of research about women in advertising — including classified advertising — is contained in "Liberating the Media: Advertising," Freedom of Information Center Report No. 290 by Muriel Akamatsu (School of Journalism, University of Missouri at Columbia, September 1972).

The infiltration of department store displays by advertising emphasizing sex was analyzed by Donia Mills in "Stalking the Sex-Lure Message" (*Washington Star*, March 6, 1977).

The view from inside Madison Avenue offices is presented in Jane Levere's interview with female ad executives in "Portrayal of women in ads defended by top ad women" (*Editor & Publisher*, June 8, 1974), and Mary Leonard's "Art Thou Sexist, Fair Adman?" (*The National Observer*, November 9, 1974).

GUIDELINES

Guidelines for Creating Positive Sexual and Racial Images in Educational Materials may be obtained from Macmillan Publishing Co., 866 Third Avenue, New York, NY 10022.

Guidelines for Equal Treatment of the Sexes in McGraw-Hill Book Company Publications is available from McGraw Hill Book Company,1221 Avenue of the Americas, New York, NY 10020.

For a copy of *Guidelines for Improving the Image of Women in Textbooks* write Scott, Foresman and Company, 1900 East Lake Avenue, Glenview, IL 60025.

A copy of the IWY Guidelines (Leaflet L-1, July 1976) is available from the *IWY Sec*retariat, U.S. Department of State, Washington, DC 20520.

The Stanford University Women's News Service *Guidelines for Newswriting about Women* are reprinted in William L. Rivers, *The Mass Media* (New York: Harper & Row, 1975, pp. 593-4).

The problems posed by the English language are discussed in *Women and Words* by Casey Miller and Kate Swift (New York: Anchor Books/Doubleday, 1976); *Language and Sex: Difference and Dominance* edited by Barrie Thorne and Nancy Henley with a 100-page bibliography (Rowley, MA: Newbury House, 1975); and in "Sexist Language or What's in a Name" by Lucy Fuchs in *Instructor,* November 1975.

Dick and Jane as Victims: Sex Stereotyping in Children's Readers is available for $1.50 from Women on Words and Images, P.O. Box 2163, Princeton, NJ 08540. The study is accompanied by tables and illustrations from some of the textbooks.

Biased Textbooks: A Research Perspective by Lenore J. Weitzman and Diane Rizzo documents sex bias in elementary science, math, reading, spelling, and social studies texts. It also recommends steps for action. It is available from the Resource Center on Sex Roles, Room 701, 1201 16th Street, N.W., Washington, DC 20036. $1.

Textbooks used by teenagers were studied by Phyllis Arlow and Merle Froschl in *Women in the High School Curriculum: A Review of High School U.S. History and English Literature Texts* (1975). It is available for $1 from The Feminist Press, Box 334, Old Westbury, NY 11568.

An action guide, *What Can You Do About Biased Textbooks?* has been prepared by the Resource Center on Sex Roles in Education, National Foundation for the Improvement of Education, 1156 15th Street, N.W., Washington, DC 20005.

An overview of sexism in schools is contained in *And Jill Came Tumbling After: Sexism in American Education* edited by Judith Stacey, Susan Bereaud, and Joan Daniels (New York: Dell, 1974).

The Racism and Sexism Resource Center for Education, established by the Council on Interracial Books for Children (Room 300, 1841 Broadway, New York, NY 10023), also prepares guidelines for judging sexist content of educational materials.

SATELLITES

The National Women's Agenda is located at the Women's Action Alliance, 370 Lexington Avenue, New York, NY 10017.

Women's Institute for Freedom of the Press

The Women's Institute for Freedom of the Press is a nonprofit, tax-exempt organization founded in 1972 for research and educational purposes and to publish works both theoretical and practical on the communication of information. For two years, 1972 and 1973, the Institute published *Media Report to Women*. In January 1974, *MRW* was spun off into a self-supporting monthly periodical based on subscriptions.

The Institute now publishes the annual *MRW Index/Directory* to increase communication among those working in women's media and to aid writers, speakers, media activists, scholars and students. Its first part is an annotated, cumulative index of women's media actions and of documents published in *MRW*; this index provides a history of women's media activities and research in over 100 subject matter categories. The second part of the *Index/Directory* is an annually updated directory of women's media that lists over 500 women's periodicals, women's presses and publishers, news services, radio-TV groups, video and cable, art/graphics/theater and music groups, bookstores and other women's media groups and individuals in the U.S. and Canada, and a few in other countries.

Long-term research by the Women's Institute is being conducted on the structure of the communication system and its relation to women. This work, based on a new theory of communication, will be published by the Institute when it is completed. Other projects include an examination of the nation's media distribution system and an analysis of its failure to serve the critical needs of women to reach the general public and particularly to reach other women. Recommendations will follow. Other activities aim to focus attention, ideas and plans on improving the communication system of the nation.

Many women throughout the country are associated with the Institute's work, either directly or by contributing time, money, ideas or their general support. The statement of views that they share with each other reads as follows:

THE WIFP ASSOCIATES STATEMENT

For our Constitutional right to "freedom of the press" to be meaningful, there must be a realistic means of exercising it — for all of us, not just for the multi-millionaires among us. In a country as intellectually and technologically creative as ours, we are sure a better way to provide a means of communication to all who need it can be devised. We do not like to be in a position of having to "beg" or "demand" access to media that belong to others, happy to be mentioned even if inaccurately. There is a very large number of women in the U.S. who are increasingly becoming dissatisfied with the inadequacies of the present structure. We are seeking improvement, both through provision of our own media and in the existing media through our inclusion at all levels equally — in employment, news coverage and a more accurate portrayal of our abilities and our options in the nation's economic, social and political life. We wish to indicate by our association with the Women's Institute for Freedom of the Press and its work on this problem that we, too, desire more national attention to the issue.

We have differences in views among us and we would propose different solutions and work at many different proposals, some of us in our existing media and some of us outside it, at different levels and in different places. But we are united in our desire to encourage meaningful change that expands the exercise of our Constitutional right to communicate in the media we find most suitable to our message, no less than the right now exercised by some Americans who presently are able to communicate their information to millions of others.

We know that changes in the structure of mass communications are going to come; too many people are now being left out. The question is on what principles is that re-structuring going to be made. We want to have something to say about how the communication system of the future is going to develop.

We want to work together in a more visible way with other women who feel as we do to register our unity and our conviction that we must aid each other in obtaining the help and funding we need for our projects and to encourage the greater total funding for all our efforts to see socially constructive changes in the nation's communication system. For women to continue to make progress, a communication system that enables us both to exchange our information and to reach the general public is essential.

THE ASSOCIATES
WOMEN'S INSTITUTE FOR FREEDOM OF THE PRESS

Dr. Donna Allen, Director
Joan Shigekawa
Flo Kennedy
Dorinda Moreno
Susan Brownmiller
Audrey Rowe-Colom
Malvina Reynolds
Florence Howe
Patricia Carbine
Martha Stuart
Eleanor Perry
Betty Medsger
Dana Densmore
Joan Levine
Phyllis Sanders
Jo-Ann Albers
Dr. Milnor Alexander
Gloria Steinem
Karen Lunquist
Dorothy Dean
Letty Cottin Pogrebin
Ellen Kirby
Eunice West
Midge Kovacs
Sandra Elkin
Charlotte Bunch
Susan Rennie
Martha Leslie Allen
Marguerite Beck-Rex
Gertrude Barnstone
Jan Zimmerman
Kirsten Grimstad
Frances K. Palmeri
Indra Dean Allen
Valerie Eads
Janice Blue
Linda Randall
Elvira Valenzuela Crocker
Karen Lindsey
Beatrice Buckler
Fran P. Hosken
Paula Bernstein
Amalie Rothschild
Alice Rickel
Susan Schiffer
Ellen Frankfort
Daisy B. Fields
Rochelle Lefkowitz
Caroline Bird
Bettye Lane
Robin Morgan
Rose K. Goldsen
Anne Braden

Ramona R. Rush
Barbara Jordan Moore
Alice Lynn Booth
Helen McKenna
Phyllis Arlow
Kim Beaman
Del Martin
Celeste Bayek
Sally Barrett-Page
Jessie Bernard
Charlotte Montgomery
Sarah McClendon
Edith Kermit Roosevelt
Carol Retz
Deborah Snow
Audrey Gellis
Gloria Kaufman
Ginny Pitt
Adele Aldridge
Kathleen Carroll
Mary P. Gardner
Hali Paul
Suzanne Pingree
Kathleen Hopfner
Peggy D. Guthaus
Marian O. Norby
Carol Clement
Jayne Marsh
Michael A. Conley
Casey Miller
Arlene Kaplan Daniels
Matilda Butler
Anica Vesel Mander
Susan Wengraf
Shirley A. Smallwood
Lisa Lian Seidenberg
Carol Lynn Yellin
Suzanne Barron
Dr. Karin Dovring
Mary Jane Lupton
Corrine B. Lucido
Dr. Mary A. Gardner
Mary R. Brown
Nona Bear
Muriel Cantor
Sheila R. Jensen
Mary Catherine Kilday
Colleen G. Patrick
Viv Sutherland
Victoria Hochberg
Mary Ellen Corbett
Andrea Dworkin
Jan Lunquist

Dr. Virginia Ramey Mollenkott
Sr. Elizabeth Thoman, C.H.M.
Ida Lewis
Susan H. Miller
Louise Lamphere
Paula S. Kassell
Louise Bernikow
Dr. Ruth N. Dowling
Dorothy Jurney
Alice Backes
Jeanne Gold Hull
Dorothy Sucher
Barbara J. Katz
Karen Wellisch
Sheila Silver
Gail Waldron
Pat McGloin
Nola Claire
Ellen Cohn
Jeanne L. Burden
Helen L. Gray
Constance Julius
Jane D. Brown
Kathleen Vogel
Dr. Maurine Beasley
Stephanie Stewart
Kathy Bonk
Joyce Maupin
Marianne Rubenstein
Leslie J. Friedman
Barbara Ann T. Motoyama
Jamie Robinson
Susan Tenenbaum
Elizabeth Stone
Mary Ellen Verheyden-Hilliard
Karen Rosenkrantz Shapiro
Gail Sheehy
Carol Mauriello
Toni "Chestnut" Mester
Dr. Sandra Brown
Claudia Dreifus
Judith Zaffirini
Rosemary Ruether
Anne Kimball Relph
Janet Lee Beals
Linda D. Hutchinson
Jean Reynolds
Blair Corning
Susan Braudy
Midge Finley
Frances Chapman
Judith Meuli
Prof. Caroline I. Ackerman

Catharine R. Stimpson
Hannelore Hahn
Brett Harvey
Jill Johnston
Mary Ann McCoy
Betsey Wright
Natalie J. Sokoloff
Lydia Kleiner
Jan Zobel
Ruth Kramer
Marian Hayes Hull
Judith Senderowitz
Kathleen M. Burns
Joann Haugerud
Gloria Serenbetz
Tina Lachowitch
Denise Levertov
Bernadette R. Finley
Julia London
Michelina Fitzmaurice
Diane T. Hand
Madge Reinhardt
Mary Jo Haverbeck
Cathy Zheutlin
Rhonda S. Griffin
Dinah LeHoven
Joyce M. Hennessee
Polly Joan
Elaine Hendrie
Freude Bartlett
Sophie Zimmerman
Dr. Morleen Getz Rouse
Rachel Field
Dr. Madonna Kolbenschlag
Toni Carabillo
Sondra K. Gorney
Lucyann Kerry
Annie King Phillips
Flora Crater
Sherry Small Sundick
Rosalyn H. Anderson
Joan E. Biren (Jeb)
Karin Lippert
Mary Anna Colwell
Martha Edelheit
Ann Stookey
Kate Swift
Edwina E. Dowell
Maxi M. Cohen
Carol A. Emmens
Maureen Honey
Madeline Lee
Betty Daniel-Green
Jacqueline Ceballos
Sondra Patrinos
Molly McIntosh
Sara Stauffer Whaley
Patricia Mainardi
Megan Wood
Helen Hinchliff-Franzwa
Silvianna Goldsmith
Marsha Kroll
Patricia B. Campbell
Betsy Warrior
Jean-Louise Landry
Harriet Molese McGovern
Sandra Shevey
Rebecca Sive-Tomashefsky
Stacey M. Franchild

Irene Tinker
Shirley Wagener
Jane Wilkins Pultz
Judy Chicago
Naomi Weisstein
Jo Freeman
Katherine Lawrence
Rebecca Kuzins
Dr. Sylvia Gonzales
Mary Lou Butcher
Elizabeth Hurlow-Hannah
Janice Goodman
Vivian Hall
Niti Salloway
Gena Corea
Mollie Gregory
Mary Reese O'Gara
Ruth J. Abram
Constance Walker
Anne M. Cooper
Laura X
Yvonne M. Perret
Harriet Gross
Melinda M. Perrin
Kathleen A. Olson
Peggy J. Durham
Dr. Edith J. Tebo
Ariel Dougherty
Dagmar E. Bubriski
Barbara Mor
Hope Snitkin
Phyllis F. Butler
Barbara Grier
Bettina Bergo
Mayri Sagady
Christina Baldwin
Fern Leaf
Jeanie Class
Anne Kent Rush
Ann Snitow
Evelyn Kaye
Karen Back
Lolly Hirsch
Jewell Jackson McCabe
Lucia Ramirez
Margaret I. Cleland
Marjory Collins
Sharon Leventhal
Celeste West
Janet Harris
June Lipton
Katherine Montague
Sara Reitz
Patricia L. Hogan
Enid Sefcovic
Charlotte Mills
Joan Chernock
Beth Rawles
Kate Daly
Judith Paulus
Judy Mathe Foley
Ellen Snortland
Ida Morris
Leonore R. Elkus
Cheryl B. Rectorschek
Sue Davidson
Ranice H. Crosby
Malissa I. Scherer
Erica Gutman

Sen. Carol Bellamy
Sherna Gluck
Susan Griffin
Sister Margaret Traxler
Jane Pierson McMichael
Boden Sandstrom
Alexa Freeman
Jayne R. Jacobs
Judy Conway Greening
Dorothy Allison
Anne B. Sayre
Carol Conn
Lynne Gallagher Stitt
Gayle Gibbons
Billie J. Wahlstrom
Bonnie Friedman
Frances K. Reid
Gloria J. O'Dell
Gerri Traina
Ava Stern
Dr. Jean Kirkpatrick
Linda M. Smith
Christine Bose
Clarissa Schaeffer
Dr. Mary E. Williamson
Jinx Melia
Allison A. Platt
Barbara Zheutlin
Anyda Marchant
Gerry Nicholson
Harriet Alpern
Ruth G. Kirsch
Barbara A. Davis
Patti Stewart
Dorothy J. Shami
Caren J. Deming
Jo Hartley
Anne L. Scott
Sue Kaufman
Judith Boone
Natalie F. Holtzman
Monica Phillips
Susan Kent Caudill
Saundra Hybels
Mary Ellen Brown
Joyce H. Newman
Sandy Hall
Ann Marie Catalano
Sallie E. Fischer
Linda Fink Matthews
Margot Burman
Carolyn Theresa Lease
Gloria Z. Greenfield
Annette Samuels
Diana Tillinghast
Marlene T. Edmunds
Jeanne Weimann
Elizabeth Stevens
Carol N. Levin
Meryl Goodman Thomas
Sandra West Whiteurs
Margaret Mansfield
Phyllis Myers
Miriam Nicholas
Nancy H. Dickerson

*WIFP is still welcoming
new Associates.*